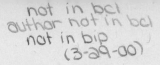

Slide Libraries

Slide Libraries

A Guide for
Academic Institutions and Museums

Betty Jo Irvine

1974

LIBRARIES UNLIMITED, INC.
Littleton, Colo.

LIBRARIES UNLIMITED, INC.
P.O. Box 263
Littleton, Colorado 80120

Dedicated to

ELEANOR COLLINS

Slide and Photograph Collection
University of Michigan
1946-1973

ACKNOWLEDGMENTS

Grateful thanks are extended to all the slide librarians and curators who assisted in the original data compilations for this work. Without the combined efforts of these individuals and the following colleagues, this publication would not have been possible: Helen Chillman, Yale University; Eleanor Collins, University of Michigan; Nicholas DeMarco, Vassar College; Gail Grisé, Indiana University; Nadine Hamilton, University of Illinois at Chicago Circle; Kaz Higuchi, Princeton University; Virginia Hotchkin, State University of New York at Binghamton; Sue Janson, Cornell University; Concetta Leone, University of Pennsylvania; Stephen Marjolies, Brooklyn College; Richard Martin, Columbia University; Margaret P. Nolan, the Metropolitan Museum of Art; Luraine Tansey, San Jose City College; Virginia Yarbro, Chicago Art Institute; and Victoria Wilson, Indiana University. Jill Caldwell assisted in the preparation of the bibliographies and directories and Debra Olken in the typing of this material. Christopher Richards prepared the diagrammatic illustrations. David Lee Carl processed and developed all photographs taken by the author.

In order to make this work financially feasible, Advanced Studies of Indiana University funded the research trip to East Coast slide libraries and the Council on Library Resources funded the period during which the first two drafts of the manuscript were prepared. This book could not have been prepared without the generous assistance of these two institutions.

The materials explosion of the 1960s has demanded formal recognition of the complex nature of visual resource libraries and of the need to establish valid criteria for their effective utilization and development. The purpose of this guide is to state these criteria for slide libraries so that they will be available to individuals in the art, audiovisual, library and instructional media fields. The chapters that follow outline standard administrative practices, classification systems, production methods, physical facilities, and supplies and equipment, indicating basic guidelines for the efficient organization and administration of these visual resource collections. In the past it took months or even years to learn to cope with the complexities of an audiovisual resource collection; it is hoped that this work will facilitate that learning process for those in academic institutions and museums.

In recognition of the lack of published information on slide libraries, a comprehensive study and survey was instituted, covering the history of the problem. the present status of slide collections, practical matters (such as equipment and photographic processing) and more formal library considerations (such as the use of classification systems, source or accession files and authority files). The base of departure for this research was art slide libraries in colleges, universities, and museums in the United States. An eight-page questionnaire was sent to the librarians and curators of these collections, and a selected number were interviewed personally.

From 1968 to 1970, 150 questionnaires were mailed to slide librarians in colleges, universities, and museums in the United States. A total of 120 (80%) responded either by writing directly or by returning the questionnaires; as a result, 101 questionnaires were tabulated for the study. Letters are included in the total number of responses but not as part of questionnaire tabulations. (See the directory of slide libraries for a list of contributing collections.)

Although initially an attempt was made to limit the size of the collections covered, the base of 25,000 was dropped because not all sources consulted (*The American Art Directory*, *The American Library Directory*, and *The Directory of Special Libraries and Information Centers*) gave the exact sizes of slide collections; moreover, in view of the tremendous growth rates of many collections, it seemed unfair to omit them under such an arbitrary standard. Thus, the frequent lack of such data, coupled with the desire to include as many academic collections as possible, negated the use of a size-limitation factor for the inclusion or exclusion of slide collections in the initial study; the size of slide libraries studied ranges from 1,000 to over 200,000 slides.

Because the emphasis in the original study was on academic collections, only a select number of museums were included. It was not considered necessary to obtain information on every slide collection in the United States in order to develop an overview of organizational and administrative procedures. The bibliographical research for this manual, however, has included all potential subject reservoirs on this topic: audiovisual, art, education, library, and science literature. Historically, art education and art history curriculums have had the greatest demand for this particular visual medium, which originated in the seventeenth century; consequently, these areas have been the primary research sources. The visual documentation of art works through the use of slides for educational purposes has been a natural function of the medium. Only recently have other disciplines discovered the advantages and flexibility of this rather "old" visual tool.

In addition to the use of questionnaires as a data base, 28 collections were directly observed and studied; in such cases each slide librarian was interviewed so that information could be collected on the day-to-day operation, organization, and general administration of each facility. Extensive photographic coverage was also undertaken of all collections directly observed. Except as noted, the photographs included here were taken by the author. Another 550 questionnaires were mailed to manufacturers and distributors of slides, equipment, and general supplies used in slide libraries. The results of this final mailing are included in the various chapters on equipment and supplies and in the directories.

Because slide libraries in the United States had never been studied in depth, the questionnaire and direct observation methods were considered critical to the formulation of guidelines for the operation of such collections. Additional research through audiovisual education, and library literature has provided the necessary supplementary information; literature from approximately the last 15 years in the audiovisual, education, and library fields was studied. Bibliographical indexes from 1876 to the present were searched specifically for the treatment of slides or lantern slides in art, education, and library literature. One of the most beneficial results of this undertaking is the extensive and comprehensive bibliographic compilations; these serve as guides to supplemental reading on related topics and, in other instances, indicate the availability of more detailed information. This work is designed not to duplicate the research and publications of others but to generate new concepts and to complement previously established ones.

One aim of this manual is to show, whenever possible, the correlation of slide library procedures with established library practices on an organizational and administrative level. Further, the guidelines and principles set forth should be useful regardless of the subject orientation of the slide library. Those working in a previously established slide library should find the guide as helpful as those interested in building a collection.

The name "library" has lost its etymologic meaning and means not a collection of books, but the central agency for disseminating information, innocent recreation, or best of all, inspiration among people. Whenever this can be done better, more quickly or cheaply by a picture than a book, the picture is entitled to a place on the shelves and in the catalog.

... A generation ago the lantern slide was little known except in magic lantern entertainments, and it required some courage for the first schools to make it a part of the educational apparatus. Today there is hardly a college or university subject which is not receiving great aid from the lantern. No one thinks of it as a course in art or discusses it from an ethical standpoint. It is needed by the engineer, physician, botanist, astronomer, statistician, in fact in every conceivable field, but of course, it is specially adapted to popular study of fine arts because they are so dependent on visual examples, and the lantern is the cheap and ready substitute for costly galleries.

Melvil Dewey
1906

"Library Pictures," *Public Libraries* 11:10 (1906).

TABLE OF CONTENTS

LIST OF PHOTOGRAPHS

LIST OF DIAGRAMS

1—BACKGROUND FOR SLIDE LIBRARIANSHIP

HISTORICAL INTRODUCTION

The earliest noted slide collections in the United States date from the 1880s to 1900 and were initiated in the following institutions: American Museum of Natural History of New York City; Bryn Mawr College; Buffalo Society of Natural Sciences; Chicago Art Institute; Cornell University; Dartmouth College; Massachusetts Institute of Technology; the Metropolitan Museum of Art; Mount Holyoke College; Princeton University; the University of Illinois; the University of Michigan; the University of Rochester; Wellesley College; and Williams College. These collections represented a vast range of subjects from architectural history to travel or geography. Other areas were archaeology, art, cultural history, design, education, general and local history, nature and science studies.

It was not until 1884 that George Eastman patented the roll film system; consequently, collections begun prior to this time solely depended upon the lantern slide which is a 3¼" x 4" glass slide with glass used as the medium upon which the image is printed. Originally, lantern slides which date from the seventeenth century were hand-painted and many were works of art in their own right. Prominent collections of these early lantern slides can be examined at the Library of Congress and the George Eastman House in Rochester, New York.

The American Museum of Natural History of New York City was one of the early promoters of museum instruction to the public and by 1900, it was providing lantern slides, filmstrips and other teaching materials to the schools, (Saettler, 1968, p. 87). By 1923, the Chicago department of visual education had built a slide library totalling 85,000 slides (ibid., p. 155).

In the 1930s color dye processes were perfected by Leopold D. Mannes and Leopold Godowsky, Jr. in collaboration with the Kodak Research Laboratory. The result of this work was the introduction of the Kodachrome three-color film process. Until the perfection of this particular technique, 35mm or 2" x 2" slides were not widely accepted. Although the period of growth of slide libraries begins in 1880, the most significant number of collections were established between 1930 and 1960. This increase was very likely due to both the added benefit of color slides and to the fact that they were, and still are, less expensive to produce than standard lantern slides. Consequently, it was financially feasible for colleges, museums, schools, public libraries, and universities to have begun their collections at that time. These birth trends might also be indicative of the steady rise of art history studies as more than a mere humanities adjunct to the liberal arts education in the United States.

The wide range of subjects of early slide collections was not unusual in light of the immediate acceptance and consequent exploitation of the full teaching potential of this medium. Moreover, the study of fine arts itself is multidisciplinary and includes research in history, literature, philosophy, religion, and the sciences. By the 1960s there were over 5,000 art, historical, and science museums in the United States and Canada and thousands of colleges and universities which included the arts in their humanities programs. Slides have readily adapted to lecture programs of all types and with the advent of the Kodachrome 35mm three-color film process, they have been well within the financial and physical constraints of

1

institutions desiring to build a slide library. Teachers, librarians, and students could easily take slides while vacationing or on research trips thereby developing art, travel, or geography collections. In addition, most science, historical and art museums have slides available of their collections and these could also be obtained by beginning slide libraries.

Today, the utilization of slides is a fundamental and integral part of every visual arts curriculum on the college, art school, and university level. The majority of art museums have slide collections which are heavily used by the curatorial staff for group lectures and by nearby academic institutions which may have inadequate collections. For example, the Chicago Art Institute and the Metropolitan Museum of Art have slide loan procedures (fees are charged on either an institutional or individual basis) for institutions within their areas. In addition, the general public borrow slides from museums and in some cases from academic institutions for community programs and for private use. Only a few public libraries have slide collections available for loan purposes. These include the Cincinnati and Hamilton County Public Library, the Enoch Pratt Free Library of Maryland, the Minneapolis Public Library and the Newark Public Library. With the exception of public libraries, the majority of educational institutions utilize slides.

Administration of the early visual resource libraries was given minimal attention. More often than not, such collections as slides, photographs, architectural drawings and maps were begun in a non-library situation by people who gathered materials in a haphazard manner. Slide collections in most United States colleges and universities were initiated by the art faculty to illustrate lectures. These collections were often small, consisting of several boxes of slides relating to only a few specialized subject areas. Because of the size of these collections and the limited demands and size of the faculty, it was generally assumed that these incipient slide libraries required minimal supervision and attention to basic library principles such as cataloging and classification. Generally, part-time students in a department aided the faculty in the performance of clerical tasks. When the collection expanded to burdensome proportions, a full-time person, usually with a visual arts background but rarely with library training, was hired. Occasionally, the collection was actually established within the library so that professional supervision was automatically instigated. Approximately 20% of the academic and museum collections surveyed indicated that their collections were initially supervised by a professional—an individual with a graduate or undergraduate equivalent degree in library science or in art history. The majority of the professionally degreed supervisors had a background in library science rather than in art. Museums were more likely to have begun their slide collections under the supervision of the library because it provided a natural location for the organization and development of a collection for the entire museum staff's use. In some instances on the academic level when the art library was physically a part of an art department, this collection was also placed under the librarian's jurisdiction. It is interesting to note that of the 101 collections returning a completed questionnaire, 19 responded that their collections began under professional guidance. The following list ranks those institutions by the beginning date of origin of their slide libraries.

Massachusetts Institute of		National Gallery of Art	1941
Technology	c. 1900	Indiana State University	1950
Princeton University	c. 1900	Miami University, Ohio	1952
University of Rochester	c. 1900	University of California,	
Chicago Art Institute	c. 1904	Los Angeles	1953
Rhode Island School of Design	1915	University of California, Davis	1955
Cleveland Museum of Art	1916	University of California,	
Grinnell College	c. 1920	Riverside	1956
Indianapolis Museum of Art		University of California,	
(formerly Herron Museum of Art)	c. 1920	Santa Cruz	1966
City Art Museum of St. Louis	c. 1925	Elmhurst College	1967
Cincinnati Art Museum	1937	School of Visual Arts, New York	1967

Although only a total of twelve museums responded to the survey, half of these noted professional administration of their collections during the initial stages of development.

Table 1 illustrates the relationships which exist among art schools, colleges, museums and universities regarding the age, initial and present staffing, and the size of the slide collection. Individual institutions are not identified because the status of an individual collection may differ from one year to the next particularly in size and professional staffing. Instead, the information provided is intended as a general indication of how collection size affects the size of its staff. Another factor which greatly affects staff size is the expansion rate of the slide library. Individual institutions tend to use different methods for recording their growth rate; consequently, such information could not also be included for comparison purposes. Moreover, a given collection may undergo rapid growth within a given year which does not reflect its normal expansion pattern. What is indicated by the table is that 50% of the institutions surveyed have a full-time professional staff (with graduate library and/or art history degrees), 85% employ a part-time staff ranging from one to twenty-one employees, and 50% maintain collections of over 50,000 slides.

Today, with the emphasis on instructional media centers, it is generally considered more desirable to administer and maintain all audiovisual collections in one location to avoid duplication of equipment, facilities and staff than to disperse them throughout an institution. With the general resistance of the librarian in the past to accept the role of nonbook materials as basic and necessary to a library, it was natural that these collections originated within the proximity of the user rather than the professional administrator such as a librarian. Although this guide is primarily concerned with slides, they cannot be divorced from their relationship to filmstrips, phonorecords and other media which can be used in conjunction with slides and which all should be housed and administered in the manner most advantageous to the user, whether a museum curator, a university professor, or a student.

LITERATURE SURVEY

Slide libraries like other audiovisual resource collections have suffered from general neglect in the literature until very recently. The earliest study in visual education was a survey by F. Dean McClusky entitled "The Administration of Visual

Relationships Between Institutional Type, Age, Initial and Present Staffing and Collection Size

TABLE 1. Collections Established from 1880 to 1930

Institution	Date Est.	Staff When Est.	PRESENT STAFF					PT No.	Size
			Professional			Clerical			
			Degree	No.	F	Degree	No.		
U	1880	F	-	-	-	BA	1	5	150,000
U	1880s	F	L	1	-	-	-	3	55,000
C	1890	F	-	-	-	BA	1	3	80,000
C	1892	F	-	-	-	BA	2	3	48,000
U	1900	PR/L	H	1	-	BA	2	3	90,000
U	1900	F	H	1	-	BA	3	-	160,000
C	1900	F	-	-	-	-	-	2	20,500
U	1900s	F	-	-	-	BA	1	1	40,000
M	1904	PR/L	H L	2 2	-	NC	2	5	82,000
M	1905	PT/CL	H	1	-	BA	2	2	70,000
C	1905-8	F	H	1	-	-	-	10	100,000
M	1907	PT/CL	H	4	-	BA	1	9	270,000
C	1910	F	-	-	-	NC	1	2	47,000
U	1910	F	-	-	-	BA	1	2	90,000
U	1911	F	H L	1 1	-	BA	2	4	135,000
U	1911	F	-	-	-	BA	1	3	100,000
U	1914	F	H L	1 1	-	BA	2	7	93,000
C	1915	CL	BA	1	-	-	-	9	60,000
AS	1915	PR/L	-	-	-	BA	2	-	46,000
M	1916	PR/L	H L	1 1	-	BA	4	9	140,000
C	1917	F	-	-	-	BA	1	4	130,000
M	1920	PR/L	L	1	-	-	-	-	22,000
C	1920	F + PR/L	-	-	-	-	-	2	22,500
U	1920	F	H	1	-	-	-	10	100,000
U	1920s	F	-	-	2	-	-	10	22,000
U	1920s	PT/CL	H	1	-	NC	1	4	90,000
C	1920s	F	-	-	-	BA	1	4	92,000
U	1923	F	L	1	-	-	-	2	137,000
U	1924	CL	L	2	-	BA	3	6	170,000
U	1925	F	-	-	-	BA NC	2 1	4	119,000
M	1925	PR/L	-	-	-	-	-	1/L	11,000
U	1926	F	-	-	-	NC	1	1	15,500
U	1927	CL	L	1	-	BA	1	4	170,000
U	1927	F	-	-	-	-	-	3 1/L	20,000
M	1930	UNK	L	2	-	NC	1	1	36,500
U	1930	PT/CL	H	1	-	-	-	UNK	200,000
U	1930s	F	-	-	-	BA	1	1	90,000

TABLE 2. Collections Established from 1931 to 1950

Institution	Date Est.	Staff When Est.	PRESENT STAFF Professional Degree	No.	F	Clerical Degree	No.	PT No.	Size
C	1931	UNK	-	-	-	NC	1	2	37,000
C	1933	PT/CL	-	-	-	BA	1	none	14,000
U	1934	F	-	-	-	BA	1	15-20	300,000
U	1935	F	H	1	-	-	-	9	100,000
U	1935	F	L	1	-	L	1	10	190,000
U	1935	F	-	-	-	BA	3	1	66,000
U	1935	F	L	1	-	-	1	3	50,000
U	1935	F	H	1	-	-	-	17	94,000
M	1937	PR/L	L	1	-	BA	1	-	20,000
C	1938	F	-	-	1	BA	1	3	95,000
U	1938	F	H	1	-	-	-	4	130,000
U	1938	F	-	-	-	BA	1	-	20,000
U	1938	F	H	1	-	BA	2	15	85,000
M	1939	CL	H	2	-	BA	2	6	89,000
U	1940	F	H	1	-	BA	1	5	34,000
						NC	1		
AS	1940	F	-	-	1	-	-	3	25,000
M	1941	PR/BA	BA	1	-	-	-	1	53,000
C	1943	F	0	1	-	-	-	4	33,000
U	1946	F	-	-	1	-	-	3	35,000
U	1947	F	-	-	-	BA	1	3	100,000
U	1947	F	H	1	-	-	1	21	106,000
U	1948	F	-	-	-	BA	1	11	35,000
U	1948	F	-	-	-	BFA	1	4	65,000
U	1948	F	-	-	-	NC	4	1	60,000
AS	1949	PR/H	-	-	-	-	-	1/L	10,000
U	1950	CL	H	1	-	-	-	3	33,000
AS	1950	UNK	-	-	-	-	-	3	15,000
U	1950	PR/O	PR/O	1	-	-	1	-	2,000
U	1950s	PR/L	L	1	-	BA	2	-	25,000
U	1950s	PT/CL	H	2	-	-	-	12	75,000

TABLE 3. Collections Established from 1951 to 1967

Institution	Date Est.	Staff When Est.	PRESENT STAFF Professional Degree	No.	F	Clerical Degree	No.	PT No.	Size
U	1951	F	H	1	-	-	-	7	70,000
U	1952	CL	L	1	-	-	-	3	55,000
U	1952	PR/L	H	2	-	-	-	2	24,000
U	1953	F	-	1	-	-	-	5	45,000
U	1953	F	H	1	-	-	-	9	60,000
U	1953	CL	H	1	-	BA	1	5	164,000
U	1953-5	F	-	-	-	-	-	2	46,000
U	1954	F	-	-	-	MFA	2	5	34,000
U	1955	F	-	-	-	-	1	12	33,000

TABLE 3. (Cont'd)

Institution	Date Est.	Staff When Est.	PRESENT STAFF Professional Degree	No.	F	Clerical Degree	No.	PT No.	Size
U	1956	PR/H	-	-	-	BA	1	5	50,000
M	1956	PR/O	-	-	-	BA	1	-	40,000
M	1957	PT/CL	H	1	-	-	-	-	11,000
			L	1					
U	1958	F	L	1	-	-	-	4	50,000
U	1959	F	L	1	-	-	-	3	10,000
U	1959	F	-	-	-	BA	1	3	37,000
AS	1959	F	H	1	-	-	2	2	95,000
U	1959	F	H	1	-	-	-	3	30,300
AS	1959	CL	-	-	-	BA	1	-	40,000
C	1959	F	L	1	-	-	UNK	UNK	16,000
U	1959	PT/CL	H	1	-	BA	1	2	12,000
AS	1960	F	-	-	1	BFA	1	-	2,500
AS	1960	UNK	L	1	-	-	-	1	20,000
U	1961	PT/CL	L	1	-	-	1	3	50,000
M	1961	CL	-	-	-	MFA	1	5	5,500
AS	1963	F	-	-	-	-	2	1	48,000
U	1964	F	-	-	-	-	-	1	15,500
C	1964	UNK	L	1	-	-	2	2	20,000
			H	1					
U	1965	F	-	-	1	BA	1	5	52,000
U	1966	PR/L	L+H	1	-	BA	1	3	58,000
U	1966	F	H	1	-	-	-	5	76,000
AS	1967	PT/CL	-	-	-	-	-	1	1,000
AS	1967	F	-	-	-	BFA	1	-	6,000
C	1967	PR/L	L	1	-	-	-	2	6,000
U	1967	F	H	1	-	-	-	5	15,000

Key to Abbreviations Used in Table

AS	art school	L	librarian/graduate library degree
C	college	MFA	master of fine arts degree
M	museum	NC	no college degree
U	university	O	other professional degree, e.g.,
BA	bachelor's degree		master's degree in education
BFA	bachelor of fine arts degree	PT	part-time
CL	clerical	PR	professional
F	faculty	UNK	unknown
H	graduate degree in art history		

Education: A National Survey" which is an unpublished report made to the National Education Association in 1924 (Saettler, 1968, p. 154). City school systems were analyzed in McClusky's report. One of the conclusions of this report was that in 1923, slides were the most widely used visual media (ibid., p. 155). Although slides were widely used by 1923 and even though Melvil Dewey had applauded their use in a 1906 article in *Public Libraries* (1906, p. 10), the literature in general did not offer an abundance of information on these early collections. Two of the earliest articles of note were by E. L. Lucas (1930) of the Fogg Art Museum Library, Harvard University, and L. E. Kohn (1932) of the Chicago Art Institute. Both discussed the classification of their respective collections. Miss Kohn especially emphasized the treatment of slides in a similar manner as books by making a title page for slides as part of the cataloging process (1932).

As a logical consequence of the development of the three-color film process in the 1930s accompanied by the widespread emergence of slide libraries, papers concentrating on the production methods for slides sporadically began to appear in the literature. In 1943, the controversy between the merits of the color 35mm slide and the black and white lantern slide was argued by two art historians in the *College Art Journal* (Beam, 1943; Carpenter, 1943). Although almost 30 years old, these articles are relevant today because many slide librarians and curators are still faced with problems of using lantern slides, dispensing with them, buying them or producing them (on roll film). The film discussed in the two papers mentioned above was Kodachrome which is the color film most commonly used in academic slide collections today.

Margaret Rufsvold pointed out in 1949 that "The literature of the audio-visual field is especially rich in its treatment of the classroom uses of media. However, little attention has been given to the reference uses of these materials in the library by individuals or groups. Also neglected is the whole field of cataloguing, organizing, and distributing audio-visual materials according to standard library practices." (Rufsvold, 1949, p. III). The slide was no exception to this pattern. The next two decades, however, would help to fill this vacuum.

By the 1950s the color 35mm slide was established as an important and necessary part of a slide library. Several articles among many discussed the relative ease of building a 35mm slide library placing special emphasis on the economy factor of these slides (Bibler, 1955; Bridaham, 1951; Ellis, 1959; Walker, 1953). Another area of concern at this time was the classification, filing, and general retrieval problems associated with slide collections (Perusse, 1954; Tselos, 1959; Walker, 1957). Several general audiovisual cataloging manuals of note also appeared at this time which included the treatment of slides, especially those by Virginia Clarke (1953) and Eunice Keen (1955). The finest general overview of the problems encountered in handling slide and photograph collections was written by Phyllis Reinhardt in 1959, who was the Art Librarian at Yale University at that time (1959). She discussed the general characteristics of these collections, the importance of developing a quality collection, cataloging and classification, methods used at Yale, and staff training. Hers was one of the first papers to stress the critical need for a properly trained professional to supervise these collections.

The major emphasis in the 1960s was on classification and cataloging problems. Slide libraries came of age as they entered the computer era. During this period, an art, history and science slide and picture classification system was devised by Wendell Simons and Mrs. Luraine Tansey at the University of

California at Santa Cruz. A preliminary edition of their work was issued in 1969; the final edition was published in 1970 (Simons and Tansey, 1970). A revised edition by Mrs. Tansey is pending publication. The Metropolitan Museum of Art slide classification is also in preparation.

While the Santa Cruz system was being developed on the West Coast, individuals on the East Coast were also making contributions to research in this field. Elizabeth Lewis (1969) of the United States Military Academy Library at West Point and Boris Kuvshinoff (1967) of Johns Hopkins University discussed two methods of establishing a visual aid card catalog that could be used manually and by machine indexing. In addition, Robert M. Diamond (1969) of the College of Fredonia, State University of New York, developed a retrieval system for 35mm slides used in the arts and humanities. Audiovisual cataloging and organization manuals that include slides also enjoyed the publication boom (Colvin, 1963; Gambee, 1967; Harris, 1968; Hicks, 1967; Hopkinson, 1963; Strout, 1966; Weihs, 1973; Westhuis, 1967).

INTRODUCTION TO MANAGEMENT, ORGANIZATION AND STAFFING

Many of the problems encountered in managing, organizing, and staffing slide libraries are endemic to audiovisual collections. Initially such materials may have been ignored but the general profundity of nonprint media and their acceptance by instructional systems have created a demand for making them accessible in a manner suited to the medium. Such modes of accessibility have not always been strictly aligned with traditional handling of print materials by libraries. The fragility of lantern or glass slides, the small size of 35mm slides, the difficulty of circulating and housing single slides and the absence of viable systems for organizing slides based upon subject content have forced many educators and librarians either to avoid slides or to treat them in a rather perfunctory manner. At the same time, however, their flexibility as a teaching tool, relatively low cost and ease of production have sustained them as a popular instructional medium. A field which has maintained consistent and heavy use of slides is the fine arts; consequently, it is not surprising that the majority of slide libraries flourish in academic art departments and museums.

Although many other audiovisual materials have been integrated within library collections (filmstrips, phono recordings and tapes in the last ten years), slides, while predating many of these media, are not commonly held and maintained by academic libraries. To compensate for the unavailability of slides, users began developing their own collections in academic departments or schools usually acquiring part-time clerical or student assistance as the collection expanded. This pattern of clerical staffing continues to present a major bottleneck in the establishment of professional management of slide libraries because it has tended to obscure the distinctions between professional, clerical and technical duties and responsibilities. By contrast, slide libraries in art museums usually come under the management of the museum librarian or a professional slide librarian.

Although a single full-time clerical employee may be in charge of a slide library, additional part-time staff are usually required to meet user demands on a daily, weekly or monthly basis. Characteristic of slide libraries is rapid expansion which allows the collection to double or triple within a period of five years or less. Commonly, such expansion is accompanied by the hiring of more part-time staff rather than by a general review and analysis of changed staffing needs required by the size of the collection and by the increase in users which usually parallels collection growth. As this pattern continues, both the slide library staff and its parent faculty (or museum curatorial staff) begin to recognize that the collection has become increasingly complex in its coverage of a single field, that the original cursory approach to cataloging and classification is no longer adequate, and that more sophisticated records and techniques are needed to maintain control of the collection. Training in the principles of administration, organization, and retrieval and storage of instructional resources is required. Unfortunately, holdings of many collections exceed 50,000 slides before an attempt is made to resolve problems created by inadequate cataloging and classification systems, by the absence of standard library techniques and tools, and by insufficient staffing. Continued management by an individual with minimal qualifications (a bachelor's degree in a subject field without professional graduate training) and by part-time rather than full-time support staff rarely provides the opportunities to overcome the problems cited. Occasionally, dedicated individuals on a clerical level will rise to the demands of both the collection and the users and develop a surprisingly sophisticated system for organizing and maintaining the library. Sound management patterns, however, should be based on more than serendipity.

Today, professional staffs manage most collections of more than 50,000 slides. Graduate degrees in library science and/or a subject field such as art history represent the backgrounds of professional slide librarians. Current trends indicate that more and more developing and established slide collections are requiring the expertise provided by advanced degrees both in library science and in a subject field. Although subject training is needed for cataloging collections focusing on a single area, such preparation does not coincidentally prepare an individual to manage a slide library. Training for slide librarianship requires a background in administration, cataloging and classification principles, handling audiovisual collections, information science, reference and selection. Computer applications and data processing techniques are being incorporated into the operations of many slide libraries thereby requiring a greater degree of information processing sophistication by individuals managing these collections. All such training is commonly available in library schools. Many library schools, however, still lack fully-developed programs on nonprint materials. In order to compensate for the absence of courses on the handling of nonprint materials, prospective slide librarians must seek courses in departments of education which emphasize the acquisition and selection of audiovisual media. The high degree of professional specialization also requires resident training in a major slide library (100,000 slides or more) under professional management. One of the major problems confronting individuals seeking training for slide librarianship is the lack of formalized programs specifically designed for special libraries coupled with the meager nonprint media course offerings by library schools. Fortunately, many schools are beginning to alter their curriculums to meet the needs of librarians who intend to work with audiovisual collections. As more and more individuals demand curricular inclusion of courses and training in handling audiovisual materials, such programs will become an integral part of preparation for librarianship. Chapter 2 provides a basis for professional, clerical and technical staff classifications for slide libraries.

Indicative of their beginnings in academic art departments, slide libraries are typically organized according to a classification based upon broad media classes, art history periods, country or geographical areas and artist entries for painting and sculpture. For architecture, after the main class divisions, buildings are usually organized by type under site or location entries. Initially, such a system sounds deceptively simple. What is generally missing, however, are authority files which prevent the misfiling of an artist under several variations of his name, under different nationalities, or within more than one historical period. Historians commonly argue about the beginning of one period, the end of another, and which artforms can be classed in one rather than another era. As long as a collection is small, broad general categories suffice but as soon as there are more than one hundred slides on a given artist, building or artform, the problems begin. Defining subject categories, dating works for chronological divisions under artist, and determining media types, particularly for contemporary artists, pose complicated questions for anyone not trained to understand theories of classifying and cataloging information. As one grapples with the major media, the decorative arts provide yet another range of possibilities for classification and cataloging. What should the main entry be—century, country, artform or media, location, i.e., libraries or museums for illuminated manuscripts and so forth.

Slide sets, as is the case with filmstrips, usually adapt to the standard systems of classification (Dewey Decimal and Library of Congress classifications) and basic subject heading lists. For in-depth collections of slides on a single topic, however, a corresponding classification and cataloging approach is needed which directly deals with the visual content of each image. In an attempt to determine systems which would adapt to the classification and cataloging of artforms, academic institutions and museums—although occasionally sharing systems—usually try to break new ground by developing their own classification schedules. As a consequence of such diverse and dispersed efforts, many institutions lack a unified and coherent classification and cataloging system. Although most do have systems which have a similar structure—media, period, artist or site arrangement—the implementation of that structure varies in sophistication from one collection to another. Chapters 3 and 4 focus on the similarities of classification and cataloging approaches and on those library techniques and tools which, if consistently utilized, offer valid alternatives and recommendations for the organization of slide libraries.

Problems in the acquisition and selection of slides reflect the absence of published selection tools and guides. Although the Metropolitan Museum of Art has provided a list of commercial and museum distributors and producers, free of charge upon request, for a number of years at least half of the individuals running slide libraries are not aware of this source. Operating in an institutional vacuum has not been a conducive environment for informed collection building. At the same time, however, the general absence of published information about slide libraries would not have generated an optimistic view toward inquiry. Fortunately, this condition is changing. Publication activity and increased communication among slide librarians through meetings of the College Art Association are helping to provide both the developing and newly established slide collections with sources which identify and evaluate slide distributors and producers. These sources are listed in the bibliography under the heading "Acquisition and Selection—Slides."

Another aspect of acquisition is the local production of slides in academic departments, campus audiovisual centers and museum photography divisions.

Although there is a plethora of publications on producing slides, much of this literature seems to have been overlooked by individuals in slide collections having responsibility for local production. All too frequently, inadequate facilities have been set up with the individual managing the collection also expected to shoot and develop slides. This diversity of roles is indicative of the previously cited lack of distinction between the character of the various functions performed in slide libraries. Many campuses have local production centers which should be more consistently utilized for slide production. What is again plaguing slide collections is their isolation within academic departments which has prevented broad-based solutions which are economical and effective. Reliance upon centralized production services may not even be considered a viable alternative to departmental slide production although it has been successfully implemented by a number of collections, e.g., Miami University, Pennsylvania State University and Yale University. The bibliography on acquisition and production of slides brings together many of the publications which will provide slide librarians a basis for making informed production and selection decisions. In addition, the text of Chapter 5 indicates the range of possibilities available for acquiring slides.

Another area which appears relatively simple at first glance is that of the selection of slide storage. This topic has received little attention in the literature and as a consequence, decisions on housing slides frequently do not take into full account the expansion schedule and organizational and use patterns which individual collections will have. Again, rather than planning the development of slide libraries on short- and long-term projections, many untrained individuals managing slide libraries make hasty decisions based upon what appear to be immediate expansion problems. The type of storage selected for slides has many ramifications for the use of the collection and can affect the implementation of organizational techniques such as interfiled shelflists and coordinated circulation systems. Unless unlimited funds are available for trying out a number of different storage facilities, the selection of slide cabinets should be based upon a critical examination of the development of a given collection and its future requirements. At the same time, however, several modes of housing may prove more practical than absolute adherence to the constraints of one type of facility. For example, a single library may have sets of slides stored in projector trays ready for classroom use, single slides filed individually in drawers, and a special collection on a given topic on visual display rack cabinets for immediate visual access.

Blame for not making informed decisions on slide storage, however, cannot be readily placed on individuals managing slide libraries. Listings of furniture for slide collections have been relatively non-existent. Except for occasional ads in photography magazines, an individual seeking information about slide cabinets was forced to conduct time-consuming correspondence surveys with other institutions to determine the various types of slide housing facilities. What may work well for one collection may not adapt readily to the needs of another. Chapter 6 and the "Directory of Distributors and Manufacturers of Equipment and Slide Supplies" provide a framework for the acquisition and selection of filing and storage cabinets for slides.

As slide collections expand, staffs enlarge, and users increase, corners of faculty or administrative offices or closet-sized spaces in museums and academic departments prove totally inadequate for a functioning collection. Requisites for designing slide library facilities in terms of standardized space needs based upon functions performed have been generally neglected in the literature. With the exception of a single paper on the slide library of the Metropolitan Museum of Art, no other publication has ever focused on this topic (Nolan, 1972, pp. 101-103). Rooms, corners, closets—any space which could accommodate a desk, viewers, and cabinets defined the physical environment of the slide library. Of course, the term "library" was rarely associated with the early modest quarters occupied by many collections. Like the acquisition, organization, staffing and storage patterns of these incipient libraries, the physical area represented as minimal an allocation as possible. Of course, such areas may have proved quite adequate during the development of the collection but like many of the other problems facing slide librarians, the physical facility for the collection in many instances remained too small with resulting inadequate arrangements to meet the demands which users place both on the staff and the slides. Guidelines for planning and designing slide library facilities are discussed in some detail in Chapter 7. The emphasis in this section is on the functions of slide libraries and the effect of user patterns on selection of furniture and equipment. A suggested building program and sample floor plans provide specific examples of slide library facilities.

Chapters 8 and 9 deal with the infinite variety of special equipment and supplies needed for slide libraries. Because of the numerous publications on projectors and projection systems, Chapter 8 is intended to complement the available literature and to offer a coherent picture of alternatives and selection considerations. Fortunately, projectors are frequently maintained by campus services or by photography departments in museums so that slide librarians are not always responsible for such equipment. At the same time, they should be aware of equipment types, and how projectors influence the general quality of projected slides. Purchasing inadequate projectors and producing high quality slides are not compatible functions for effective use of slides.

Various types of viewers, light tables, and magnifiers are necessary for slide preview in the slide library. Slide mounts, file guides, portable screens and carrying cases are also among the variety of supplies and equipment utilized. Such equipment and supplies are within the acquisition jurisdiction of the slide librarian who needs to be aware of the market options in all areas which affect slide library management.

The designing, equipping, managing, organizing and staffing of any library are not simple tasks but problems encountered in traditional libraries are compounded in audiovisual collections. Certainly, these problems are not insurmountable. First, a general recognition and examination of operable procedures currently practiced is necessary. Second, an explanation of how such operations and procedures can be standardized making use of standard library techniques and tools should be provided. Third, through the subsequent realization of the complexities involved and expertise necessary to manage a slide library, professional, clerical and technical staffing patterns can be developed. Fourth, the increase in and use of published guides for slide librarians will offer a basis for informed decision making which is critical to the effective management of these collections. Fifth, and outside the scope of this work, is the need for a strong professional association, affiliated with existing organizations, which will provide a forum for presenting issues and recommendations affecting the management, organization and staffing of slide libraries.

REFERENCES

BEAM, P. C. "Color Slide Controversy." *College Art Journal*, 2:35-38 (January 1943).

BIBLER, Richard. "Make an Art Slide Library." *Design*, 56:105, 128 (January 1955).

BRIDAHAM, L. B., and MITCHELL, C. B. "Successful Duplication of Color Slides; Results of Research at the Chicago Art Institute." *College Art Journal*, 10:261-263 (Spring 1951).

CARPENTER, J. M. "Limitations of Color Slides." *College Art Journal*, 2:38-40 (January 1943).

CLARKE, Virginia. *Non-Book Library Materials: A Handbook of Procedures for a Uniform and Simplified System of Handling Audio-Visual Aids, Vertical File, and Other Non-Book Materials in the School Library.* Denton, Texas: Labratory School Library, North Texas State College and North Texas State College Print Shop, 1953.

COLVIN, Laura C. *Cataloging Sampler: A Comparative and Interpretive Guide.* Hamden, Connecticut: Shoe String Press, 1963.

DEWEY, Melvil. "Library Pictures." *Public Libraries*, 11:10 (1906).

DIAMOND, Robert M. *The Development of a Retrieval System for 35mm Slides Utilized in Art and Humanities Instruction.* Washington, D.C.: Bureau of Research, Office of Education, U.S. Department of Health, Education, and Welfare, 1969. (Final Report, Project No. 8-B-080).

ELLIS, Shirley. "Thousand Words About the Slide." *A.L.A. Bulletin*, 53:529-532 (June 1959).

GAMBEE, Budd L. *Non-Book Materials As Library Resources.* Chapel Hill: The Student Stores, University of North Carolina, 1967. (Bibliographies for Chapters 1, 2, 4, and 5 were revised June 1970).

HARRIS, Evelyn J. *Instructional Materials Cataloging Guide.* Tucson, Arizona: Bureau of Educational Research and Service, College of Education, the University of Arizona, 1968.

HICKS, Warren B., and TILLIN, Alma B. *The Organization of Nonbook Materials in School Libraries.* Sacramento, California: California State Department of Education, 1967.

HOPKINSON, Shirley L. *The Descriptive Cataloging of Library Materials.* San Jose, California: San Jose State College, Claremont House, 1963.

KEEN, Eunice. *Manual for Use in the Cataloging and Classification of Audio-Visual Materials for a High School Library.* Lakeland, Florida: Lakeland High School, 1955.

KOHN, L. E. "A Photograph and Lantern Slide Catalog in the Making." *Library Journal*, 57:941-945 (1932).

KUVSHINOFF, B. W. "A Graphic Graphics Card Catalog and Computer Index." *American Documentation*, 18:3-9 (January 1967).

LEWIS, Elizabeth M. "A Graphic Catalog Card Index." *American Documentation*, 20:238-246 (July 1969).

LUCAS, E. Louise. "The Classification and Care of Pictures and Slides." *A.L.A. Bulletin*, 24:382-385 (1930).

NOLAN, Margaret P. "The Metropolitan Museum of Art—Slide Library." *Planning the Special Library*. Edited by Ellis Mount. New York: Special Libraries Association, 1972.

PERUSSE, L. F. "Classifying and Cataloguing Lantern Slides." *Journal of Cataloguing and Classification*, 10:77-83 (April 1954).

REINHARDT, Phyllis A. "Photograph and Slide Collections in Art Libraries." *Special Libraries*, 50:97-102 (March 1959).

RUFSVOLD, Margaret I. *Audio-Visual School Library Service: A Handbook for Librarians*. Chicago: American Library Association, 1949.

SAETTLER, Paul. *A History of Instructional Technology*. New York: McGraw-Hill, 1968.

SIMONS, Wendell W., and TANSEY, Luraine C. *A Slide Classification System for the Organization and Automatic Indexing of Interdisciplinary Collections of Slides and Pictures*. Santa Cruz, California: University of California, 1970.

STROUT, Ruth French. *Organization of Library Materials II*. Madison, Wisconsin: University Extension Division, University of Wisconsin, 1966.

TSELOS, Dimitri. "A Simple Slide Classification System." *College Art Journal*, 18:344-349 (Summer 1959).

WALKER, Lester C., Jr. "Low Cost Slide Production for Teaching Aids." *College Art Journal*, 13:39-41 (Fall 1953).

WALKER, Lester C., Jr. "Slide Filing and Control." *College Art Journal*, 16:325-329 (Summer 1957).

WEIHS, Jean Riddle, LEWIS, Shirley, and MacDONALD, Janet. In consultation with the CLA/ALA/AECT/EMAC/CAML Advisory Committee on the Cataloguing of Nonbook Materials. *Non-Book Materials: The Organization of Integrated Collections*. 1st ed. Ottawa, Canada: The Canadian Library Association, 1973.

WESTHUIS, Judith Loveys, and DeYOUNG, Julia M. *Cataloging Manual for Nonbook Materials in Learning Centers and School Libraries*. Rev. ed. Ann Arbor, Michigan: Association of School Librarians, The Bureau of School Services, The University of Michigan, 1967.

2–ADMINISTRATION AND STAFFING

INTRODUCTION

The administration and staffing of a slide library varies depending upon whether the collection is under the jurisdiction of an instructional materials center on the academic level, a departmental or library system of a college or university, or an art school or museum. Because the instructional materials center concept has not been fully implemented as an efficient *modus operandi* for media organization, it is still necessary to discuss the administration and staffing of a slide library within varying institutional contexts. What are the functions of the chief administrator and his staff? Before administration and staffing can be discussed, this question must be answered.

According to Robert De Kieffer, Director of the Bureau of Audiovisual Instruction at the University of Colorado, there are "five primary functions and four secondary functions in any educational program:

Primary functions:	Secondary functions:
1. Informing	1. Reporting
2. Educating and training	2. Recommending
3. Supplying	3. Cooperating
4. Producing	4. Evaluating"
5. Assisting	(1965, p. 100).

Informing is the process of making teachers and other users aware of "the types of audiovisual materials, equipment, facilities, and services available to them." The second function involves *educating* teachers and users in the use of media. *Supplying*, and *producing* audiovisual materials, and *assisting* users or teachers in how to use media are the remaining primary functions outlined by De Kieffer. The secondary functions include *reporting* on present and long-term needs, *cooperating* with the various areas within a system so that coordination of objectives is possible, and *evaluating* methods of operation and the overall effectiveness of a program (ibid., 1965, pp. 101-103).

If a slide library is part of an instructional materials or media center within a larger organization such as a college, the general director of the center will be assuming the functions defined by De Kieffer, and will be delegating his authority to accomplish those functions when appropriate. If slides are located within a department or branch of a library, academic complex or museum, the individual in charge of that branch or department may be responsible for these functions and for their delegation to subordinate staff members. Of course, there is always the possibility of a collection growing and expanding without any directional guidance so that its functions often reflect its haphazard expansion pattern. In the majority of academic slide libraries in the United States, the collections began in such a manner. Slides were necessary to support the teaching of art, thereby forcing the faculty to develop their own private or departmental collections which they initially organized or turned over to clerical or student supervision. As a consequence, if any of the functions defined by De Kieffer were performed, it was more by chance than by design. Accidental collection building of this type may have sufficed at the turn of the century but today it is both economically inefficient and administratively unwise. Museum collections have usually developed under the aegis of the museum library although this has not necessarily been the case in art schools which frequently do have their own library facility.

Because of the materials explosion and rapid development of technological competence which has occurred over the past two decades, a collection of slides can double or triple within a year or less. This rapid expansion potential contributed to the immediate need to establish patterns of administration and staffing that both provide short- and long-term solutions to the fulfillment of a collection's primary and secondary functions. For the academic campus system that is working to develop or to maintain an instructional media program, the literature offers both questions and solutions through publications including *Administering Instructional Media Programs* (Erickson, 1968), *Developing Multi-Media Libraries* (Hicks and Tillin, 1970), *Library Uses of the New Media of Communication* (Stone, 1967), *Media Milestones in Teacher Training* (De Kieffer, 1970), and others. Such works have contributed to this chapter's objective to define the professional and supportive staffs of slide libraries and to offer recommendations on administration and staffing.

COLLEGES AND UNIVERSITIES

The majority of slide libraries in the United States were faculty initiated and supervised in academic institutions. As the collections expanded, they became too cumbersome for the faculty to administer on a part-time basis. Full-time staff, usually on the clerical level, was hired to supervise the collection; occasionally, a professional staff member took over the collection. In rare instances, the collection was begun under the direction of a librarian. Although art collections were the primary focus for this study, they do not vary from the general supervision patterns of slides in other academic disciplines. For example, a survey taken at Indiana University revealed the separate development of ten slide collections in addition to the one in the Fine Arts Department. All of these were initiated without professional library supervision and are under part-time faculty or clerical guidance. The demand for slides as a teaching tool speaks for the need to consolidate as much as possible in order to make materials widely available in the most efficient and economic manner. Consolidation through instructional materials or learning resource centers perhaps will be the most advantageous solution to the problem. Particularly in academic communities, large slide collections have developed which are searching for answers to the administrative and staffing problems engendered by their haphazard birth. As C. Walter Stone points out:

> It would seem that the most significant work being done with new media on the college or university campus takes place outside libraries and that, when all types of libraries have been surveyed, only those school programs which have followed an instructional materials center philosophy are demonstrating any significant gains. (1967, p. 179).

As early as 1960, the Standards for Junior College Libraries stressed the importance of audiovisual materials as part of the junior college library concept

(Christensen, 1965). In the same paper on the Standards, the author points out, however, that the concept of incorporating audiovisual materials into the college library program goes back to 1946, "when a postwar planning committee of college and university librarians recommended the library as the 'logical agency to handle these teaching aids.' " (ibid., p. 121). The Standards also include the administration of audiovisual services under the auspices of the library (ibid., p. 128). In an article appearing in the *Junior College Journal* in 1970, the author notes that the 1960 Standards are being revised and that the *Standards for School Media Programs* will certainly be considered as useful for standardization of "terminology, staffing, organization, and services" for library-college media centers (Fusaro, 1970, p. 42). Administration and staffing guidelines have been set forth for public schools in the *Standards for School Media Programs* prepared jointly by the American Library Association and National Education Association (1969). The second chapter of this publication outlines the "Staff and services in the media programs" from the professional staff which includes the "Head of the Media Center" and "media specialist" to the "Supportive staff" which includes "media technicians and media aides" (ibid., 1969, pp. 7-17). In addition, the School Library Manpower Project, *Occupational Definitions for School Library Media Personnel* (1971) and *Jobs in Instructional Media* by the Association of Educational Communications and Technology of the National Education Association (1970) should be examined.

If a college or university is developing a media program or center, then the proper administration of the slide collection belongs to this program under the jurisdiction of the professional and supportive staff. The *Standards for School Media Programs* (1969) amply describe the functions and duties of each type of position and also indicate the training required. With slight modification, many of the principles outlined can be applied to the university or college media center concept. *The Occupational Definitions. . . .* (School Library Manpower Project, 1971), and *Jobs in Instructional Media* (Association for Educational Communications and Technology, 1970), should also be utilized with the Standards. *The Occupational Definitions. . . .* does prefer the use of the term "school library media" rather than "media" so that the "Head of the School Library Media Center" is discussed in the Definitions, while "Head of the Media Center" is used in the *Standards for School Media Programs*. The coordination of this differentiation is left to others but the basic terminology pattern should be recognized and used when applicable.

Large university libraries are rarely involved in the administration of a slide library or for that matter, in the administration of any type of media facility. The following statement represents the conclusions of Fred F. Harcleroad, President of California State College at Hayward, in his article "Learning Resources Approach to College and University Library Development":

> Although the large libraries may have to be separate because of their large book collections and enormous problems of storage and retrieval, ideally there should be some relationship between the other learning resources on the campus and the basic part of the learning resource of any campus, the book and magazine collections. At the present time, however, the most promising organizational developments for using learning resources are taking place outside the library in large research universities, and in a new division of educational services or learning resources which includes the library in smaller, instructionally-oriented colleges and community colleges. (1967, p. 239).

The implications of this splintering of educational resources have certainly played a role in the diversified administration of slide libraries in colleges and universities on the faculty, professional library, and clerical levels. At the present time, however, it is significant that 50% of the more than 100 academic slide libraries documented, indicate that their staffs include individuals on the professional level having graduate library or art degrees administering the collection and receiving commensurate library or administrative rank as part of their positions. For academic collections having more than 50,000 slides, the probability of a professional staff administering the collection is higher with 59% of these larger collections reporting a professional staff while only 31% of collections under 50,000 slides have a professional staff. Institutions such as art schools or colleges also follow this same pattern of staffing dependent upon the size of the collection. At the present time, 35% of the total number of surveyed collections maintain only a clerical staff with a remaining 15% administered by faculty or part-time staffs. Supportive staffing is present in 85% of the collections studied, and includes either full- and/or part-time staffing in addition to the full-time professional and one full-time clerical or supportive staff member with a number of these indicating staffs larger than one professional and one supportive member.

One of the major staffing controversies existing in academic slide libraries is the question of qualifications based on library versus subject versus media training. Should the slide librarian have a graduate degree in a subject area rather than in library science if the collection is composed of slides on a single topic? One of the reasons that this question is frequently asked is that traditional library school programs do not yield much helpful information to individuals desiring to administer media collections of any type. As one prominent professional who heads a slide and photograph library pointed out, "Library school grads usually want to work in a general reference library rather than a slide and photo collection and there is usually not any direct relationship to the program of library science schools and media handling." Many slide librarians or curators lament that "no one will treat it like a library." This is indicative of the casual birth and awkward adolescence which most collections have experienced when professional administration was not present from the collection's inception. Generally, if the collection was started on a professional level by a professional staff, the collection and the staff enjoy a commensurate level of respect.

Another aspect of the nebulous professional and non-professional role of the slide librarian is the profusion of titles given to this individual and to what he is supervising: bibliographic specialist; audiovisual curator; curator of the slide collection; curator of visual resources; director of the section of slides and photographs; slide curator; slide librarian; and slide room supervisor. The collection of slides itself varies in title from slide room to visual resource collection. Frequently, slides and photographs are administered by the same individual so that both slides and photographs are included in the title of the collection and its administrator. The rather strange title, "bibliographic specialist," was used by one institution (University of Pennsylvania) where the slide collection was under the jurisdiction of the university library system. Even in those cases in which a media title is applied, the individuals are rarely under the supervision of a campus media center or program. Although the term curator is most commonly associated with museum staffs, this title was more common to the academic slide library administrator than to the museum slide librarian.

How can these titles be adjusted to the national patterns developed through the Standards and the School Library Manpower Project? In the *Junior College Journal* article which discussed the Standards and the "library-college media center," a pattern of organization and staffing is diagrammed using the Standards staffing terminology when applicable (Fusaro, 1970). The combined title "slide library media specialist" is redundant while "slide librarian" signifies the logical coordination of library plus media expertise necessary to administer a slide collection. If the slide collection is within an academic media center, a media specialist would be the primary supervisor unless slides composed such a major portion of the collection that a specialist in slides only is necessary; therefore, the following administrative hierarchy would prevail: head of the media center, media specialist, slide librarian. Supportive staff for a single slide library could be termed slide library aides and slide library technicians while these individuals functioning in a media center which housed a variety of media including slides would maintain their titles, media technicians and media aides.

ART SCHOOLS AND MUSEUMS

In art schools and museums, the logical location for the administration of the slide collection is within the library. If the institution is unable to hire a full-time slide librarian, the collection should be under the supervision of the professional library staff. Even if the collection is small—less than 50,000 slides—it should be established within the framework of professional administration. Occasional faculty or curatorial supervision is inadequate and places responsibilities and duties on those frequently not qualified and without ample time to administer a visual resource collection. It is the responsibility of the librarian in a museum or art school to be informed about and prepared to administer all learning resources within that institution. If the library and library staff are sufficiently large in relationship to the size of the institution, a professional staff member or members should be made responsible for the slide and photograph collection. It is quite common to have slides and photographs considered as a single collection and administered by the same staff members. As much coordination as possible should be encouraged between the slide and photograph collections. Many of the problems relating to cataloging and classification, authority, source and subject files, and so forth, are common to both media. The same status and benefits of the professional library staffs in art schools and museums should be provided for the professional slide library staff. Qualifications, training and general management functions of slide librarians are the same for academic institutions and for museums.

QUALIFICATIONS FOR PROFESSIONAL STAFF

Training in library science is a necessary aspect of preparation for slide librarianship. Slide collections are highly sophisticated instructional resource libraries which need to be managed and organized for maximum retrieval and utilization. Professional programs in library and information science provide much of the expertise needed for efficient administration and organization. Subject area or clerical training alone are inadequate backgrounds for competent management of a slide library. The library science program should be complemented by courses on the handling of audiovisual materials. Unfortunately, many library schools still have inadequate curriculums on nonprint media. For individuals attending library schools deficient in this area, additional instruction should be acquired through the audiovisual program, offered by schools or departments of education. The majority of library schools, however, do provide curriculum on data processing and computer applications to information management—an area becoming increasingly important to slide librarians. In addition, resident training in a major academic or museum slide library (100,000 slides or more) operated by a full-time professional staff, should be arranged through the library school as part of the specialized professional expertise required for slide librarianship. For collections focusing on a single subject area such as the fine arts, either a bachelor's degree or an additional master's degree in the subject field is desirable. The following is a summary of the training recommended for an individual to qualify as an academic or museum slide librarian:

> master's degree in library science with emphasis on audiovisual materials and information science;
> resident training in a major academic or museum slide library;
> bachelor's degree in relevant subject area or an additional master's degree in a subject area (if applicable).

For large single subject collections requiring several full-time catalogers, the emphasis may be placed on in-depth knowledge of a single field; consequently, a master's degree in a subject area complemented by coursework in library science may be adequate in some instances. If a collection has either a single full-time professional position or a head of the slide library who supervises the work of other full-time staff, these positions should be filled by individuals having the qualifications outlined.

STAFF FUNCTIONS AND STATUS

As noted above, the professional staff should have a coordinated training program providing subject expertise if necessary, and library school and media coursework. The professional staff is responsible for the primary and secondary functions outlined by De Kieffer and those in the *Standards* and *Occupational Definitions.* The supportive staff performs clerical routines such as typing slide labels and guidecards, plus technical tasks such as producing slides. The professional staff includes the following positions: head of the slide library; cataloger(s); and reference librarian(s). Each should be identified as a "slide librarian" with the appropriate position title added to this basic title, e.g., slide librarian, reference. The following titles should be given to the supportive staff: binders; filers, photography technicians, projectionists, and typists. Based upon the tasks performed, each is identified as either a slide library aide or technician.

The professional staff of the slide library should have the following responsibilities and duties:

cataloging and classification of slides which includes:
    development of catalog headings
    development of authority file
    development of shelflist and auxiliary catalogs to the collection
    revision of cataloging and classification system and/or revision of a section or entire
        collection

educating, training and informing the users of the services and equipment available from
    the slide library

providing reference service to the users of the collection

determining and planning the activities of the clerical and technical staff

directing the production of slides by the slide library

selecting and evaluating commercial and museum sources of slides

evaluating the methods of operation

selecting equipment for the slide library

reporting on the long-term and short-term needs of the slide library and recommend-
    ing changes and policy decisions on the operation of the slide library

developing channels of cooperation and communication within a department, college,
    museum or university

The professional staff should have faculty status and salary equivalent to that for
the professional library and/or administrative staff of the college, museum, or
university. The standards for the professional staff and benefits should be no less
than those specified by the new American Association of Junior Colleges and the
Association of College and Research Libraries guidelines for two-year college library
learning resource centers:

> Every professional staff member has faculty status, together with all faculty benefits
> and obligations.
>
> Faculty status for professional staff includes such prerogatives as tenure rights, sick
> leave benefits, sabbatical leaves, vacation benefits, comparable hours of duty, retire-
> ment and annuity benefits, and inclusion on the same salary scale which is in effect
> for faculty members engaged in classroom teaching. Where academic ranks are recog-
> nized, ranks are assigned to the professional staff independent of internal assignments
> within the center based on the same criteria as for other faculty. (AAJC-ACRL Guide-
> lines. . . ., 1971, p. 271).

At the present time, of the 101 collections surveyed and reporting on staffing arrangements, 47 are staffed by a full-time professional. Collections having
100,000 slides or more are staffed with from one to four full-time professionals
having either a graduate degree in library science or in art history. Over 50% of
the major collections have a full-time staff of two or more individuals with one or
more being a professional. Of the 60 collections initiated and staffed by faculty,

27 are now professionally staffed. The progression in these collections has been from faculty to clerical to professional staffing. Although art slide libraries were used to exemplify this trend, collections beginning in other subject areas do not differ radically.

The supportive staff of the slide library should have the following responsibilities and duties:

Slide Library Technicians

making of all materials for the slide library, e.g., color and black and white slides (this individual may be a professional photographer who is on contract to perform this function or a student or part- or full-time employee skilled in slide production; or campus audiovisual services or museum photography departments may perform this function)

maintaining and making available equipment for showing slides (this may be performed by an audiovisual department of a college or university or by the staff of the slide library solely or with the assistance of the campus audiovisual center, and in museums by the photography department)

training slide projectionists, binders, and filers (this function may be performed by the slide library technicians or by slide library aides)

Slide Library Aides

performing circulation routines and record keeping

typing slide labels, correspondence, purchase orders and other slide library records

binding, filing and projecting slides

If the slide library supportive staff is small, there may be an overlap between tasks performed by technicians and aides, although aides should only be expected to assist in such duties normally expected of technicians on a minimal level. If the slide library does not handle its own production and maintenance of equipment, a full-time technician may not be necessary. For every full-time professional, there should be a minimum of one full-time slide library aide. The necessary number of staff members will, of course, depend upon the size of the collection and production and expansion rates.

Unfortunately, at least 50% of the academic collections surveyed are still under the sole administrative supervision of a clerical staff member although many of these individuals have undergraduate degrees in fine arts. An individual with such training, however, cannot be expected to make short- and long-term administrative decisions and guidelines such as those outlined under the duties and responsibilities of a professional staff member should be followed. If the individual hired on a clerical level is able to perform these responsibilities, then the collection, department, and college or university have momentarily enjoyed a propitious staff selection. To expect every clerical hired and paid on a clerical scale to perform on a high professional level is an unreasonable and invalid expectation. A position should not be based upon the qualifications of a temporary staff member but upon an accurate and appropriate job description which defines a position thereby placing it on a professional, clerical, or technical level but *not* on all three simultaneously.

SUMMARY

Whether a slide library exists in an art school, college, museum or university, it should be placed within the logical jurisdiction of other learning resources within that institution. In schools and museums having unified media programs both for print and nonprint materials, slides should be circulated, housed and organized under the general administration of the program's staff. In centralized academic library systems, the slide collection should be administered within a general library setting. For decentralized or branch library systems, the slide collection should function as a branch library under the immediate jurisdiction of a corresponding subject library, i.e., an art slide collection within a fine arts branch library. Although the preceding options are recommended for the administrative placement of a slide collection within academic institutions or museums, organizational patterns which work well for one institution may not be readily adapted to another; consequently, variations to the administrative structure mentioned are possible. For example, a slide library might function on a co-equal basis with other libraries in a given system. In any case, each member of the staff with professional credentials should be titled a slide librarian with commensurate salary, status and benefits provided other professional staff and should be provided the necessary supportive staff to expedite the effective and efficient operation of the library.

REFERENCES

"AAJC-ACRL Guidelines for Two-Year College Library Learning Resource Centers." *College and Research Libraries News*, No. 9:265-278 (October 1971).

American Association of School Librarians and the Department of Audiovisual Instruction of the National Education Association. *Standards for School Media Programs*. Chicago and Washington, D.C.: American Library Association and the National Education Association, 1969.

Association for Educational Communications and Technology. *Jobs in Instructional Media*. Washington, D.C.: Association for Educational Communications and Technology, 1970.

CHRISTENSEN, R. M. "Junior College Library as A-V Center." *College and Research Libraries*, 26:121-128 (March 1965).

De KIEFFER, Robert E. *Audiovisual Instruction*. New York: The Center for Applied Research in Education, Inc., 1965.

De KIEFFER, Robert E., and De KIEFFER, Melissa H. *Media Milestones in Teacher Training*. Washington, D.C.: Educational Media Council, 1970.

ERICKSON, Carlton W. H. *Administering Instructional Media Programs*. New York: The Macmillan Company, 1968.

FUSARO, J. F. "Toward Library-College Media Centers; Proposal for the Nation's Community Colleges." *Junior College Journal*, 40:40-44 (April 1970).

HARCLEROAD, Fred F. "Learning Resources Approach to College and University Library Development." *Library Trends*, 16:239 (October 1967).

HICKS, Warren B., and TILLIN, Alma. *Developing Multi-Media Libraries*. New York: Bowker, 1970.

School Library Manpower Project. American Association of School Librarians. *Occupational Definitions for School Library Media Personnel.* Chicago: American Library Association, 1971.

STONE, C. Walter, ed. "Library Uses of the New Media of Communication." *Library Trends*, 16 (October 1967).

STONE, C. Walter. "Introduction." *Library Trends*, 16:179-180 (October 1967).

3–CLASSIFICATION AND CATALOGING

INTRODUCTION

The necessity for an acceptable system organizing knowledge for book libraries providing coherent and utilitarian accessibility is no longer argued. But what has happened to the so-called "nonbook materials"? The reasons for organizing slides or any other type of media are the same as those for books and to submit that one is more or less ephemeral than the other thereby deserving less organizational attention is to deny the usefulness and need for more than one medium of communication.

A noted authority in the field of classification, W. C. Berwick Sayers has written several manuals explaining how and why classification is utilized. The following statements have been selected from one of these manuals to provide some cursory background of the principles which he so wisely and yet succinctly provides the reader:

> When the librarian uses the word "classification" he means the work of sorting and arranging the material—books, manuscripts, documents, maps, prints—with which he has to deal. His primary business is to select books and other printed and graphic records for the use of others; and he is successful if he is able to marshal this material so effectively that it can be placed before his readers in the least possible time. In short, to save the time of readers in their pursuit of knowledge, information or even amusement, is his ultimate work as a librarian. (Sayers, 1958, p. 2).

> Nothing can be more confusing than a disorderly, unrelated mass of books, unless it is a mass of pamphlets, cuttings, prints, photographs and the other ana of civilized life. Anyone who has tried to find something in the lumber room of a library which has been merely a place where things are collected in the hope that some day someone will arrange them, understands the waste of effort and the futility involved in disorder. It is to bring system out of the confusion of things that classification has been devised. (ibid).

Sayers further states that:

> In order to make a classification scheme a practical instrument for the arranging of books, the nature of books themselves must be recognized. Books are not subjects, but may be statements of subjects. (ibid., p. 13).

This observation is particularly relevant to a discussion of the classification of visual resource materials because the immediate and yet simple difference between much book and nonbook material is set forth. Pictures or slides are in most instances, the "subjects" themselves which communicate instantly to the individual whether he is able to read or not. His intellectual interpretation of that visual communication may differ from that of other individuals' as with textual material, but the initial differences in the information transfer process vary because the actual information medium is not the same. For example, a written or verbal picture of a bucolic scene including various forms of rural architecture and domesticated animals can evoke a wide range of intellectual conceptions while the actual picture provides some semblance of a concrete reality which is not so easily conjectured. To say that the "subjects" themselves can be classified in exactly the same manner as the verbal renderings is highly debatable. The point is not, however, to say that one is less valuable than the other—book versus visual image—but to say that "the nature of books" as opposed to visual images "themselves must be recognized."

In light of the preceding discussion, the reader is asked to keep the differences between books and visual images in mind while reading the following passages from Sayers:

> Likeness governs classification and the likeness we choose we call the characteristic of classification. (ibid., p. 8).

> A natural classification is one that exhibits the inherent properties of the things classified: an artificial classification depends upon some arbitrarily chosen characteristic or accident of the things classified and has no direct relation to their inherent properties. (ibid., p. 34).

> Practically the whole history of the classification of knowledge is a gradual working forward from the artificial schemes of arrangement to more and more natural ones. In describing the difference between natural and artificial classification, the scientist tells us that artificial classification is classification by *analogy*, that is to say, things are classified by their external likeness and apparent purpose; while natural classification depends upon *homology*, the likeness that resides in the structure and function of the things classified. (ibid., p. 35).

In the most current and up-to-date publication on the classification of slides and pictures, Simons and Tansey defend their development of a distinct classification of visual media by emphasizing and explaining the basic differences between the printed concept and the visual one. They particularly emphasize the need for a separate classification for collections of individual slides and pictures as visual material that already has a pre-determined sequence such as filmstrips or motion pictures can readily be adapted to standard book schemes (Simons and Tansey, 1970, pp. 2-3). The basic crux of the problem is to recognize the essential differences in the nature of slides or pictures and books. One of the most useful and yet confounding aspects of a unitary image collection is the fact that each individual unit can be classified, cataloged, stored, and retrieved individually and then re-assembled according to a specific teaching function without regard to the previous organization of the file. A filmstrip, or motion picture, however, cannot be adapted to this type of re-definition of utilization patterns without destroying the original function and continuity of the sequenced material.

There are three basic methods of organization of a slide collection: accession number order; classified order; and subject order. The arrangement of slides in sets can be used in any of these three systems. In *accession number* order, the slides are filed numerically according to the sequence of acquisition with the internal subdivisions based upon the numerical sequence of the slides, e.g., every twenty or thirty slides might have a subdivision guide card with the accession number sequence indicated. Useful with this type of filing system are contact prints of the slide image on catalog or subject cards providing the user with an immediate visual record of the slide without first checking the slide files. *Classified order* depends upon a formal classification system such as the Dewey Decimal, Library of Congress, a modification of these systems, or a specially devised scheme with a correlated notation. In order to provide for efficient use of the collection, however, auxiliary catalogs or indexes should be used. *Subject order* is based upon the alphabetical organization of subject classes and divisions. Using this arrangement, a collection is considered self-indexing and does not include supplemental catalogs or indexes. Even with this system of organization, there are a restricted number of access points to an individual slide. If the user is not familiar with the terminology upon which the subject classes and divisions are developed, then he may have difficulty locating specific types of information.

The following represent the major elements of a classification. These terms will be used throughout this chapter to indicate the hierarchical levels of each system.

> Main classes.
> > Divisions.
> > > Sub-divisions.
> > > > Sections.
> > > > > Sub-sections,
> > > > > > etc. (Sayers, 1958, p. 12).

MEDIA STUDIES, HANDBOOKS AND MANUALS

If there is one consensus of opinion on the cataloging and classification of audiovisual materials, it is the proliferation of approaches and the lack of standardization. As William J. Quinly, Director, Educational Media Center, Florida State University, has pointed out, "One of the major bottlenecks in getting educational media from the producer to the patron has always been the cataloging and catalog production process. . . .Furthermore, the majority of audio-visual specialists have fallen into the practice of cataloging their own material, duplicating the almost identical efforts of other cataloguers " (1967, p. 276). In the same publication, Jay E. Daily, Professor, Graduate School of Library and Information Sciences, the University of Pittsburgh, stated that ". . . there are no books which tell a librarian precisely how best to process non-book materials nor which provide a better rule of thumb than the general one of treating each collection of nonbook materials as a separate and special entity " (1967, p. 287). This latter comment was made in a paper analyzing the relevance of the 1967 edition of the *Anglo-American Cataloging Rules* to nonbook materials. Even though the acceptance of audiovisual materials by most education institutions is considered a *sine qua non* of their teaching functions, "Educational specialists lament the deplorable lack of organization of 'media' for utilization in the learning process" according to Pearce Grove, Library Director at Eastern New Mexico University (1969, p. 299).

Louis Shores, Dean Emeritus of the Library School, Florida State University, succinctly summarized the scope of materials organization when he wrote that, "For the first time in the history of education, instructional materials are so many and so varied that individual differences in students can be matched with individual differences in media" (1968, p. 11). A pioneer in media education, Dr. Shores has been a primary force in the movement toward the total integration of all library materials. To him, "What audio-visual really means is an extension of the means of communication between learner and environment; consequently, the librarian must make himself as knowledgeable in these other formats of the generic book as he now is with those which are lumped together under the heading of print" (ibid., p. 15).

How are the preceding comments relevant to the individual administering a slide collection? To ignore the problems of the organization and retrieval of audiovisual media on a broad level is to operate in a vacuum regarding the optimal possibilities of media utilization and standardization potentials. As Dr. C. Walter Stone, Director of the Center for Library and Educational Media Studies and Director of the University of Pittsburgh Libraries points out,

> ... in the future our concern is going to be with information, not with its possession, processing, and distribution. In many parts of the United States the definition of a librarian, audiovisual specialist, or media specialist tends to be an individual whose concern is to buy packages of material. But in the future we are not going to care about the form in which information is packaged; we shall seek the information itself. (1969, p. 5).

The operation and administration of any media collection whether it is specialized or generalized in terms of subjects or by types of materials covered should be approached in the context of contemporary research and models for development. If the slide librarian or curator faces his daily tasks submitting to whatever organization vagaries impinge upon him, then he is compounding the complexity of his tasks and duplicating and wasting effort, expense, and time. What is mandatory is that the primary forces—directors of instructional media centers, museums, and chairmen of academic departments—effecting the organization of slide libraries recognize the value of standardizing procedures for handling materials no matter what their "form" may be. The remainder of this chapter examines organizational alternatives that are available to a slide collection at the present time and recommends guidelines on the use of these alternatives.

What progress has been made in the past twenty years in the literature on the cataloging and classification of audiovisual materials? This section provides a general survey of existing publications with an emphasis on the organization of slides.

In 1948, a survey of the cataloging, arrangement and storage of motion pictures, filmstrips and 2" x 2" slides was undertaken by a student as part of her thesis requirements at Florida State University with Louis Shores acting as one of the consulting professors for this project (Daughtry, 1948). Questionnaires were mailed to 88 audiovisual centers throughout the United States with 61 responding. The following conclusions resulted from her study:

> Eighty-four percent of the surveyed audio-visual centers include 2" x 2" slides in their collection. The methods of cataloging 2" x 2" slides used by the surveyed a-v centers are similar to those used for motion pictures and filmstrips. The two methods most frequently used for indexing 2" x 2" slides are (a) subject and title and (b) subject only. Fifty-one percent of the surveyed audio-visual centers index 2" x 2" slides by subject and title; thirty-three percent index by subject only. Ten percent index by title only. (ibid., p. 45).

> In contrast to the relative uniformity of cataloguing and classification, there is no system of shelf order or rack arrangement used by more than approximately one-third of the surveyed audio-visual centers. The two most frequently used methods of shelf

order or rack arrangement of 2" x 2" slides are (a) alphabetically by subject and (b) Dewey Decimal classification. Thirty-five percent of the audio-visual centers surveyed arrange 2" x 2" slides alphabetically by subject and thirty-one percent arrange them by Dewey Decimal classification. (ibid., p. 49).

The third most frequently used shelf arrangement was by accession number (ibid., p. 50).

The following year, Margaret Rufsvold of Indiana University published one of the standard works in the audiovisual field, *Audio-Visual School Library Service: A Handbook for Librarians* (1949). She attempted to fill the vacuum existing in the "whole field of cataloging, organizing, and distributing audio-visual materials according to standard library practices" (ibid., p. III). She recommended the use of title main entries and added entries when important for audiovisual materials and that units or sets of materials should be entered under the title of the set (ibid., p. 58). For slides she offered the following guidelines:

> To process slides assign one classification or one identification number to all slides in a unit or series and form the call number by placing SL or SM before this number.
> . . . Catalog by unit using title or subject of the entire series as the main entry;
> . . . Make added cards for subjects only . . . and file all cards in the public card catalog. (ibid., p. 61).

Summarily, she recommended the same type of cataloging as is used for print or book materials and discussed the use of Dewey Decimal or "identification" (accession) numbers as possibilities for classification (ibid., p. 55). Her final statement in the section on "Classification" still proves critical to media accessibility: "In the final analysis it becomes apparent that only through the card catalog can all materials on a subject be brought to the attention of the library patron" (ibid., p. 56).

In 1952, 1953, and 1955, respectively, Dixie Thompson (1952), Virginia Clarke (1953), and Eunice Keen (1955), published their manuals on handling audiovisual materials in the school library. In order to allow for the lack of background of the Dewey Decimal classification by library personnel, Miss Thompson advised the use of accession numbers for shelving material and a symbol system for classification so that a media symbol combined with the accession number formed the call number (1952, p. 2). Slides would be cataloged by set or unit using a title or subject main entry with added entries made for subjects only (ibid., p. 23). Miss Clarke recommended the inclusion of all materials—book and nonbook—in one subject catalog, their arrangement by media code and accession numbers, the main entry under title, and the use of Sears *List of Subject Headings for Small Libraries* (1953). Miss Keen stated that the call number should be a symbol for lantern or 2" x 2" slides over the Dewey number, the main entry, a subject entry (if the slides did not have a distinctive title), title, imprint, collation, and notes should be on the catalog card in that order (1955, p. 10).

In a *Primer of Non-Book Materials in Libraries* that appeared in 1958, Mason stated that "Slides can be arranged in alphabetical subject, classified, or accession order. While the first two methods appear to be ideal the accession number method with its fixed location does avoid constant moving of the slides and thus lessens the risk of breakage" (1958, p. 46). The problem of breakage so commonly associated with lantern or 3¼" x 4" slides was still used to pre-determine the organization of slides in many libraries at this time.

By the end of the decade, the Descriptive Cataloging Division of the Library of Congress published a preliminary edition of the *Rules for Descriptive Cataloging in the Library of Congress: Pictures, Designs, and Other Two-Dimensional Representations* which was superseded by the 1967 edition of the *Anglo-American Cataloging Rules* (1967). Both editions make the same general entry recommendations that maintain as much consistency as is feasible with those rules designed for book materials with main entries under artist (or studio), architect (or architectural firm), and anonymous works under title.

During the 1960s the universality of the organization problems inherent in media collections was generally recognized by most individuals handling these materials; consequently, a proliferation of solutions was offered. The following manuals have been selected to demonstrate both the diversity and similiarity of suggested standards during this ten-year period.

Instructional Materials, written by Louis Shores, was published in 1960 (1960). Although Shores indicated the cataloging entry sequence for slides as "(1) Title, format. (2) Imprint. (3) Number, size" (ibid., p. 25), he did not make any definite suggestions for their classification except by the following: "In the Materials Center books are universally arranged by DC. Periodicals usually are arranged by title. Some centers also arrange disk recordings, filmstrips, and films by DC . . . but as a rule film collections are not arranged by DC numbers" (ibid., p. 18). He did, however, recognize the trend at that time to interfile the catalog cards for all library materials (ibid., p. 21).

The Descriptive Cataloging of Library Materials, published in 1963 (Hopkinson, 1963), followed basically the *Rules for Descriptive Cataloging* for the Library of Congress. The author recommended that title main entries be used either for individual or sets of slides and the use of a media code preceding the call number (ibid., pp. 40-41). In a guide intended for use in a library science course at the University Extension of the University of Wisconsin, Department of Library Science, the author stressed the use of title main entries for slides, filmstrips and motion pictures except when a set of slides were by the same artist. In this latter instance, the slides would be entered under the artist or the compiler. When a compiler was absent and more than one artist was included, then the title main entry was used. If a title was not supplied, then one was created for the main entry.

In 1967, Warren B. Hicks, Director of Library Services, Chabot College, Hayward, California, and Alma M. Tillin, Technical Services Librarian, Library Center, Berkeley Unified School District, California, wrote *The Organization of Nonbook Materials in School Libraries* (1967). In the introduction they state that, "The decisions on cataloging procedure are based on the fundamental principle that the organization of printed and audio-visual materials by subject reinforces the learning and extension of experiences and skills already acquired by pupils and teachers" (ibid., p. 1). They also indicated that a State Department of Education survey revealed that the accession number and Dewey Decimal systems were the two systems used in school libraries for audio-visual materials (ibid., p. 7). Briefly, they outlined the advantages and disadvantages of these two methods. For the most part, they support the use of the Dewey Decimal over the accession number system because it directly relates to the classification of the books thereby preventing the total separation of book and media materials and maintains the same subject approach through the classification system to all materials (ibid., pp. 7-8). They also indicate the shelving advantages of different media by using the DDC but point out the slower cataloging rate involved in the assignment of call numbers. Title main entries are recommended for all materials in addition to a media code plus a number (accession, DDC, or LC) and a Cutter number for the call number (ibid., p. 15). Their thorough approach to the various types of classification systems and methods of cataloging that can be used for nonbook materials make this publication one of the most useful published during this period. The trend throughout the publications on this topic has been toward a total materials center concept whereby all types of materials are available through the same retrieval device—the card catalog.

The *Instructional Materials Cataloging Guide* was written by Evelyn Harris, the Instructional Materials Librarian at the University of Arizona (1968). She recommended the use of Sears for subject headings but did not really offer advice regarding the classification of materials except for the following: " . . . choice of classification scheme is largely dependent on physical facilities available for housing materials in some kind of consistent order. The Dewey Decimal classification for all forms of materials is often unworkable because of space problems and other difficulties" (ibid., p. iv). She did, however, recommend the use of a classified listing in a separate card catalog of all materials (ibid., p. 25). Consequently, whenever an item was accessioned it would also have to be assigned the DDC number in order to be placed in this catalog—this catalog was in addition to a regular shelflist for books (ibid.). If Dewey numbers are assigned, it would seem advisable to use them both as classification and as shelving tools. Intershelving of different forms of media, which does present storage problems as Miss Harris indicated, is not mandatory. For general slides, title main entries are suggested and for art slides, "artist and title analytics should be made for individual works represented, as listed in a contents note, unless separate entry is made for each individual slide" (ibid., p. 16). She recommended the AAC *Rules* as main entry authority.

As indicated earlier in the Daughtry survey, access by subject and title, and by subject only were the two most common indexing methods for slides in 1948. In fact, the strict subject arrangement has probably been the most frequently used method by most collections because of the directness of the retrieval approach. In 1968, *The Picture Collection Subject Headings* for the Newark Public Library was published (Newark Public Library, 1968). Although this same method could be used for slides, other subject approaches tend to dominate. For example, the slide collection at the Newark Public Library is classified by Dewey with Cutter numbers (ibid., p. vi), thus providing a subject approach which also groups works of one artist together although separating one form of artistic medium from another by the same artist. The geographical arrangement under medium (architecture, graphic arts, engraving, painting and sculpture) with further subdivision by artist is characteristic of both the DDC and LC systems.

Although Sayers third edition of *A Manual of Classification* (1955) was completely revised and partly rewritten by Arthur Maltby in 1967, Maltby did not deem it necessary to alter Sayers comments on the organization of lantern slides (Sayers, 1967). Sayers noted the importance of classifying slides and any other type of picture and indicated the feasibility of using the UDC (Universal Decimal Classification), (1955, pp. 306-307; 1967, pp. 327-328). He also stressed the use of subject cataloging. At the same time, however, he recognized the inconvenience of keeping individual slides in strict classified order when they would be continually removed from this set order to be used for lectures. He reluctantly reinforced their logical organization in "lecture sets" because this conformed best to their use patterns (1955, p. 307; 1967, p. 328). Filing slides by set versus the filing of slides individually will be discussed in detail in the next chapter.

By 1966 the Department of Audiovisual Instruction (now called the Association for Educational Communications and Technology, AECT) of the National Education Association organized a task force to develop "(1) standards for cataloging education media and (2) coding standards for computerized cataloging and scheduling" (National Education Association, 1968, p. iii). A revised and third edition of the *Standards for School Media Programs* were also published (Association for Educational Communications and Technology, 1971; 1972). The *Standards* provide for a ten-entry sequence ranging from title main entries to the use of tracings (subject added entries or others when relevant). In addition a classification number using the LC or DDC numbers to allow for subject organization of materials is recommended (ibid., p. 8). Whether slides were cataloged individually or in sets, the main entry would be under title (ibid., p. 1). Tracings would provide an artist or a subject approach to a slide.

In 1969 Virginia Clarke published a revised edition of her handbook for non-book materials (1969). This later edition includes thirteen pages on the handling of art slides (ibid., pp. 63-75). She also included a bibliography of books suggesting lists of headings that may provide some authority for establishing subject lists. In addition to the standard practice of main entry under title, she suggested added entries to satisfy the need for information on the medium, nationality, period and visual content or subject of the slides. A list of headings for the art history periods and a list taken from Sears, 9th edition, is also included (ibid., p. 74).

Akers' *Simple Library Cataloging*, 5th ed., has one chapter devoted solely to "Audio-visual Materials" (1969, pp. 199-222). The author indicated that she does not think it worthwhile to use a classification system for audiovisual materials because of the lack of integrated storage or shelving and instead suggested the common use of accession numbers plus media codes (ibid., p. 200). For slides like other materials, she recommends title main entries (ibid., p. 219), and stressed the use of a catalog for access to the materials.

In Wetmore's general guide to the organization of library materials, she recommended the use of accession order filing and title main entries (1969, p. 128). *Special Libraries* by Silva also noted the widespread use of accession order or alphabetical subject filing and title main entries (1970, p. 52).

The *Standards for School Media Programs* was issued jointly by the American Association of School Librarians and the Department of Audiovisual Instruction (now AECT) of the NEA (American Association of School Librarians. . . ., 1969). The two-page section on the "Organization of Materials" is, unfortunately, not as specific in its recommended standards as are other sections of the guide (ibid., pp. 26-27). The use of some classification scheme is recognized but not strongly advocated and the intershelving of book and other media is noted as working well in some schools (ibid., p. 26). They do, however, strongly defend and promote the cataloging and processing of materials by an outside source so that staff time need not be spent on housekeeping rather than user-related tasks (ibid.).

Two of the most recent publications intended for school libraries were published by the Canadian Librarian Association and Audiovisual Catalogers, Inc.

(Weihs, 1973; Johnson, 1971). Perhaps one of the most innovative cataloging decisions represented in the former work is the elimination of a media code or symbol as part of the call number. The author asserts that the media symbol does not serve a valid function (Weihs, 1973, p. 6). Preference for the commonly used DDC system over that of accession number arrangement and the use of Sears and *A List of Canadian Subject Headings* is advocated. Main entry is under author in accordance with the AAC *Rules* including the allowance for artist or composer main entries. In the section on slides title main entries for general material with art slides under artist is stipulated (ibid., p. 69). In general, the same rules apply to stereo-scope and to microscope slides (ibid., pp. 56-57, 68). The Johnson publication also recommended the use of DDC and Sears and title main entries when possible, and included general advice on the accessioning, processing, and cataloging of slides (Johnson, 1971, pp. 177-186).

In another recent publication, Hicks and Tillin again joined forces in *Developing Multi-Media Libraries* which provides a great deal of practical information on the development of media collections within a library (1970). They discuss the widespread use of an accession number or subject classification (DDC or LC) for media materials and title main entries with art materials under artist (ibid., pp. 62, 73).

Along the lines of Dr. Stone's comments regarding our primary concern in the future with the information itself rather than its form or package, several articles have been written about the concept of uniterming a slide collection or audiovisual library. An article by Drucilla Motley explains how to "Find Your Slides—Fast" through the use of "descriptors" which can be adapted to either a manual or mechanical indexing system (1970, p. 19). A mechanical indexing system is recommended for a slide collection having more than 4,000 to 5,000 slides (ibid.). Whether the terminology uses "uniterms," "keywords," or "descriptors," the concept is still the same. A thesaurus of terms is developed which describes the content of the material to be indexed. The material can be retrieved by these terms without the necessity of a formal classification system or a previously devised rigid subject heading list. Thomas H. Ohlgren of the English Department at Purdue University, has been working on an archival index to medieval manuscript illuminations based on content descriptions capable of computer generation and retrieval. Eugene Fleischer has described a project at the Audio-Visual Resources Division at Brevard Junior College using the uniterm system for their entire media collection which includes slides (1969). A retrieval system developed specifically for slides based upon the descriptor concept which is not a filing but a retrieval device—the filing order can be in simple numerical order—was developed at the Instructional Resources Center at the State University College in Fredonia, New York, by Robert M. Diamond (1969). This system can be used in conjunction with the computer manipulable classification system for slides and pictures developed at the University of California at Santa Cruz.

In summary, the guidelines that have been proposed primarily focus on the school library system or the instructional materials center having a rather broad subject orientation. For these set-ups, the general recommendations are for title main entries with some allowance for artist or composer main entries and preference for the Dewey Decimal Classification over an accession number arrangement. The integrated subject catalog approach for all materials is also recognized as the critical retrieval device for all materials allowing both for a multi-media approach and for specific item retrieval by subject. This overview has demonstrated both the simplicity and multiplicity of handbooks and manuals for the library materials collection. With the exception of the latest edition of Clarke's handbook, however, and a handful of articles and other publications, allowances have rarely been made for art slide libraries. Paradoxically, the largest slide libraries in the United States are composed of art slides in museum and academic institutions. The next section analyzes the outlines of a selected number of heretofore unpublicized classification systems designed for slides.

SYSTEMS DESIGNED FOR SLIDES

The existance of subject catalogs or indexes to the slide files which are necessary when using a DDC, LC, or accession number arrangement is uncommon in most academic institutions and museums. Art slide libraries prefer a self-indexing file arrangement which is the same as the classification system and functions as an alphabetical subject index to the collection. The subject access is, of course, limited by the number of main classes, divisions, subdivisions, sections, subsections and so forth. Basic to this different approach to the organization or classification of slides is the concept of the specialist versus the general user. In the majority of academic institutions, art slide libraries were begun by faculty who have a specialized subject background in the arts. Because of their subject training, they have usually preferred a slide collection organized within the historical framework of artistic periods or styles, while individuals outside the art field have preferred a subject access to art materials to compensate for their lack of knowledge of individual artists or architects. For example, the art historian preparing a lecture on seventeenth century landscape painting knows immediately which artists worked in this area. On the other hand, the general user desiring slides on this topic would find it quite difficult to extract those slides from an art historically classified collection without knowing beforehand the nationality and names of the artists in the seventeenth century who painted landscapes as their major occupation.

In order to clarify exactly what is meant by an art history classification scheme, the basic outlines of those used and devised at the following institutions will be examined: College of Architecture, Art, and Planning, Cornell University; Corning Community College; Department of Art History and Archaeology, Columbia University; Fogg Art Museum Library, Harvard University; the Metropolitan Museum of Art; the National Gallery of Art; the University Library, University of California at Santa Cruz; Department of the History of Art, the University of Michigan; Department of Art History, the University of Minnesota; and the Art Library, Yale University. These collections range in size from the largest academic collection at Columbia University having approximately 285,000 slides to less than 20,000 slides at Corning Community College, and are representative of the major art history collections in the United States. Whether collections have more than, or less than 50,000 slides, their classification systems tend to be quite similar although the smaller the collection, the frequently less refined, detailed, and extensive are the classification divisions, subdivisions, sections, subsections and so forth. Unfortunately, most collections do not have formal classification systems which have been completely and accurately recorded in staff handbooks for classifying and cataloging information; consequently, the only method by which complete comprehension of the total classification and organizational system can be obtained is by direct observation and study of the slide files themselves.

Columbia University

Although a complete guide to the classification system at Columbia University used in the Department of Art History and Archaeology is not available, a brief outline of their scheme is posted for the user. The following represents their user's guide to the collection:

I   Initial letters designate media [Main Classes]
- A   Architecture (Architecture is subdivided by country with sites arranged alphabetically under country and designated by a code number.)
- S   Sculpture
- P   Painting
- MINOR ARTS
- B   Stone objects (generally prehistoric)
- C   Ceramics (including vase painting)
- D   Design, Perception, & Organic Form and Perspective
- F   Furniture
- G   Gems, Seals, Cameos, Jewelry
- H   Glass
- J   Ivories
- K   Metal Work
- L   Stained Glass
- M   Manuscripts (Typography is a subdivision of design.)
- N   Numismatics: Coins, etc.
- T   Maps
- V   Views
- W   Textiles
- X   Topography
- Y   Gardens & Garden Design
- Z   Social Customs (e.g., dance, ritual, literary texts)

II   Numbers following the initial letter designates periods and countries [Divisions]
- 1   Prehistoric
- 2   Egypt
- 3   Mesopotamia and Assyria
- 4   Western Oriental (Asia Minor, Syria, Persia, etc.)
- 5   Pre-Hellenic (Minoan, Mycenean, Cycladic, etc.)
- 6   Greece
- 7   Etruscan
- 8   Rome
- 9   Ancient European
- 10   Early Christian and Byzantine
- 11   Coptic
- 14   Pre-Romanesque (Merovingian, Carolingian)
- 16   Romanesque
- 17   Gothic

21-29	Renaissance (to 1700):	
	21	England
	22	France
	23	Germany, Austria, Switzerland
	24	Italy
	25	Low Countries
	26	Spain and Portugal
	27	Central and North Europe, Russia
	28	Latin America
	29	North America
31-39	Eighteenth-Nineteenth Century (By country in same order as Renaissance.)	
41-49	Twentieth Century (By country in same order as Renaissance.)	

III   Special Categories

AP: Architectural Techniques, Construction, Diagrams, etc.; precedes Architecture. Architectural Treatises are cataloged under Architecture by country; they appear in the slide drawers before the monuments proper.

ARC: Archaeology. Greek, large slides only

E: Examination, technical analysis, forgeries, etc.

EP: Painting; ES: Sculpture. EP precedes Painting, ES precedes Sculpture.

NE: Ancient Near East (designates small slides only)

O: Oriental (designates small slides only)

OM: Islamic (designates small slides only)

PM: Mosaics (designates small slides only). In large slides, Mosaics are cataloged under painting, but appear in the slide drawers after other forms of painting.

If an architectural monument were being classified, it would be treated according to the following schedule:

> Medium (main class)
> > Country (division)
> > > Period (subdivision)
> > > > Site (section)
> > > > > Type of building (subsection)

Another alternative to classifying architecture by site is to class it by architect although site locations are usually easier to handle unless the collection is used solely by an architectural historian. The architectural sites and names of the buildings are designated by a Cutter number.

Painting and sculpture would be classed by medium, period or country, by artist and then by iconography or subject content.

> Medium
> > Period or country
> > > Artist
> > > > Subject

The manuscripts collection of slides is quite extensive at Columbia and are classified according to the following system:

        Medium
            Period
                Site (city and name of owning library)
                    Shelf number
                        Folio number

A sample slide label illustrates how this system of cataloging and classification is applied:

```
RODA BIBLE.  M53-P218
DANIEL.             LAT.6
                     f.66
11th century.

Paris,BN,Lat.6,f.66
Neuss,Katalan Bibel 33.
```

Slide Label 1

Line 1.	RODA BIBLE.	M53-P218
Line 2.	DANIEL.	LAT.6
Line 3.		f.66
Line 4.	11th century.	
Line 5.	Paris,BN,Lat.6,f.66	
Line 6.	Neuss,Katalan Bibel 33.	

Line 1: manuscript title; M for manuscripts; 53 for Romanesque; P218 for Cutter number for Paris
Line 2: initial or title of illustration; LAT.6 for shelf number
Line 3: f.66 for folio number
Line 4: date or approximate date
Line 5: city and name of owning library with shelf and folio numbers
Line 6: source of slide

For painting, sculpture or works having a known artist, the main entry would be under artist, for architecture under the site or name of the location of the building, and for manuscripts under the title of the manuscript.

Corning Community College

Corning Community College bases their system for art slides on the one used in the *American Library Color Slide Catalogue of World Art, Teachers Manual for the Study of Art History and Related Courses* (1964), the Metropolitan Museum of Art, and at Yale University. In addition they use the *Outline of the Library of Congress Classification* (Library of Congress Processing Department, 1970). Both art history and general history slides are filed according to the same period divisions so that all material is historically related in the files no matter what the subject matter may be. For non-historical slides, Corning uses the relevant LC class and divisions. The Enoch Pratt Free Library of Baltimore also utilizes LC classification in their Films Department. In their guide to the cataloging system, Corning provides the following broad outline:

All Historically-Oriented slides:
    I.   WESTERN (This term is understood but not used on labels or cards.)
        A   Architecture
        B   Sculpture
        C   Painting
        D   Minor Arts
        E/F History

M	Music	
P	Language & Literature	According to *Outline of Library of*
U	Military History	*Congress Classification*
Z	Bibliography	

II.   PRIMITIVE
III. ORIENTAL
IV.   ISLAMIC
V.   LATIN AMERICAN & PRE-COLUMBIAN

(Roman Numerals not used allow for later possible additions)

X.   NON-HISTORICALLY ORIENTED SLIDES
      E
      to   (according to *Outline of Library of Congress Classification*)
      Z

After the preceding main classes, Corning uses basic time or period divisions for art, history, music, language and literature, military history and bibliography:

1. 500,000-1500 B.C.
2. 1500 B.C.-approx. 500 A.D.
3. 500 A.D.-approx. 1400 A.D.
4. 1400 A.D.-1600 A.D.

5. 1600 A.D.-1800 A.D.
6. 1800-1900 A.D.
7. 1900- . . . or undated

After these basic divisions for western civilization, subdivisions are used for the periods from medieval through the twentieth century, i.e., from 3 through 7 as decimal numbers, e.g., 3.1 is Frankish or Merovingian within the medieval time division. Lower case letters are used for country designations.

Slide Label 2

Line 1.	Architecture.Med.Fr.Rom.
Line 2.	Moissac, Abbey.
Line 3.	1115-30 A.D.
Line 4.	South Portal.
Line 5.	IA3b.6 Loc.: Moissac,
Line 6.	Moissac France.
Line 7.	1

Line 1:   medium, general time period, country, subdivision period, Rom. for Romanesque
Line 2:   site, name of building or type of building
Line 3:   date
Line 4:   section of building illustrated
Line 5:   call number, I for Western civilization, A for architecture, 3 for 500 A.D.-approx.
          1400 A.D., b for French, and .6 for Romanesque; location of site
Line 6:   second line of call number which gives site location; country
Line 7:   accession number, 1 is for the first slide in this category

Main entries are similar to those used at Columbia University. A card file similar to a standard library card catalog is also maintained for this collection.

Cornell University

In a format similar to that of other institutions, the College of Architecture, Art and City Planning of Cornell University provides a general guide to the classification of their slide collection. It is primarily devised for architectural history although it does allow for fine arts slides which are classified by the following categories:

Media
    Country and/or period
        Geography (or country)
            Artist

Architecture and city planning slides are classified and cataloged by the following categories:

Medium (architecture)
    Country or geographical location
        City (alphabetically within a country)
            Building type
                Name of building (alphabetically within type)

The major classes which are primarily of a media type are the following:

A MAPS
B ARCHITECTURE
C SCULPTURE
D Numismatics (coins, medals, seals)
E PAINTING
F Mosaics
G Manuscripts
H Book Arts
I Prints
J Photography
K Landscape
L Military (military camps, military organization, etc.)
M
N Portraits
O THEORY
P Ornament
Q Ceramics
R Glass and Enamels
S Jewelry, Jewels, Metalwork
T Wrought Metal, Arms, Armour
U Furniture
V Tapestry, Textiles, Wallpaper, Embroidery
W Culture and Civilization
X Tools and Inventions
Y Transportation
Z Government

The classes comprising the most significant sections of the collection have been capitalized. As is immediately apparent, this system and Columbia's are quite similar. For additional information on the categorization of architectural types, consult the *American Institute of Architects Filing System for Architectural Plates and Articles.*

Harvard University and the University of Michigan

The classification system utilized at the University of Michigan is based upon that of Harvard University's lantern slide and photograph classification schedule, with the latter being derived from the Metropolitan Museum of Art's scheme. Because these two systems are almost identical, they will be outlined together with differences indicated by brackets. Although this system is actively used by Michigan for both their lantern and 2" x 2" slides and photographs, Harvard has restricted its use to the lantern slide collection because its application was considered too time-consuming within the last five years. Rather than change completely from one classification system to another for the entire collection, a new simpler scheme was devised for the 2" x 2" slides which does not include the use of a decimal notation system. The University of Michigan's slide and photograph collection has a large professional staff which is able to handle the application of an elaborate and complicated classification system while Harvard does not. The Harvard lantern slide and Michigan classification schemes are discussed as one system.

In this system, the arts are divided into nine main classes:

```
000   Maps [Harvard only]
100   Architecture
200   Sculpture
300   Painting and drawing
400   Work in mineral stuffs
500   Work in metals
600   Work in wood
700   Work in ivory, leather, etc.
800   Textiles, embroideries, lace, etc.
900   Prints
```

A combination of numerical, decimal, and alphabetical tables are provided for chronological divisions, geographical or country subdivisions and subject content or architectural type sections. To include all these tables in their entirety would be to include the entire classification system which is not the intent of this chapter. Instead, the following summary of the subject content divisions is given:

```
a.  Architecture
    1  General views, bridges, public squares, etc.
    2  Religious buildings
    3  Palaces, villas, etc.
    4  Manor houses, etc.
    5  Educational buildings
    6  Museums
    7  Public amusements
    8  Governmental and municipal buildings, etc.
    9  Other buildings not easily classifiable
```

b. Sculpture
1-3	Religious subjects
4	Mythological subjects
5-6	Portraits
7	Ecclesiastical sculpture
8	Monuments and tombs

c. Painting
1-3	Religious subjects
4	Mythological subjects
5-7	Portraits
8	Landscapes and marines
9	Animals
90	Genre [Harvard only]

d. Minor Arts (separate sections by specific type of material or craft are used for each of the classes from 400 to 900; class 400, Work in mineral stuffs, illustrates a sampling of this section)
1	Stone and marble (not sculpture)
2	Gems and precious stones (crystal, jade, etc.)
3	Mosaics and Cosmati
4	
5	Enamels, Cloisonne
6	Glass, stained and painted
7	Glass
8	Pottery (includes faience, lustre, majolica, etc.)
81	Stucco
82	Terracotta
83	Tiles
9	Porcelain

Basically, this system can be summarized as follows:

Medium
   Period (Ancient—all art till the beginning of the Christian era; Modern—art from the beginning of the Christian era)
      Country, geography or culture
         City (architecture)
            Artist or school and century (painting, drawing, sculpture, prints)
               School and century (minor arts)
                  Architectural type (architecture)
                  Subject content (painting, drawing, sculpture, prints)
                  Specific type of material or craft (minor arts)

The major difference between the Harvard and Michigan use of this system is their treatment of manuscripts which fall under class 700, Work in ivory, leather, etc. Harvard classifies their lantern slide manuscripts by collection (city, museum, manuscript number or shelf number, and folio number) in a format similar to Columbia's. Michigan classifies them by century, chronology or country and then by manuscript type, e.g., gospel, evangeliary, missal and so forth. Michigan retains the use of the 700 class number while Harvard uses a Cutter number for the city and letters or initials for the name of the library or owning body.

In order to clarify precisely how this system is used, the following example of a painting slide is analyzed:

Slide Label 3

Line 1.	Gogh, Vincent Van	375
Line 2.	Self-portrait at an easel	G553
Line 3.	1888.	5G(n)
Line 4.	Amsterdam,Stedelijk Mus.	

Line 1:   Gogh for artist main entry; 300 for painting and drawing and 075 for modern France represents 375

Line 2:   title of painting; G553 is Cutter number for Gogh

Line 3:   date; 5 is portraits of men; G for portrait of Gogh, i.e., self-portrait; (n) distinguishes different representations of the same subject by the same artist

Line 4:   location

The new classification system used at Harvard for 2" x 2" slides was devised in 1968 to expedite the cataloging and classification of slides. For the most part, it is based directly on the scheme which utilized decimal notation. Verbal transliterations are used instead of call numbers. The class, division, subdivision, section, and subsection arrangement follows the original system. Rather than being divided by decimal notation, the slides are arranged alphabetically by city, geographical area, or by materials (for minor arts). A broad outline of the new main classes and divisions and subdivisions are indicated:

Maps
    Country or geographical area
Charts
    Type or country
Pre-Historic
    Medium
        Date or age
Primitive
    Country
        Medium
Pre-Columbian
    Medium
        Geographical-cultural area
Ancient (before beginning of the Christian era)
    Geographical-cultural area
    Medium
Architectural Projects (drawings and plans of buildings which have not been built. . .)
    Artist
Architecture
    Country
    State
        City or site
Sculpture
    Period (for Early Christian to Byzantine)
    Country
        Artist*

Painting (see sculpture)
Drawing (see sculpture)
Prints
    Country
        Artist*
Photographs
    Artist*
Manuscripts
    City of collection
        Museum or library
Minor Arts
    Material
        Country
Oriental
    Country
        Medium

*Anonymous works precede all artist divisions.

Unlike the decimal notation system, the abbreviated system is not consistent in its main class designations. The former's main classes were all basically of a media nature describing a type of artform whereas the latter mixes artforms, cultural divisions, and period classes within the same main class structure; consequently, the following two variations are possible when summarizing the system:

1. Medium (charts, maps, architecture, drawing, sculpture, painting, prints, manuscripts, minor arts)
   Country or geographical area (charts, maps, architecture, drawings, prints, manuscripts)

   Material (minor arts)
   Period (painting, sculpture)

2. Culture or period (pre-historic, primitive, ancient, pre-Columbian, oriental)
   Medium (pre-historic)
   Geographical-cultural area (pre-historic, primitive, pre-Columbian, ancient)

With this abbreviated system, the Van Gogh slide label would appear as follows:

Slide Label 4

Line 1.	PTG. FRANCE GOGH,
Line 2.	VINCENT VAN 287
Line 3.	Self Portrait at an Easel,
Line 4.	1888
Line 5.	Amsterdam, Stedelijk
Line 6.	Museum
Line 7.	Leymaire: Van Gogh
Line 8.	Pl.57

Line 1:   medium (abbreviated); country; last name of artist
Line 2:   first name of artist; accession number
Line 3:   title
Line 4:   date

Line 5:   location
Line 6:   location
Line 7:   source of slide, book by Leymaire on Van Gogh
Line 8:   plate number in book

Basically, the same cataloging information is provided on both slide labels but a notation code is not available for filing purposes in the simplified scheme. This system also includes the source information directly on the slide label. The use of the shelflist card for additional cataloging information is still used by Michigan but only for lantern slides at Harvard.

Princeton University has a classification system similar in complexity to that used for the Harvard lantern slides and for the entire collection at Michigan. A decimal notation system is used accompanied by Cutter numbers for cities and for artists' names. The summaries of these systems are identical, e.g., medium, period, country, artist or site.

The following institutions base their systems upon either the Harvard lantern slide classification or upon a combination of the Michigan and Harvard systems: Skidmore College; University of California at Los Angeles; University of California at Riverside; University of New Mexico; University of Pennsylvania; University of Rochester, New York; University of Texas; and the University of Wisconsin. Please refer to the directory of slide libraries for information on the departments involved at these various institutions.

The Metropolitan Museum of Art

The Metropolitan Museum of Art slide classification is pending publication. In the meantime, a two-page outline is available upon request. The Metropolitan does not use a notation system for slides. Accession numbers are used only as an inventory check. The Western arts are classified by medium or what the Metropolitan Slide Library refers to as "art form," then by country, and finally by chronological period for architecture and sculpture. Standard subdivisions follow the main classes and divisions. For Ancient arts and other than Western arts such as Far Eastern, Near Eastern, and so forth, the divisions under the geographical areas are first by country and then by medium. The primitive arts of Africa, Oceania, and North America, are classified by geographical or cultural area, tribe, and medium. One of the unique features of the Metropolitan system is the use of museum locations as a filing device. For example, a collection of paintings by a single artist might be filed by their museum locations rather than by subject content or by date which in most instances are more commonly used for this purpose. Using the owning institution as a source for locating objects may not be the most practical method for academic institutions; however, for a museum, it is useful in consolidating the works of a particular artist in its own collection.

The Cleveland Museum of Art, Ohio State University, and Pennsylvania State University base their systems upon that of the Metropolitan. The Massachusetts Institute of Technology utilizes a combination of the Harvard lantern slide system, the Metropolitan, and the Yale University classification schedules.

National Gallery of Art, Washington, D.C.

Although the National Gallery of Art has a medium-sized collection of about 52,000 slides, it has one of the most complicated classification systems. The guide to the Gallery's classification contains 174 pages of explanation which includes the outline of the system, alphabetical symbols for culture and country, cultural and chronological tables, subject content designations, an alphabetical list of art schools and centers, and a list of museums and libraries with alphabetical code abbreviations. Cutter numbers are used for artists' names and for city names. This system has been modified and adapted from the one used at the Chicago Art Institute.

Primarily, the main classes, divisions, and subdivisions are represented in the following outline:

A   Architecture
        Country or cultural area
           Location (cite site) or century

D   Diagrams (only those that cannot be classified with specific objects or countries or cultures)

A	Architecture	M	Minor Arts
AE	Aesthetic Analysis	P	Painting
CO	Cosmology	PS	Psychology
CR	Criticism	S	Sculpture
D	Decoration	TH	Theater
LI	Literature		

(G)   Graphic Arts (G is always followed by a 2nd upper case letter to indicate the kind of Graphic Art)
      GD   Drawings
            Country or cultural area
              Artist or country or century
      GP   Prints (same as drawings)

M   Maps (this section is arranged in two main divisions)
      1. General maps
         a. Maps of the *World* as a whole and those that include part of both hemispheres
         b. Maps of the *Eastern Hemisphere*
         c. Maps of the *Western Hemisphere*
         d. Maps of the *Northern Hemisphere* (used only when "Eastern" or "Western" hemispheres are not appropriate)
         e. Maps of the *Southern Hemisphere* (used only when "Eastern" or "Western" hemispheres are not appropriate)
      2. Maps of individual *countries*. Within this section the countries are alphabetically arranged, and disbanded countries, i.e., Flanders, etc., are included in this section under their original names.

(M)   Minor Arts (M is always followed by an Arabic number to indicate the specific Minor Art)
        Type of minor art, e.g., M1   Arms and Armour
           Country or cultural area
              Century or subculture

MU   Museum Techniques
     ED   Education
     EX   Exhibitions
     HA   Handling of objects
     LA   Laboratory processes

P   Painting
       Country or cultural area
         Artist (if known) or century (if artist unknown) or culture, subculture,
         site of discovery, or century (prehistoric, ancient, or primitive cultures)
           Subject

PH   Photography
       Country or cultural area
         Photographer or century
           Subject

S   Sculpture (same as painting)

T   Techniques
       Type of art to which the technique belongs (major divisions used for type of
       art)
         Specific technique or material, the minor art division, the word *materials*,
         or the word *tools*.

The following slide label illustrates how this system is applied:

Slide Label 5

Line 1.	A IT	ROME. S.AGNESE,
Line 2.	R763 RC	FACADE(BY RAINAL-
Line 3.	AG E 1	DI,1652-53;BORRO-
Line 4.		MINI,1653-55;
Line 5.		OTHERS,1655-66).
Line 6.		EVANS TRIP 1966

Line 1:   A for architecture; IT for Italian; name of city; name of church
Line 2:   R763 for Cutter number for site or city of building; RC for cathedrals, churches,
            etc. or type of building; section of building illustrated; name of architect
Line 3:   AG for initials of building; E for exterior; 1 for sequence of slides dealing with a
            particular part or area of a single building; names and dates of architects or
            architect
Line 4:   name and date of architect, i.e., period during which architect worked on the con-
            struction of the building
Line 5:   continuation of Line 4
Line 6:   source information for slide; slide made by a staff member in Rome in 1966

This system has ten main classes and with the exception of diagrams, maps, museum techniques, and techniques, can be summarized as follows:

Medium
     Country, geographical or cultural area
         Artist or century
            Subject

University of Minnesota

Dimitri Tselos of the Department of Art History at the University of Minnesota is preparing for publication the system which he devised for the slide library at Minnesota. At the present time, an article by Mr. Tselos can be examined for a basic description of how this scheme works (1959).

Unlike the Harvard, National Gallery of Art, or Princeton schemes, this system does not include a decimal notation code but instead art terms or alphabetical abbreviations. Rather than being a classified system, it is based upon alphabetical subject order. The following is a broad outline of the system:

(A) Primary Divisions:
    Aboriginal
    Far East
    Near East
    West
    XYZ
(B) Eras:
    Ancient
    A-Mod (ancient through modern: Aboriginal, Far East)
    M-Mod (Medieval through Modern for Islamic)
    Medieval
    15-16c
    17-18c
    19c
    20c
(C) Countries: constituent countries alphabetically.
(D) Major Art Types:
    For all primary division except XYZ: Architecture, Painting, Sculpture, Varia (minor arts). For XYZ: Elements, Photography, Prints, Varia (20c minor arts) (ibid., p. 346).

Examples of abbreviations used include the following: 20c for twentieth century; ARCH for architecture; FR for France; and ABOR for aboriginal. For slide libraries not utilizing a decimal notation code in conjunction with their classification system, this type of abbreviated code is commonly used as a filing device which expedites slide filing. It is not necessary to read the entire label in order to determine where the slide belongs within the classification scheme. Two samples are provided; one with and one without such a code (these do not belong to any specific institution):

Slide Label 6	Slide Label 7
WITHOUT CODE	WITH CODE

Painting.19th Century.France.	P19FR	Cezanne, Paul.
Cezanne, Paul. Figure Groups.	.C425	The Cardplayers.
The Cardplayers.Date.Size.	m	Date.Size.Collection.
Collection.		

The code includes a Cutter number for Cezanne and a small letter "m" for figure groups. The use of a code also allows for an abbreviated label which involves less staff preparation but without the loss of complete cataloging information.

The Minnesota system can be summarized as follows:

Geographical or cultural area
    Period
        Country
            Medium

As is apparent from the summary of this scheme, it varies from the majority of the systems noted thus far in its main class emphasis on geographical or cultural areas as opposed to medium which has been moved to a section ranking in the overall scheme.

Yale University

Although a complete schedule of the Metropolitan Museum of Art's classification system has not yet been published, their scheme is used or modified by a significant number of academic institutions so that its broad outlines are not difficult to determine. Another system which is similar to the Metropolitan's—if not actually derived from it—is Yale University's Slide and Photograph Collection classification system totalling 75 pages.

The four main classes are as follows:

Architecture
Painting (including Drawing)
Sculpture
Minor Arts

Each of these main classes are then arranged by the following divisions, subdivisions, sections and subsections:

Periods (chronologically)
    Country (alphabetically—exceptions are noted)
        City (architecture)
            Building
        Artist (painting and sculpture)
            City
                Museum

The following periods are used:

General	Ancient world		Romanesque
Prehistoric	Early Christian		Gothic
Primitive	Byzantine	Early Medieval	Renaissance
Pre-Columbian	Merovingian	(alphabetical by city)	XIX-XX Centuries
Oriental	Carolingian		Latin America
Islamic	Ottonian		North America
Mudejar	Pre-Romanesque		

A rapid perusal of this list indicates an integration of geographical, cultural and chronological division designations so that Yale's use of the term "period" as applied to these terms is not totally consistent.

Exceptions to the period, country, city or artist classification are made for early medieval, African, and manuscript slides. Early medieval is classified by city first rather than by country. African slides are classified by medium (architecture, painting, sculpture, and minor arts), then by geographical region (African West, African Central, African South, African North, and African East), and by tribe. *An Outline of African Art* by William Teel, written as a Supplement to the African art series of University Prints, is a useful guide for geographical divisions and for the tribes of Africa (1970). Manuscripts are classified under Minor Arts and are divided by period, e.g., Early Christian, or by geographical area, e.g., Oriental, or by country. Within these divisions, the subdivisions of school, century, or artist are used.

Yale utilizes an abbreviated alphabetical code for their slide labels. The following slide label illustrates how the slides are cataloged:

Slide Label 8

Line 1.	Arch. XIX-XX U.S.
Line 2.	North Dartmouth, Mass. Schools
Line 3.	Southeastern Massachusetts Technical
Line 4.	Institute,
Line 5.	Paul Rudolph, Arch.
Line 6.	Arts and Humanities Building, 1966-67
Line 7.	Int: main hall
Line 8.	Y67-094 A-V Center March 1967
Line 9.	Architectural Record, March, 1967, p. 148

Line 1: Arch. for architecture; XIX-XX for nineteenth through the twentieth century; U.S. for United States
Line 2: name of city; name of state; subject or building type represented by Schools
Line 3: name of academic institution in which the building is located
Line 4: continuation of line 3
Line 5: name of architect
Line 6: name of building illustrated; building dates
Line 7: view of building; int. for interior
Line 8: Y67-094 is the negative or sequence number; A-V Center means that the slide was made by the Audio-Visual Center at Yale University; month and year when slide was made.
Line 9: source from which slide was made; name of the journal; date; plate number

As indicated by this label, Yale includes complete source information on all slide labels. The inclusion of this type of information for slides will be discussed in Chapter 4.

Summary

In order to select the preceding classification systems, approximately twenty-five different schemes were examined ranging from those devised for a slide collection of 15,000 slides to over 250,000 slides. The most salient aspect of all of these systems is their similarity. Whether developed for a large or a small collection, these classification systems all exhibited the basic utilization of medium, period, country or culture, artist or century, and subject format. The following outline of classes, divisions, subdivisions, sections and subsections for the major artforms is representative of the classification system utilized in most academic institutions:

> Medium (architecture)
>> Period
>>> Country, geographical or cultural area
>>>> Site (city or geographical area)
>>>>> Type of building

> Medium (painting or sculpture)
>> Period
>>> Country, geographical or cultural area
>>>> Artist
>>>>> Subject (or chronological order by date of work)

> Medium (decorative arts)
>> Country, geographical or cultural area
>>> Century

The major classes may be reversed with period preceding medium, but for the most part, the systems are all basically the same. Some use a decimal notation code (Harvard University, National Gallery of Art), while others do not (Metropolitan Museum of Art, University of Minnesota). One system is over 170 pages in length (National Gallery of Art) while another is less than 15 pages long (Cornell University). The examination of these different classifications reveals several important patterns. First, the absence of a coordinated approach to classifying slides in one area—the arts—has been a predominate theme for these visual resource collections because of their relatively isolated beginnings throughout academic institutions. Second, each collection has been organized with the intention of satisfying individual institutional idiosyncracies and yet, at the same time, each has been repeating the work of the other. Although the Harvard and Metropolitan systems have predominated as guides to other collections, in the majority of the collections throughout the United States, the similarity is only coincidental and not planned. Finally, the literature on the classification and cataloging of slides has either been completely absent or so widely dispersed throughout periodicals, journals, or handbooks that it has not been readily accessible to slide collection staffs.

University of California, Santa Cruz

Fortunately, for the slide library in the humanities or the sciences, a major breakthrough has been made in the consolidation and standardization of a classification system. This system has been devised at the University Library at the University of California, Santa Cruz, by Wendell Simons, Assistant University Librarian, and Mrs. Luraine Tansey, Slide Librarian (Simons and Tansey, 1970).

Basic to the conception and realization of this system is the difference between the concept of *visual* as opposed to *verbal content* as the fundamental drawback to the application of previous knowledge systems such as Dewey or the Library of Congress to a visual materials collection.

The following outline is a summary of the classification schedule provided by Mrs. Tansey:

HISTORY (Regional)
Field 1: Major time period
        2: Country (alphabetical)
        3: Major subject area
        4: Sub-category of subject area
        5: Person, place, or other term of major importance
        6: Person, place, or term Cuttered
        7: Subdivision
        8: Title of image in slide
        9: Detail or total image denotation
      10: Additional sequence of details

ART
Field 1: Major time period
        2: Country
        3: Art form
        4: Style
        5: Artist, place, or sub-period indicator
        6: Subject matter
        7: Optional subdivisions of Subject matter
        8: Title
        9: Total or part image
      10: Sequence code for details

SCIENCE
Field 1: Scientific discipline
        2: Country
        3: Subject area
        4: Subdivision of Subject area
        5: Major category
        6: Subdivision of major category
        7: Additional subdivision of major categories
        8: Specific title of image on slide
        9: Total or detail code for sequence
      10: Additional sequencing code letter

Included within this system are chronological period tables for arts, country and geographical divisions, subject divisions and subdivisions, style designations, and a complete nomenclature for science divisions and subject subdivisions. An authority list giving artists' names, their Cutter number, nationality, medium, and birth and death dates is also provided. A numerical and alphabetical code is used to compose the call numbers.

In addition to the ten fields for each topic from which the call number is derived, five more fields are included for cataloging data. The latter fields give the data in natural language rather than in coded alphabetical or numerical form: main entry, e.g., name of artist; title of item illustrated; date; present location of item illustrated; and the source for the slide. For each slide a punch card is made which includes all 15 fields. From these punch cards it is then possible to generate machine-readable indexes to the collection by call number, by each of the ten fields represented by the call number, and by any of the remaining five fields. For example, if a patron wants to know which slides in the collection are from the National Gallery of Art in London, then an index by present location or museum could be generated or scanned. It is, of course, possible to utilize the system manually without ever producing machine automated indexes. However, the University of California at Santa Cruz irregularly produces automated indexes to the slide collection which then updates the previous year's data base. A shelflist or call number index, an artist or place index, a subject matter index, an alphabetical title index, a date index, and a place name or location index comprise possible computer print-outs to the slide collection. As of 1973, approximately 37,000 (out of 75,000) slides had been classified, cataloged and indexed using this system.

As is apparent from the summary schedule, this scheme draws heavily upon the inherently natural and visible order of artistic, historical and scientific materials. The previous endeavors to classify pictorial materials have by no means been neglected, but instead have been incorporated into the system and have refined it. Even if the entire system is not used by a collection, aspects of it such as the subject divisions or the artist authority file may be practical for integration into a previously established collection. In order to make the system function both as an indexing and retrieval device, slides could be placed on aperture cards and mechanically retrieved but this approach is awkward for a large collection. The Medical School at the University of California at San Diego has used aperture cards as a master slide file from which they have duplicate slides made for faculty use. These cards are retrieved according to a keyword system based upon the publication *Standard Nomenclature of Diseases and Operations* (National Conference on Medical Nomenclature, 1961), which is also recommended as a source for fields 5, 6, and 7 of the Tansey system. Other published thesauri are also noted by Simons and Tansey in the section on the sciences.

A retrieval system for 35mm slides used in the arts and humanities has been developed by Robert Diamond (1969) of the College of Fredonia under a grant from the Bureau of Research, Office of Education, of the U.S. Department of Health, Education, and Welfare (Diamond, 1969). This system is primarily concerned with the full exploitation of the retrieval potential inherent in a visual image while the Tansey Slide Classification System (formerly called the Santa Cruz System) is based upon a formal classification approach to visual data. Mr. Diamond has developed a system of identifiers by which the user can retrieve an item by the standard methods such as by artist or by period and by his scheme which includes the date of the subject in addition to the date of the painting or object, the types of buildings depicted, battle sites illustrated, and other content approaches to the image. The scheme is directed toward both the general and the specialized user so that subject expertise is not a prerequisite for retrieval. At the present time, most collections are arranged for the subject specialist in academic institutions. The computer-produced indexes to the Santa Cruz collection allow for a wide range of user backgrounds in order to locate material but most academic collections do not have catalogs available to the patron. In Mr. Diamond's final report, he shows the application of the system to the art, history, and literature of the seventeenth century. His system of identifiers could be used in conjunction with the Tansey system in the same manner as any keyword or thesaurus approach to provide terms for the various sort fields such as the subject fields.

The following label illustrates the application of the Tansey classification system:

Slide Label 9

Line 1.	L474F	MICHELANGELO
Line 2.	M623V	SISTINE
Line 3.	S632VC	CUMEAN SIBY
Line 4.		1508
Line 5.	Rome:SC	
Line 6.	ET1.CS0106	

Line 1:   L for Renaissance (15th-16th centuries); 474 for Italy; F for painting

Line 2:   M623 for Cutter number for Michelangelo; V for Old Testament and Apocrypha (subject content); Sistine for title of work.

Line 3:   S632 for Cutter number for title; V for detail number and C for additional detail number (indicates that slide is a detail of a detail); Cumean Siby for the title of the detail

Line 4:   date

Line 5:   location, Rome, Sistine Chapel

Line 6:   source code

The following figure demonstrates how this same information appears in printed form at the top of a punch card. The numbers above the card indicate the 15 sort fields. Fields not used for the call number are blank, i.e., 4 and 7.

Slide Label 10—Punch Card

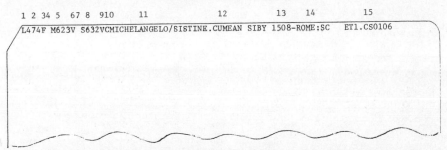

The first label is a sample from the history section and the second is from the science section of the Tansey classification.

Slide Label 11

Line 1.	G630L.J	FORD
Line 2.	F699Y.M	STAGECOACH
Line 3.	S7790	RINGO KID
Line 4.		1939
Line 5.	Wayne, John	
Line 6.	368.38.448	

Line 1:   G for twentieth century; 630 for United States; L for "Recreation outside the Home, Sports"; .J for motion pictures
Line 2:   F699 for Cutter number for Ford; M for model, three-dimensional representation; Stagecoach for title of work
Line 3:   S779 for Cutter number for Stagecoach; 0 for detail
Line 4:   date
Line 5:   present location of the work
Line 6:   source code

Slide Label 12

Line 1.	V73OG	LEGUMINOSAE
Line 2.	L521	LUPINUS NANUS
Line 3.	L969B	SKY LU
Line 4.	Santa Cruz	
Line 5.	URK1.2.8	

Line 1:   V for life sciences; 730 for Cutter number designating a state, local community or institution; G for Botany
Line 2:   L521 for Leguminosae which designates the arrangement for botany by taxonomic family
Line 3:   L969 for Cutter number for Lupinus Nanus (taxonomic binomial—genus species)
Line 4:   present location
Line 5:   source code

The Tansey Slide Classification System has been used by approximately one hundred institutions including the following: Ball State University, Indiana; the California Institute of the Arts, Los Angeles; Georgia Institute of Technology, School of Architecture Library; Sacramento State College; San Fernando State College; and the University of Houston, Audio-Visual Center. In 1971, Mrs. Tansey automated the Harvard (lantern slide) system utilized at the State University of New York at Buffalo.

Conclusions

For the slide collection composed solely of sets, adaptation of the Dewey Decimal Classification, Library of Congress, Universal Decimal Classification, or other formal classification schedules can be easily accomplished. This allows for complete integration of all print and nonprint material in one central catalog, a logical filing arrangement, and a subject arrangement reflective of the classification system. The single or unitary image collection cannot be logically adapted to the majority of classification systems devised for printed materials; therefore, the application of the Tansey Slide Classification System either directly or in modified format is recommended. The Metropolitan Museum of Art system, when it is published, should provide a useful supplement and complement to the Tansey System. In addition, the University of Michigan adaptation of the Harvard lantern slide system, best developed fine arts classification to emanate from an academic institution, is also recommended as a supplement to the Tansey System. When keyword or uniterm indexing is possible in conjunction with machine retrieval, this approach should be used either alone or in correlation to the Tansey System. The function of the collection, the needs of the users, and the potential for expansion should effect the classification, cataloging, or retrieval method selected by each collection. Within this framework, every attempt should be made to utilize standard approaches to the organization of slide libraries.

REFERENCES

AKERS, S. G. *Simple Library Cataloguing.* 5th ed. Metuchen, New Jersey: Scarecrow Press, 1969.

American Association of School Librarians and the Department of Audiovisual Instruction of the National Education Association. *Standards for School Media Programs.* Chicago and Washington, D.C.: American Library Association and the National Education Association, 1969.

American Library Colored Slide Catalogue of World Art. Teachers Manual for the Study of Art History and Related Courses. New York: American Library Color Slide Company, Inc., 1964. (Sixth printing, 1970).

Anglo-American Cataloging Rules. North American Text. Chicago: American Library Association, 1967.

Association for Educational Communications and Technology. Cataloging Committee. *Standards for Cataloging Nonprint Materials.* Rev. ed. Washington, D.C.: Association for Educational Communications and Technology, 1971.

Association for Educational Communications and Technology. The Information Science Committee. *Standards for Cataloging Nonprint Materials.* 3rd ed. Washington, D.C.: Association for Educational Communications and Technology, 1972.

CLARKE, Virginia. *Non-Book Library Materials. A Handbook of Procedures for a Uniform and Simplified System of Handling Audio-Visual Aids, Vertical File, and Other Non-Book Materials in the School Library.* Denton, Texas: Laboratory School Library, North Texas State College and North Texas State College Print Shop, 1953.

CLARKE, Virginia. *The Organization of Nonbook Materials in the Laboratory School Library.* Rev. ed. Denton, Texas: Laboratory School Library, 1969.

DAILY, Jay E. "Selection, Processing, and Storage of Non-print Materials: A Critique of the Anglo-American Cataloguing Rules as They Relate to Newer Media." *Library Trends,* 16:283-289 (October 1967).

DAUGHTRY, Bessie. *Cataloguing, Arrangement and Storage of Motion Pictures, Filmstrips, and 2" x 2" Slides.* M.A. Thesis, Florida State University, 1948.

DIAMOND, Robert M. *The Development of a Retrieval System for 35mm Slides Utilized in Art and Humanities Instruction.* Washington, D.C.: Bureau of Research, Office of Education, U.S. Department of Health, Education, and Welfare, 1969. (Final Report, Project No. 8-B-080).

FLEISCHER, Eugene B. "Uniterm Your A-V Library." *Audiovisual Instruction,* 14:76-78 (February 1969).

GROVE, P. S., and TOTTEN, H. L. "Bibliographic Control of Media: The Librarian's Excedrin Headache." *Wilson Library Bulletin,* 44:299-311 (November 1969).

HARRIS, Evelyn J. *Instructional Materials Cataloguing Guide.* Tucson, Arizona: Bureau of Educational Research and Service, College of Education, the University of Arizona, 1968.

HICKS, Warren B., and TILLIN, Alma B. *Developing Multi-Media Libraries.* New York: Bowker, 1970.

HICKS, Warren B., and TILLIN, Alma B. *The Organization of Nonbook Materials in School Libraries.* Sacramento, California: California State Department of Education, 1967.

HOPKINSON, Shirley L. *The Descriptive Cataloging of Library Materials.* San Jose, California: San Jose State College, Claremont House, 1963.

JOHNSON, Jean T., FRANKLIN, Marietta G., McCOTTER, Margaret P., and WARNER, Veronica B. *AV Cataloging and Processing Simplified.* Raleigh, North Carolina: Audiovisual Catalogers, Inc., 1971.

KEEN, Eunice. *Manual for Use in the Cataloging and Classification of Audio-Visual Materials for a High School Library.* Lakeland, Florida: Lakeland High School, 1955.

Library of Congress Processing Department. Subject Cataloging Division. *Outline of the Library of Congress Classification.* 2nd ed. Washington, D.C.: Library of Congress, 1970.

MASON, Donald. *A Primer of Non-Book Materials in Libraries.* London: Association of Assistant Librarians, 1958.

MOTLEY, Drucilla. "How to Find Your Slides Fast!" *Educational Screen and AV Guide*, 49:18-20, 31 (May 1970).

National Conference on Medical Nomenclature. *Standard Nomenclature of Diseases and Operations.* 5th ed. New York: McGraw-Hill, 1961.

National Education Association. Department of Audiovisual Instruction. *Standard for Cataloging, Coding, and Scheduling Educational Media.* Washington, D.C.: National Education Association, 1968.

Newark Public Library. *The Picture Collection Subject Headings.* Hamden, Connecticut: Shoe String Press, 1968.

QUINLY, W. J. "Selection, Processing, and Storage of Non-Print Materials; Aids, Indexes and Guidelines." *Library Trends*, 16:274-282 (October 1967).

RUFSVOLD, Margaret I. *Audio-Visual School Library Service, A Handbook for Librarians.* Chicago: American Library Association, 1949.

SAYERS, W. C. Berwick. *An Introduction to Library Classification.* 9th ed. London: Grafton and Company, 1958.

SAYERS, W. C. Berwick. *A Manual of Classification for Librarians.* 4th ed. Completely revised and partly rewritten by Arthur Maltby. London: Andre Deutsch, Ltd., 1967.

SAYERS, W. C. Berwick. *A Manual of Classification for Librarians and Bibliographers.* 3rd ed. rev. London: Grafton and Company, 1955.

SHORES, Louis. *Instructional Materials.* New York: Ronald Press Company, 1960.

SHORES, Louis. "The Medium Way; Librarian's Methods, and Media in the New Learning Mode." *The Library-College Journal*, 1:10-17 (Winter 1968).

SILVA, Manil. *Special Libraries.* London: Andre Deutsch, Ltd., 1970.

SIMONS, Wendell W., and TANSEY, Luraine C. *A Slide Classification System for the Organization and Automatic Indexing of Interdisciplinary Collections of Slides and Pictures.* Santa Cruz, California: University of California, 1970.

STONE, C. W. "Image for the Future." *California School Libraries*, 41:4-7, 37-40 (November 1969).

TEEL, William. *An Outline of African Art.* Cambridge, Massachusetts: University Prints, 1970. A supplement to University Prints Series N, Section I, African Art.

THOMPSON, Dixie. *Organization of Audio-visual Materials.* Tempe, Arizona: Curriculum Laboratory, Arizona State College, 1952.

TSELOS, Dimitri. "A Simple Slide Classification System." *College Art Journal*, 18:344-349 (Summer 1959).

WEIHS, Jean Riddle, LEWIS, Shirley, and MacDONALD, Janet. In consultation with the CLA/ALA/AECT/EMAC/CAML Advisory Committee on the Cataloguing of Nonbook Materials. *Non-Book Materials: The Organization of Integrated Collections.* 1st ed. Ottawa, Canada: The Canadian Library Association, 1973.

WETMORE, Rosamond B. *A Guide to the Organization of Library Collections.* Muncie, Indiana: Ball State University, 1969.

4—USE OF STANDARD LIBRARY TECHNIQUES AND TOOLS

INTRODUCTION

Most slide curators and librarians are fairly sophisticated users of library techniques and tools. In fact, the title "slide library" might be a more informative and valid nomenclature than slide "collection." For the purposes of this chapter, a library tool is defined as a referral or reference device utilized by librarians to locate information. Those tools used heavily by both the library staff and the patron include author-title and classified card catalogs, various types of standard reference works such as dictionaries and encyclopedias, and a variety of indexing sources. Remaining are the tools restricted more frequently for the direct use of the library staff rather than general user including acquisition, accession, authority, circulation, and shelflist records. The library's maintenance of these latter records may indirectly affect the efficient use of the library by the patron while the former provide immediate access for him to the library's reservoir of information.

Whether or not the individual in charge of the slide library identifies his index to artists' names as an authority file, for all practical purposes, it is. The lack of standardized terminology has led to many variations of basic library techniques and tools for slide libraries because the majority of these academic collections were not begun under the direction of the library. In schools and museums, the slides usually found their natural location for organization within the library although they frequently received limited attention during their initial growth period. The relatively recent abundance of publications on the organization of audiovisual materials for school and public library systems is indicative of the rather late concern shown for the standardized organization of these materials within the library context.

For the benefit of those unfamiliar with the various terms used to define library organizational methods and tools, the purpose of this chapter is to clarify and to establish a basic nomenclature for slide libraries based upon that used by libraries in general. In most instances, the terminology is not new or original but instead represents a synthesis of methods and terms used at the present time in many slide libraries throughout the United States.

CARD CATALOGS

Subject Catalog

As the majority of academic slide libraries are arranged in subject order based upon a classification system without notation, the use of a subject catalog is usually considered unnecessary because the collection is self-indexing. *Sears List of Subject Headings* (Westby, 1972) and the *Subject Headings Used in the Dictionary Catalogs of the Library of Congress* (U.S. Library of Congress, 1966) are the standard sources of subject heading format for most libraries. How do these standard headings relate to the classed slide file? If an individual is looking for nineteenth century French painting books in a library, he would check under the heading, "Painting, Modern—19th century—France" which utilizes the following order:

> Medium (painting)
>> Period (modern, 19th century)
>>> Country (France)

The books entered under this subject heading would then be in main entry, or title order depending upon the filing rules of the particular library. In the classed slide library, the patron would go directly to the slide files and check under painting, 19th century, France.

> Medium (painting)
>> Period (19th century)
>>> Country (France)

After country, however, the slides would be arranged alphabetically by artist. In contrast to the classed slide file, monographs on artists would be arranged separately in the subject catalog for book libraries directly under the artist's name. The slide file for a particular period would be arranged by the artists who defined the styles rather than by broad stylistic periods. Within each artist subsection, the slides would be classed by the subject orientation of that particular artist, e.g., portraits, landscapes, secular or religious works and so forth. This type of self-indexing arrangement, however, can present problems for the non-specialist who would not necessarily know by name and nationality, or by period, all the landscape artists whose work he would like to examine. This function provided by the general library card catalog heading, "Painting, Modern—19th century—France," is not possible for the classed slide file because of its internal class structure. A subject or classed slide file can operate fairly efficiently in a specialized academic departmental collection, in a museum or in an art school context but once the collection must provide multi-disciplinary access, then exhaustive reference service must be given to the user whose field is outside the subject orientation of the slide collection.

In the school, public library, and centralized academic library system, a collection of slides by individual artists or on any specific topic would necessitate the use of a subject catalog to locate materials. It is unfair to expect the non-specialist to utilize such a collection without the added expense of extra staff to accommodate this use pattern. The non-specialist should not be expected to know the country, medium, period or style in which an artist worked or in which a given historical concept or trend was established. For example, the historian interested in the changing patterns of costume styles should be able to approach his topic directly from this subject rather than through given historical periods or incidents. The ability to locate information in this manner is one of the primary advantages of the Tansey classification because it has a built-in capacity for generating its own indexes. Each keyword or concept designated by the numbers which compose a given field has an indexing potential. Several articles have also been written about the uniterm or keyword concept for slide or media retrieval in general (Diamond, 1972; Fleischer, 1969; Lewis, 1969; Motley, 1970). Although a classed and structured system, the Tansey scheme incorporates aspects of the uniterm or keyword method and can be expanded to unlimited possibilities as Mr. Diamond has indicated in his report. Unless a great many subject headings are made for each slide or visual image in a collection of this type, the specific pictures can receive only limited use. Utilization of a subject approach is mandatory for multi-disciplinary retrieval.

When an instructional materials center is being developed so that a media collection can service an entire campus, school or library system, it is impractical to devise a limited-use system. If such a collection is to have a central catalog which is a necessity for the total media approach, the materials should be integrated in the subject catalog but not on the shelves unless materials have been developed to be used only as packages or sets. To intershelve records, slides, and photographs is inefficient and wasteful of space. Storage for slides alone is quite complicated (see Chapter 6). What must be kept in mind is the difference between unitary image collections and packaged or set collections. For example, a set of slides (boxed), photographs (boxed), and records may conform enough in size to be intershelved without a loss of convenience. What happens, however, when an individual wants to mix various media from these sets? If the collection is indexed only by set, as it is shelved, then the ability of the user to integrate materials in novel ways might be seriously impeded if not destroyed. The most desirable system would provide for machine indexing of all print and nonprint material so that sound, image, and word could be retrieved without regard to physical format.

Very few academic collections have subject catalogs to their slide collections although this is the rule rather than the exception in school library systems. For examples of the application of standard subject heading rules, consult the following audiovisual cataloging manuals (Clarke, 1969; Harris, 1968; Hicks and Tillin, 1967; Weihs, 1973; Wetmore, 1969). Harvard University once maintained a contact print catalog alphabetically by artist, school or city for the lantern slide collection. It no longer does so for 35mm slides because of the time and labor involved in its development. Moreover, the self-indexing nature of the collection does not encourage use of such catalogs except by users outside the particular subject discipline of the collection. The Chicago Art Institute maintains a dictionary catalog for painters, architects, buildings and subjects in the collection. At Pratt Institute where the collection is housed in the general library rather than a departmental one, an attempt is being made to index the collection on a limited basis. When a collection begins to receive a great deal of use by various departments, as is the case at the Cornell University College of Art, Architecture and Planning, a need for thorough subject indexing is manifested. However, staff to do the indexing is frequently not available. The following examples, one for art and one for geology, illustrate how such a catalog might be devised. (See Slide Labels 13 and 14.)

Author-Title Catalog and Authority File

If a collection of slides is biographical, a standard author catalog is appropriate using entry format consistent with the *Anglo-American Cataloging Rules* (1967). If the collection includes art, the author catalog would be an artist catalog—painter, sculptor, architect, craftsman and so forth—leading the user to materials by the same artist under a uniform name whether his artform or medium is of one type or a variety of types. For collections arranged by historical period

Slide Label 13—Art Slide Subject Card (4" x 6")

```
                Waterfalls--United States--New York
    Call    Niagara Falls
    No.         American Falls.  n.d.
            View from Goat Island.  Aerial view.


            Color slide.  Purchased May 1965.
            From:  Ward's Natural Science
            Establishment, Inc.  Rochester, New York.
            173 W 1714.
```

Slide Label 14—Geology Slide Subject Card (4" x 6")

```
                Painting, Modern--19th century--France
    Call    Matisse, Henri, 1869-1954
    No.         Red Studio.  1911.
            New York, Museum of Modern Art.


            Ektachrome.  A-V Center.  February 1955.
            From:  Barr, A.  MASTERS OF MODERN ART.
            New York, Simon and Schuster, 1954.  p. 49.
```

or by medium, this catalog would provide invaluable access to all the works by one artist. This is the same function the author catalog provides for books.

Sets of slides can be assigned a title main entry card with artist added entry cards if appropriate. Locating slides solely by title, however, should be avoided and instead combined with some form of subject, author or artist catalog to insure a variety of access keys to an individual item or set of slides. The various manuals mentioned thus far provide adequate information on this catalog form and should be consulted if a title main entry approach to slides is used.

If the collection is small or if a consolidation of catalogs is desirable, the authority file can be combined with the author or artist catalog. The authority file gives the accepted format of an author's or artist's name which will be used consistently throughout a single collection. Cross references are included for pseudonyms and for complicated name forms.

For artists and architects, standard authorities include the following sources:
American Architects Directory. New York: Bowker, 1955-1962.
Art Index. New York: H. W. Wilson, 1930– .
Benezit, Emmanuel. *Dictionnaire critique et documentaire des peintres, sculpteurs, dessinateurs et graveurs.* . . . Nouv. ed. Paris: Gruend, 1948-1955.

Bryan, Michael. *Bryan's Dictionary of Painters and Engravers.* 1905, reprint ed., New York: Kennikat Press, 1971.

Catalog of the Avery Memorial Architectural Library of Columbia University. 2nd ed. Boston: G. K. Hall, 1968.

Catalogue of the Harvard University Fine Arts Library. The Fogg Art Museum. Boston: G. K. Hall, 1971.

Fletcher, Sir Bannister Flight. *A History of Architecture on the Comparative Method, for Students, Craftsmen, and Amateurs. . . .* 16th ed. London: Batsford, 1954.

The Metropolitan Museum of Art. New York. Library Catalog. Boston: G. K. Hall, 1960. Supplements: 1962, 1965, 1968, and 1970.

Thieme, Ulrich, and Becker, Felix. *Allgemeines Lexikon der bildenden Kuenstler von der antike bis zur Gegenwart.* Leipzig: E. A. Seemann, 1908-1954.

Vollmer, Hans. *Allgemeines Lexikon der bildenden Kuenstler des XX. Jahrhunderts.* Leipzig: E. A. Seemann, 1953-1962.

For additional dictionary and encyclopedia authorities consult the *Guide to Reference Books* by Constance Winchell (1967) for general materials and *Guide to Art Reference Books* by Mary Chamberlin (1959) for art books. English language reference books published since 1969 can be located in *American Reference Books Annual* edited by Bohdan S. Wynar. The above mentioned German work by Thieme and Becker is the most comprehensive dictionary of artists available. This basic source is supplemented and updated by Vollmer. Neither of these volumes, however, is particularly useful for contemporary artists. The *Art Index* or the Metropolitan Museum of Art library catalog are valuable sources on contemporary artists. Library catalogs are helpful for name or entry verification; those of the Bibliotheque Nationale, the British Museum and others cited above should be used when necessary. When the exact form of a name cannot be verified in such sources, strict adherence to the *Anglo-American Cataloging Rules* is recommended (1967).

When possible, the authority file card should, in addition to the standard name entry, provide birth and death dates, nationality, and the source of the name as used. Cross reference cards would also appear in this file. The mobility of the contemporary artist has posed nationality attribution problems for many collections. As a consequence, some collections file all artists in one alphabet without country divisions, while others follow the place of birth as the authority even though the legal nationality of an artist may have changed. Included in the Santa Cruz system is an authority for approximately 4,000 artists which gives birth dates, Cutter numbers, and nationalities. This list is based upon the strict use of place of birth for all nationality attributions. The major drawback to having the single integrated nationality arrangement for all artists is the size and awkwardness associated with using it. For example, many book libraries have a divided rather than a dictionary catalog in order to separate the author and title cards from the subject cards. This reduces the bulk of a single catalog and makes it easier to use. Another disadvantage of the integrated artist file is the fact that distinctions are not made with regard to period or chronology. It further divorces the user from a subject approach to the catalog because he cannot locate material by nationality or by historical alignment. Individuals who would normally be interested only in Renaissance slides would conflict with the user desiring to use only nineteenth and twentieth century materials. Moreover, unless a refined subject approach is available, the non-specialist would have a great deal of difficulty finding, for example, the religious art which dominated during the Renaissance. Historical or nationality divisions within the files yield more readily to browsing. For collections basing their system upon one similar to the Santa Cruz classification where nationality divisions are integral to the system, an authority file is mandatory.

The authority file functions to prevent the entry of an artist or author under different name forms or nationalities in the files which could cause dispersion of his works throughout the files. The following is a complete set of authority cards for a single artist including cross references:

Slide Label 15—Main Authority Card (3" x 5")

```
Cornelis Van Haarlem
Also called:  Cornelis Cornelisz
1562-1638
Netherlands                        Born:  Haarlem


Thieme-Becker
```

Slide Label 16—Cross Reference Cards (3" x 5")

```
            Cornelisz,  Cornelis
                  see
            Cornelis Van Haarlem
```

```
      Haarlem, Cornelis Van
            see
      Cornelis Van Haarlem
```

The use of authority files is relatively common in slide libraries. Forty percent of the academic and museum collections surveyed have authority files either for painters, sculptors, or architects or for all of these. Among these are the following institutions: Chicago Art Institute; Elmhurst College, Illinois; Indiana University; Rhode Island School of Design; School of Visual Arts, New York; Stanford University; Sterling and Francine Clark Art Institute; University of California at Los Angeles; University of Illinois; Winterthur Museum, Delaware; and Yale University. Princeton and the State University of New York at Binghamton, in addition to having painter, and architect authority files, also have authority files for the names of buildings.

Shelflist Catalog

The majority of the slide libraries studied have either an interfiled or a separate shelflist. The University of California at Santa Cruz and the California Institute of the Arts, Los Angeles, have machine-printed shelflists. As the use of machine indexing becomes more common, the availability of shelflist print-outs for holdings will also enjoy this convenience. An investory check system such as the shelflist is an invaluable aid to slide libraries in the same manner that it is to a book collection.

An interfiled shelflist refers to the placement of a shelflist card in front (the most common method) or behind each slide in a drawer storage file. This card is approximately the same size as the slide, 2" x 2", and has a copy of the slide label information typed directly upon the card. For example, the University of Illinois at Chicago Circle has an interfiled shelflist which is made by typing carbons of all labels (Slide labels 17 and 18). The sheets used for the carbons are the same label sheets used for the slides and are self-adhesive so that the identical label information typed on a label can be adhered to a shelflist card.

Slide Label 17	Slide Label 18
Slide with Label	Shelflist Card

Some collections include additional source data on the shelflist card although frequently the shelflist and slide label are the same. It is not immediately apparent on the University of Illinois at Chicago Circle label or shelflist card but source data is indicated by the "599a2" code on the third line. This code refers to a job order number, and the year during which this slide was made. As each slide is made, it is entered on a job order sheet which has a discrete number. These sheets are kept in loose-leaf notebooks as source and accession records.

An interfiled shelflist has both advantages and disadvantages. With the removal of a slide from the file which has an interfiled shelflist card for each slide, the staff and users immediately know that a particular slide is in the permanent collection but has been temporarily removed. With the separate shelflist, it is necessary to check an auxiliary record to determine the existence of a given item within the collection. Circulation controls are also possible with an interfiled shelflist and these will be discussed in the section on this topic in this chapter. The shelflist card also functions as a filing aid making more precise the exact location where the slide must be correctly re-filed. Where group filing of slides is maintained without call number order, an individual slide will not have a discrete filing location except as part of a group of slides. The major disadvantage is the added time it takes to remove slides individually and to re-file them individually rather than by groups. Moreover, the removal of these cards by the patron may also present problems which can be overcome by using a rod within the drawers similar to standard card catalog drawer rods with the slides resting above the rods. For example, if a standard card catalog such as the Library Bureau catalog, is used for slide filing, a diagram for the internal design of the drawer might look like the diagram on the following page (courtesy of the Winterthur Museum, Delaware). Blocks a, b, c, d, and e have been inserted into a standard card file in order to accommodate slides, shelflist cards, and rods. Various institutions including the University of Louisville, Vassar College, University of New Mexico, University of Michigan, and the Chicago Art Institute which have interfiled shelflists do not use rods. The use of rods or the need for rods will depend upon each institution's ability and desire to use this system. Indiana University is developing an interfiled shelflist using rods but, unlike the custom-designed drawer interiors for the Winterthur Museum, in drawers designed for this purpose. (See Chapter 6 for further information on storage systems.)

A separate shelflist is basically the same as a standard book shelflist merely duplicating the shelf or file location for each item in card form. Frequently, when separate shelflists are used (standard library-size cards are used), additional information such as the type of film, size of slide, source, and whether or not it is the duplicate of another slide already in the collection is noted. The size of the interfiled shelflist card will somewhat restrict the amount of information which can be given that is supplementary to the label data in addition to the format of the card. The following format is recommended for shelflist cards which are interfiled:

Slide Label 19

```
Call        Main entry.
No.         Title. Date.
            [Det. or View]
            Location.

Source.
Date acquired or made.

Accession number (if used).


            ◯
```

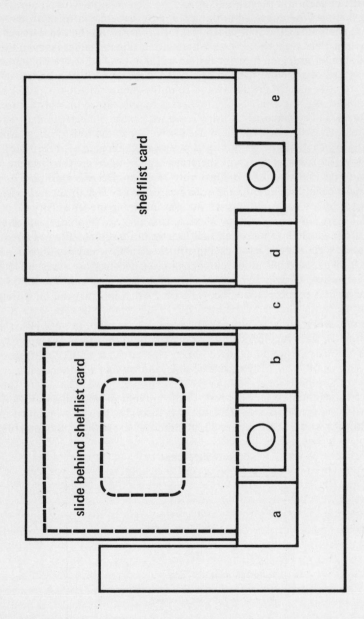

Diagram 1—Cross-section of drawer showing shelflist cards, slide position and location for drawer rods

The main entry could be an artist, author, title, or a word or phrase which describes the content of the slide. Detail or View is bracketed because it would not appear on every shelflist card.

A shelflist filed apart from the slide file does not function as an immediate circulation aid but can still be used to provide information on the slide library's holdings in a given area or in general. If consolidation of files is desired, however, an integrated or interfiled shelflist can be useful in a collection not composed solely of slide sets. Slides filed by sets should have a separate shelflist.

Conclusions

Although individual slides may be considered expendable because of their low production and purchase costs and may not, according to some, merit the creation of a two or three-phase card catalog system—author-title plus authority or separate authority and shelflist files—the information which the individual slide yields is not! The same applies to sets of slides. If the individual slide or set of slides is misplaced, as long as there is a convenient and complete record of that item or set within the library, it can in some form be replaced and again be made available to the user. The replacement form may be in black and white rather than in color or in 35mm rather than 3¼" x 4", or a duplicate rather than an original slide but these are minor points of differentiation. What is important is insuring the highest possible level of use and accessibility of information whether it is recorded orally, printed, or visualized as an image. Accomplishing this function efficiently is impossible without the use of the catalogs described.

ACQUISITION RECORDS

Approximately 75% of the slide libraries studied utilize acquisition records. Acquisition records record the date of acquisition, the vendor or source of the slide, and basic entry information which identifies the specific slide acquired or the dealer code number or a reference to a book from which the slide was made. These records may be of a temporary nature or of a permanent one depending upon how they are used. For some collections, the acquisition or source records and the order forms are the same. If the majority of slides are being made from books, it is not unusual for the request form to be kept as a permanent record of all slides made with the slides having a code which refers back to its original order sheet. For slides commercially purchased, standard institutional order forms are usually utilized and these may or may not provide the permanent record for slides purchased.

One of the most important aspects of the acquisition record is the notation of the vendor or source for each slide. This is critical for the replacement of slides and for supplementing the collection with similar types of material from a given source that has proven useful. A majority of slides made in academic institutions are copied directly from book plates so that an acquisition or source record can function as a bibliographic aid referring a user to specific texts relating to the slide image. Frequently, the entire record of the source is included on the slide label, e.g., Yale University, see Chapter 3, Slide Label 7, so that it is not necessary to refer to a supplementary acquisition file to find this information. It is, however, rather time-consuming to include complete bibliographic citations or source data on each slide label so that some abbreviation or code may be more desirable. At the same time, a complete reference to the original source should be maintained in some form. The author has developed the following form which is in use at Indiana University at the present time:

Slide Label 20—Acquisition or Source Record Format (4" x 6")

Author or vendor name.   Name of requester.
Date acquired.   Call number or book owner.
                                               (leave blank if vendor)

Title of book. Imprint (place, publisher, date).   OR
Name and date of catalog. Street address. City. State. Zip code.

Plates, figures, or pages copied listed numerically.   OR
Vendor number for each slide (if unavailable, the page and item number from vendor's catalog).

Slide Label 21—Sample from Book. Acquisition Card (4" x 6")

Murdock, George Peter.   Professor R. Sieber.
12/1870.   Personal copy.

Africa: Its Peoples and Their Culture. New York: McGraw-Hill, 1959.

Page (black and white): 353

The code on the slide label referring to this card (last line on label): 353.Murdock.12/1870.

The cards would be arranged alphabetically by author or vendor name; each slide would have a discrete code having the plate, page, or figure number first, author or vendor name second, and date of acquisition third. The year is abbreviated using only the last two digits so that this particular slide was made on December 18, 1970.

Slide Label 22—Sample from Vendor. Acquisition Card (4" x 6")

Ward's.   Mr. J. Whitehead
7/1369.

Ward's Color Slides Identification List. "Early Embryology of the Frog (Rana Pipiens)." Ward's Natural Science Establishment, Inc. P.O. Box 1712. Rochester, New York.   14603.

171 W 1000 (Set of eight slides).   171 W 1011 - 171 W 1018.

The code on the slide label referring to this card (last line on label): 171 W 1011.Ward's. 7/1369.

The code, 171 W 1011 refers to the first slide's number in this set purchased from Ward's, July 13, 1969. For convenience, vendor and book sources should be interfiled. A 4" x 6" card is recommended as it is an excellent size for indicating complete acquisition data.

There are numerous advantages to using this particular type of record as opposed to sheet, accession or log books. First, the information is in a convenient format which demands a minimum of space and can be conveniently placed in standard-sized cabinets while sheet records which may be kept in loose-leaf binders or in accession books become bulky and awkward to handle as they are amassed. In addition, if the staff or patron needs to know the extent of purchases from a specific source or the number of plates copied from a book, he can go directly to the acquisition card filed according to the author or vendor's name without consulting the slide files. Unless an index to the accession or sheet records is kept, this is not possible. For inventory or accession records on an annual basis, the new acquisition cards for each year may be kept separate for that year, inventoried at the end according to the number of slides acquired, and then interfiled with the main file or, as the new cards are added to the file, a note could be made of the number of slides acquired and then totalled at the end of the year. An accession card file would serve a similar purpose although again, it would not integrate all slides being acquired from a given source.

For slides being added to the original source card at a later time, the new date would be placed after the original date on the second line and a slash would be placed between the original page numbers and the second group or number acquired on the second date.

Slide Label 23—Additions to Original Book Acquisition Card (4" x 6")

Murdock, George Peter.   Professor R. Sieber. H. Smith.
12/1870. 1/1371.   Personal Copy. DT14.M97.

Africa: Its Peoples and Their Culture. New York: McGraw-Hill,
1959.

Page (black and white):   353; / 272; 343

If necessary, the notation of the person requesting slides could be continued on the reverse of the card. For the vendor card, a new card would be made since all the slides in the particular set illustrated were purchased. More than one card for a single vendor would be arranged in date order with the most recent acquisition card first.

Another possible method for keeping acquisition records is to type the source or acquisition data directly on the interfiled shelflist card or on a separate shelflist card. Unfortunately, the concept of maintaining an acquisition record arranged by the original source or vendor has not been commonly practiced in most academic collections because the shelflist or accession record sheets have been the standard location for this information. As is apparent from the system suggested, however, such data need not be restricted to one location, e.g., a code may be typed on the label, or shelflist card, but should be organized in the manner in which it will be needed which is according to the name of the source.

Institutions recording their acquisition or source data directly upon the slide label include the following: Emory University, Georgia; Johns Hopkins University; Smith College; San Jose State College; University of California at Berkeley; University of Florida; and the University of Iowa. The following indicate source data on separate shelflist cards: Harvard University; University of Illinois; University of Oregon; and the University of Pennsylvania. Source data is indicated on interfiled shelflist cards by Toledo Museum of Art; University of Louisville, and the University of Michigan. Accession or log books are used at the following institutions: Chicago Art Institute; Miami University, Ohio; University of Chicago; University of Illinois at Chicago Circle; University of New Mexico; University of North Carolina; University of Washington; and Wellesley College.

Conclusions

Order or acquisition records function for a slide library in the same manner as for book libraries and depend upon institutional formats in use at the time the order is placed. Book libraries like slide libraries also maintain vendor catalogs and, for a limited time, the original copies of order forms. These are used to check prices or identify vendors for the original purchases. In addition, if there are questions regarding the misplacement of an item when it is in the processing stage, the original order slip can be used to verify purchase. These same functions are provided by order, or acquisition forms for slides ordered commercially and for those made from books. Indigeneous, however, to the slide library—and to many photograph collections—where material frequently is made from book plates is the need for bibliographic reference to the corresponding text and to the original book plate. The large number of commercial dealers specializing in specific topics also makes it advantageous to have direct reference to these sources. A formal acquisition record designed to perform this function is mandatory for the efficient use, replacement, and supplementation of the slide library in any type of institution.

CIRCULATION RECORDS

Approximately 80% of the academic collections in the United States and the majority of museums use some form of circulation control. The most common circulation system used is based on charge sheets on which a patron lists each slide individually giving either a full subject description, call numbers, accession numbers or an alphabetical code combined with descriptive data. These sheets generally require information similar to that written on standard book charge forms.

Standard 8½" x 11" pages are used for charge sheets rather than cards because an individual may charge out 20 or more slides at a single time. By using a sheet of corresponding size to the number of entries or slides charged at one time, it is possible to determine all material charged to a single patron without checking an entire charge file. With this system, priority is placed on the name of the individual rather than on the item removed, as would be the case with book libraries. Consequently, it is necessary to know the name of the borrower before specific items can be traced for location. An example of the basic format of such a sheet is illustrated in Diagram 2.

The utilization of charge sheets of this type for circulation control has obvious disadvantages although the type of collection for which it is most commonly used must be considered if criticism of the method is to be valid. It functions fairly efficiently for those collections composed of one subject used by a limited number of faculty members within the subject orientation of the collection. For example, in the majority of art departments or schools where this system is used, the majority of the users work according to specific areas of art history study thereby automatically classifying their charged material by their area of specialization. For example, the medieval history professor would probably have the major portion of the Romanesque and Gothic architecture slides charged from the files. In order to locate specific slides which are in circulation, his charge sheet could be checked. As soon as a collection becomes widely used, however, this system collapses unless it is accompanied by a subject index to the slides charged out to each patron. Needless to say, this becomes a rather complicated and time-consuming effort necessitating additional staff time to maintain such an index. In fact, when the charge sheet type of circulation control reaches or is beginning to reach the point when it is not feasible, an alternative method should be selected. The charge sheet method of circulation control is commonly used by academic institutions for

Diagram 2—Slide Library Charge Sheet

SLIDE LIBRARY CHARGE SHEET

Name: _____   Title: _____

Address: _____   Phone: _____

No. of 2″ x 2″ slides: _____   Date Charged: _____

No. of 3¼″ x 4″ slides: _____   Date Due: _____

Call No. or Access. No. or Abbreviated Code.	Artist or Subject.	Title.

two reasons: it allows adequate space for the recording of information on individual slides, and most academic collections receive use by a limited number of subject specialists in a single discipline. This pattern is changing as academic collections become more in demand by other users.

For many academic collections, the application of rigid circulation methods is rather difficult because of the heavy faculty use patterns and the feasibility of checking out a large number of slides at a single time. This prohibits the slide librarian or curator from imposing complicated charging procedures for individual slides. Consequently, the faculty or staff may not be using the charge sheet method but another simpler charging process or, in some instances, none at all. The latter may apply when the collection and number of users is quite small, e.g., fewer than five users and fewer than 5,000 slides.

An example of a relatively simple method of circulation control is operative at the University of Michigan where all of the faculty keep their slides in the slide library in trays or cases until they are removed for class presentation. Thus, all slides remain in the slide library unless they are in use, and are available to all patrons who may remove them temporarily. At Michigan, these trays or cases are kept on standard storage shelves in the workroom. As would be apparent, keeping all slides separated in lecture order ready for immediate use requires adequate space allotted for this function based upon the total number of users or potential users of the slide library. This system works relatively well for users making slide presentations in the same building as the slide facility but presents transportation problems for individuals who may need their slides for a presentation outside the immediate building or institution. Again, as soon as slides are being used by a large number of individuals in various teaching stations and buildings, this procedure becomes inadequate.

If the collection has been properly organized from its inception, then an interfiled shelflist has been developed. The interfiled shelflist can be an invaluable aid to circulation control. For collections used in a departmental situation by a constant group of patrons, each faculty member or patron is assigned color-coded cards or white cards with his name printed across the top of each card. A chart of names or of color codes could be posted in the slide library for everyone's use. As each patron removes a slide, a color card or card which identifies the user is placed in the slide's slot. These circulation cards should be ¼" to ½" higher than the inter-filed shelflist cards. The circulation cards are visible above the interfiled shelflist cards and immediately show which slides have been removed from the file. The following illustrates how these cards would appear in the file:

Slide Label 24

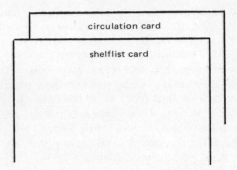

This method also informs the staff or user who has removed the slide. How is the irregular user handled? A single color-coded card may identify all outside (outside the immediate department) or irregular users who then fill out a charge card or sheet indicating the total number of slides removed. Individual identification of each slide is not necessary because it has already been identified within the slide file by the color card. The major disadvantage of this system is the need for a dual circulation system for inter-departmental or regular users and extra-departmental or irregular users. Another alternative available to the irregular user would involve signing his name on each card which he inserts to replace each slide removed. His name would then refer to a charge card indicating the total number of slides charged, his address and phone number. This latter method is a more precise means of distinguishing exactly which irregular user has charged out slides. In addition, the process of refiling slides is also simplified. The exact location of each missing slide is flagged by the circulation card.

How do large museums handle circulation control? Many, including the Boston Museum of Fine Arts, the Cincinnati Art Museum, the Cleveland Museum of Art, the City Art Museum of St. Louis, and the Philadelphia Museum of Art, use charge sheets or cards for circulation records. These are filed alphabetically by the name of the patron. The Chicago Art Institute and the Metropolitan Museum of Art require that a microfilm copy be made of all slides charged out. They both have a Recordak microfilmer. The patron fills out a charge card or form giving his name, address, and number of slides to be charged. A Recordak machine microfilms this card at the beginning and end of the group of slides which are loaned. Referral to the microfilm is necessary only when a slide is lost and the patron cannot identify it or when he returns the incorrect number of slides. The microfilm copy can then be used to acquire information for replacement purposes. Patrons are usually fined for lost or damaged slides. The charge cards are filed alphabetically by the name of the patron. This method of charging out slides usually applies only to the public; the curatorial staff may use a simple charge card or sheet method without the use of the Recordak microfilmer. The major advantage of the microfilm charge record is that it involves a minimum of user time to check out slides.

If slides are to be charged out in sets, standard book cards can be used and interfiled in the circulation file for books. Interfiling of all media and book circulation records, however, is based on the assumption that all materials have been classified according to the same system. If this is not the case, separate files should be maintained and labelled so that there is not confusion regarding each file's function. Charging by slide set refers only to those slides which have been classified as a set. Sets of slides or individual slides which have been assigned discrete classification numbers or an alphabetical code system combined with numbers such as the Dewey, Library of Congress, or Santa Cruz schedules can be charged on standard library charge cards and filed according to notation system used. Slide Label 25 is an example of a library charge card demonstrates its use for charging out a slide classified according to the Santa Cruz system.

Using a circulation system that readily conforms to standard library procedures and materials is the most convenient method if the collection has been developed to adapt to this type of circulation pattern. Most collections, however, do not have a classification system which relies on the use of discrete call numbers for each slide or use an accession number which could also be used as a charge number. The disadvantages of maintaining only a file according to the name of the patron who has charged out the slides has already been noted. The dual system of circulation control using an interfiled shelflist charge or circulation card and a charge card filed alphabetically by the name of the patron is certainly the most efficient method for a unitary image collection. The charge card used could be a standard library card. The microfilm record, although an efficient method for maintaining accurate circulation records, would be awkward for patrons and staff to use on a regular basis in order to identify individual slides that have been charged out.

Whether the slide library is an independent one developed for the use of a single academic department, for the use of more than one department or school, for the use of a museum curatorial staff, the public, or for an instructional materials center designed for multi-disciplinary use, the user patterns will affect the type of circulation system selected. The circulation system chosen for a given institution can be flexible depending upon the function of the collection but it should be as consistent as possible for all users in order to avoid confusion. A combination interfiled shelflist and charge card system is recommended for academic collections having inter- and extra-departmental use. A standard library charge card should be

Slide Label 25—Charge Card

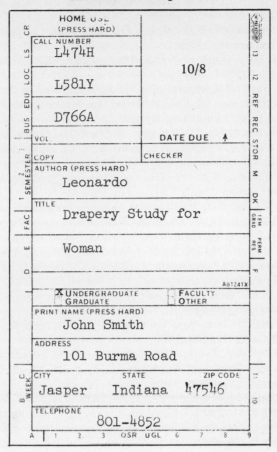

used by collections of classified slide sets. For a unitary image collection of slides in a museum, public library or school, either the combination interfiled shelflist and charge card system, a microfilm system, or a standard library charge card system with each slide charged out individually (one per card) can be used.

Summary

Standard library tools and techniques should be utilized in the slide library as frequently as possible. This basic principle will decrease arbitrary standards and procedures, will allow for the logical expansion of the collection, and will provide consistency and standardization in the use of all library materials. Most standard library procedures and tools have already benefitted from a great deal of reform and revision. If such procedures or tools can be directly adopted by the slide library with a minimal amount of change, then the general maintenance and organization of the collection should benefit by the adoption process.

REFERENCES

Anglo-American Cataloging Rules. North American Text. Chicago: American Library Association, 1967.

CHAMBERLIN, Mary. *Guide to Art Reference Books.* Chicago: American Library Association, 1959.

CLARKE, Virginia. *The Organization of Nonbook Materials in the Laboratory School Library.* Rev. ed. Denton, Texas: Laboratory School Library, 1969.

DIAMOND, Robert M. "A Retrieval System for 35mm Slides Utilized in Art and Humanities Instruction." *Bibliographic Control of Nonprint Media.* Edited by Pearce S. Grove and Evelyn G. Clement. Chicago: American Library Association, 1972.

FLEISCHER, Eugene B. "Uniterm Your A-V Library." *Audiovisual Instruction,* 14:76-78 (February 1969).

HARRIS, Evelyn J. *Instructional Materials Cataloguing Guide.* Tucson, Arizona: Bureau of Educational Research and Service, College of Education, the University of Arizona, 1968.

HICKS, Warren B., and TILLIN, Alma B. *The Organization of Nonbook Materials in School Libraries.* Sacramento, California: California State Department of Education, 1967.

LEWIS, Elizabeth M. "Graphic Catalog Card Index." *American Documentation,* 20:238-246 (July 1969).

MOTLEY, Drucilla. "How to Find Your Slides Fast!" *Educational Screen and AV Guide,* 49:18-10, 31 (May 1970).

U.S. Library of Congress. Subject Cataloging Division. *Subject Headings Used in the Dictionary Catalogs of the Library of Congress.* 7th ed. Washington, D.C.: Library of Congress, 1966.

WEIHS, Jean Riddle, LEWIS, Shirley, and MacDONALD, Janet. In consultation with the CLA/ALA/AECT/EMAC/CAML Advisory Committee on the Cataloguing of Nonbook Materials. *Non-Book Materials: The Organization of Integrated Collections.* 1st ed. Ottawa, Canada: The Canadian Library Association, 1973.

WESTBY, Barbara M., ed. *Sears List of Subject Headings.* 10th ed. New York: H. W. Wilson, 1972.

WETMORE, Rosamond B. *A Guide to the Organization of Library Collections.* Muncie, Indiana: Ball State University, 1969.

WINCHELL, Constance. *Guide to Reference Books.* 8th ed. Chicago: American Library Association, 1967.

Supplements to the 8th ed. published in 1968, 1970, and 1972.

WYNAR, Bohdan S. *American Reference Books Annual.* Littleton, Colorado: Libraries Unlimited, 1970– .

5-ACQUISITION, PRODUCTION METHODS AND EQUIPMENT

INTRODUCTION

Ninety percent of the academic institutions and museums documented in the United States are engaged both in making and purchasing slides. It is possible to make slides institutionally for a relatively small expenditure per slide while commercially acquired slides may be double or triple the cost. Although the majority of academic institutions both purchase and make their own slides, the budget allotment for commercial purchasing is usually smaller than that for internal production on a cost-per-slide basis, i.e., even if the budgets are the same, fewer slides can be acquired commercially because of the higher costs. At the same time, however, the cost range varies so radically (from about $0.30 to $3.00 per slide) that in many instances, even the cost factor is not significant enough to prevent commercial purchasing. Moreover, an institution may prefer not to invest in the staff, cameras, film, copystands, and processing materials and equipment necessary to make slides. For some institutions, it is less expensive to purchase slides mounted, labelled, and ready to use from commercial sources.

Under a Ford Foundation Grant in 1961/62, the College Art Association undertook a study which touched on every aspect of visual arts education in academic institutions and museums. Andrew C. Ritchie's study, *The Visual Arts in Higher Education* (1966), briefly notes the problems of supplying quality slides for lectures and also the vast sums expended in this area in 1961/62.

> In 1961-62 the total slide budget for 264 departments, our questionnaire revealed, came to $172,600, to meet an annual demand of 233,000 slides. Since by no means all departments answered our questionnaire it is conservative to estimate that at least a quarter of a million dollars is being spent annually in America by art departments for slides alone. (Ritchie, p. 43).

Based on the present study, with 91 institutions out of 101 supplying information on slide production rates, a total of 572,643 slides were produced and purchased during 1968/69 in the United States by less than one-third the number of schools reporting to the College Art Association survey. The range was from 500 slides per year at Denison University, to 16,000 slides annually at Columbia University. The annual average per school was 6,293 slides for both purchases and institutional production. Eight institutions supplied figures for the total acquisition annually of commercial and produced slides so that it was not possible to determine the percentage of purchased as compared to produced slides for this group. For the remaining 83 institutions, slightly more than 50% of the slides acquired were commercially purchased so that approximately 177,141 slides out of a total of 347,803 slides were commercially purchased.

Institutionally produced	347,803 (83 institutions)
Commercially purchased	177,141 (83 institutions)
Produced and purchased	47,699 (8 institutions)
Total	572,643 (91 institutions)

In comparison to the College Art Association study, these figures which document fewer institutions than CAA included, indicate acquisition levels which more than double the amount of slides acquired in 1961/62 by academic departments. The CAA figures reveal an average cost for slide acquisition of $0.74 per slide in 1961/62. If this same figure were used today to determine the total budgets for 91 slide collections, $4,237,550.02 would be the resultant expenditure for these institutions. If CAA were estimating a quarter of a million spent for over 264 departments in 1961/62, then a modest estimate for 1968/69 would be close to ten million dollars for over 200 schools using their base figures. These figures, however, may vary greatly because of increases in overhead, supplies, equipment, and staffing from 1961 to 1969. At the same time, however, slides are actually less expensive to acquire today because of mass commercial production methods. At the beginning of 1960, more schools could have still been purchasing 3¼" x 4" slides than 2" x 2" which also could have caused higher per-slide cost. [Although somewhat dated, the results of the CAA study are provided to illustrate the fact that the acquisition of slides by academic institutions and museums is a major undertaking involving vast expenditures. Budgets necessary to acquire slides are rarely understood because of the relatively low per unit cost of slides in relation to that of other media, i.e., filmstrips, phonorecordings, tapes, and so forth.]

Certainly, on the academic level, the commercial distributor and producer plays an important role in collection building even though significant quantities of slides are produced institutionally. The figures discussed apply only to colleges, universities and a small number of museums. A large number of institutions, particularly on the public school level, have not been identified in terms of the extent of their acquisition of slides. As is apparent from the directory of slide distributors and producers outside the art field (see Appendix), this is not an insignificant market for either business or educational institutions.

There are obvious advantages and disadvantages to both methods of acquisition. Each institution should decide which method or combination of acquisition methods is most economical and efficient based upon its needs and budget.

TYPES OF SLIDES

The most common slide used in slide libraries is the 2" x 2" slide produced by using a 35mm camera. In addition to this format, there are "super slides" or square 2" x 2" slides, 2¼" x 2¼" slides and 3¼" x 4" or lantern slides. The square 2" x 2" slide which uses 126 film results from using the Instamatic cameras and are frequently called Instamatic slides. All of the standard 2" x 2" size slides can be used in 2" x 2" slide-filmstrip projectors. Lantern or 3¼" x 4" projectors can project the lantern slide, 2" x 2" (all formats), and 2¼" x 2¼" slides with appropriate slide carriers or masks. The general range of sizes derived from 2¼" x 3¼" film is 2½" x 2¼", 2-3/4" x 2-3/4", and 3¼" x 4" slides.

Slide collections which were established before 1940 still have relatively large quantities of lantern slides. Many of these collections have withdrawn lantern slides from daily use, while others maintain them as part of their active library. Large lantern slide collections are still actively used at Cornell University, College of Architecture, Art and Planning (90,000 lantern slides), Harvard University (80,000 lantern slides), University of Michigan (61,000 lantern slides), University

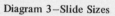

Diagram 3—Slide Sizes

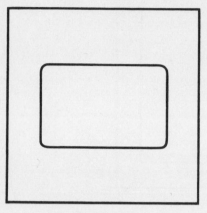

2″ x 2″ (135 size film)

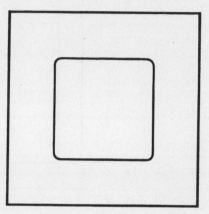

2″ x 2″ (126 size film)

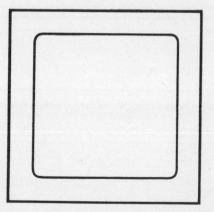

"Super" (127 size film)

Diagram 3—continued

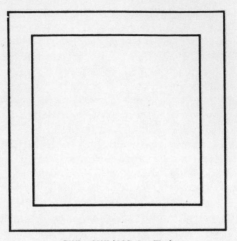

2¼″ x 2¼″ (120 size film)

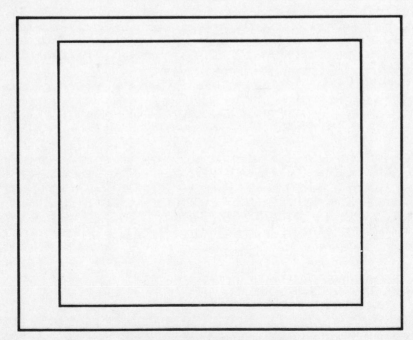

3¼″ x 4″ Lantern (2¼″ x 3¼″ size film)

of Minnesota (60,000 lantern slides), and Princeton University (105,000 lantern slides). Although many academic institutions still have lantern slides, a relatively small number are actively engaged in making them for their collections. These schools include the following: Harvard University; Howard University; Oberlin College; Smith College; the University of Minnesota; the University of Iowa; Vassar College; and Yale University. Less than one-fourth of the academic collections surveyed reported that they are producing and purchasing lantern slides.

The lantern slide may not enjoy the widespread use which it did at the turn of the century and for the first three decades of the twentieth century, but the "hand-made" lantern slide is still noteworthy particularly for schoolroom use and for production by both students and teachers. A publication useful in this area by Holland, Hartsell and Davidson describes five different types of handmade 3¼" x 4" slides: cellophane typewritten slides; frosted cellophane or plastic slides; etched or ground glass slides; gelatin slides; and silhouette slides (1958, pp. 60-63). Using 2" x 2" cover glass, miniature slides can be made from laboratory specimens such as hair or wood slivers. Students can also make their own slides using paints and felt markers. Several articles have appeared on various types of 2" x 2" handmade slides in *Arts and Activities* (Gruber, 1969; Moody, 1966). For additional literature on this topic see the bibliography on "Slides Made Without Film" in the Appendix.

Until the advent of Polaroid Land film within the last ten years, the lantern slide played a less prominent role in slide library collection building because of its cost, fragility, size, and weight as compared with 2" x 2" slides. As indicated earlier, these slides were printed upon glass plates and bound with another glass plate of the same size covering the emulsion side of the slide to protect it from damage. Even with standard photographic processing and film available, the lantern slide has not held its own with the miniature slide. Now, using a Polaroid Land camera with 46L (for continuous tone) or 146L (for line copy), a Polaroid process can be used for 3¼" x 4" or 2¼" x 2¼" slides providing rapid projection material for less than $0.75 per slide (Wiesinger, 1964).

MAKING SLIDES FROM
REPRODUCTIONS AND PHOTOGRAPHS

Although there is an adequate amount of literature on various types of slides and basic production methods, an area that has not enjoyed widespread publication is the copying of slides from reproductions or book plates and from photographs—possibly because of the copyright issue which will be discussed later in this chapter. Most reproductions in books have been produced by offset or letterpress with offset being the less expensive process for the printing of large quantities of plate material. Several books have been published on the photographic processes involved in the reproduction of works of art—the reader is advised to examine this material, some of which is included in the bibliography on the "Photography of Art and Architecture" in the Appendix.

Notwithstanding the complexity of the techniques of photographic reproduction, a slide librarian should become familiar with the basic principles for judging the quality of a reproduction or photograph in order to insure that slides made from such reproductions are of the highest quality possible. The majority of academic collections make their own slides from book plates or photographs so that it is imperative to establish selection standards for these reproductions in order to control slide quality. Some schools may have large photograph collections which provide a source for slides along with picture and vertical file materials.

Black and White Slides

Whether the slide library has its own photographic equipment for making slides or the campus audiovisual center or museum photography department is responsible for this task, the slide librarian always should examine critically material submitted for copy work. A poor quality reproduction or photograph will result in a low quality slide. The following questions should be asked when judging the quality of black and white reproductions or photographs.

1. **Is the image in focus or are the edges of objects fuzzy?**
2. **Is there a wide range of contrasts including darks, middle tones or greys, and whites or is the image "washed" out?** If it is a high contrast reproduction or photograph, it will have limited or negligible middle tones or greys. Detail is frequently lost entirely during the copying process. If it is low contrast, the entire reproduction will have a grey or faded quality.
3. **Does the reproduction have an overall grey cast and if so, is it characteristic of the original image?** Many graphic reproductions of drawings, or prints, may actually have this monotone quality from the outset so that it is indicative of the original image and not of inferior photographic techniques. Frequently, the immediate response to this question is, "How can I know the quality of the original if I have never seen it?" Unfortunately, this is the case for many individuals who are faced with copy work of this type. A good source of expertise is from teachers or persons who have had the opportunity to travel and to examine firsthand paintings, drawings, prints and other objects d'art. The other method for judging is provided by this outline.
4. **Is the reproduction or photograph too small to be copied and then projected successfully?** If the image is small and of inferior quality, it is doubtful that when projected on a large scale that even original quality will be retained. In its pamphlet *Artwork Size Standards for Projected Visuals* (1968), the Eastman Kodak Company recommends a simple technique for determining whether an image to be copied for projection is of adequate size. Rooms designed for projection usually have a maximum viewing distance that is about six times the width of the screen image (ibid., p. 1). This same relationship can be used when examining reproductions for copy work.

> For typical (6W) viewing, the material size can be judged by looking at the area to be copied from a distance of six times its width. (ibid., p. 2).

Using this formula, take a reproduction in a book which is 4" wide, multiply four times six which equals twenty-four, and examine the image from a distance of 24". If the image and relevant details are visible, the reproduction size should be adequate for copying and projection. This technique is particularly useful for judging projection clarity of highly detailed monochromatic images.
5. **What is the general quality level of the rest of the plates in the book?** Most publications are fairly consistent in their reproduction qualities as this has been

predetermined by the process used and papers selected for optimal printing of black and white plates. Many books having the highest quality plates will require the use of different papers and printing methods for color, black and white, and line reproductions such as maps or fine drawings or prints. This added expense of plate reproduction is indicative of the generally high cost of "picture" books. If the book demonstrates relatively high quality throughout, then the plate in question is probably fairly accurate at least in terms of reproduction potentials. From the beginning it should be remembered that any reproduction is automatically removed from the fidelity of the object itself and therefore will minimally suffer from distortion of one form or another. What needs to be determined is the severity of that distortion.

6. **If the item reproduced has been placed against a backdrop, e.g., a cloth, paper, or board, does the background detract from the object itself?** If so, an attempt should be made to find another reproduction which has a simpler background. A fine scientific specimen or an art object can be greatly enhanced by the proper background. For example, the color of a background can affect the color of the item photographed against it.

Many researchers and teachers prefer monochrome or black and white slides or reproductions to color ones because monochrome plates can be better controlled in terms of their quality. The color process is less flexible. John Lewis and Edwin Smith (1969) discuss this problem in their book on graphic reproduction. For classroom and student use, however, the color plate is frequently more effective for nature, science or art studies and other subjects that are enhanced by the use of color images.

Color Slides

Whether the image projected is a painting, a butterfly, or a scene of the Grand Canyon, the reality of the projection is heightened with color slides. Certainly, if the color slide is of high quality, even the most demanding user would prefer it to a monochrome one depending upon the subject matter illustrated. There are cases where color slides are simply not necessary or do not satisfy the demands of a given image or user. For example, for line drawings, topographical maps or architectural diagrams, the black and white slide is preferred because of the greater resolving power of black and white film. An excellent explanation of this concept is provided in a book on the history of photographic research by C. E. K. Mees in a chapter entitled, "The Structure of the Developed Image" (1961, pp. 87-98).

Criteria for judging photographs using supplementary equipment other than direct visual examination are also discussed by Mees (ibid.). For the purposes of this chapter, however, criteria based solely upon direct eye-to-image evaluation are elucidated. In the majority of slide libraries, this type of direct examination of film and images will be the only available guide for qualitative judgments. In order to determine the quality of color plates or slides, some basic information on the color theory of photography is necessary. Again, if the reader is interested in a detailed discussion of this topic, Mees' book, *The Encyclopedia of Photography* (1965), and other publications are readily available.

The three primary colors in photography are red, green, and blue as compared to red, yellow, and blue in color theory. The three complimentary colors are cyan, magenta, and yellow in photography as compared to orange, green and purple in color theory.

Photography	Color Theory
Primary Colors	
red	red
green	yellow
blue	blue
Complimentary Colors	
cyan	orange
magenta	green
yellow	purple

In order to judge the accuracy of the standard photographic image, e.g., an indoor or outdoor scene with people, the skin tones and whites should be examined as they are good indicators of the faithfulness of the overall photograph to the original color scheme—this assumes that color filters were not used intentionally to distort the colors of the original scene. If the skin tones or whites have a red, green, blue, cyan, magneta, or yellow cast, then the remainder of the picture probably demonstrates corresponding levels of color error.

Light, of course, is an important factor affecting the potential for color error or accuracy of a photograph as are background and foreground colors for a given subject. Mid-morning or mid-afternoon lighting is the preferred lighting for making color slides using only natural light because at these times, the distortion level caused by early morning, noon, or late afternoon lighting is lowest. Using only natural light, a copy stand and camera, it is possible to make good slides from color reproductions. As it is rather awkward to do such work outside, a table placed near a window that is receiving adequate natural lighting will prove satisfactory. Needless to say, this type of set-up is not desirable for copying large quantities of material on a regular basis but is offered simply as an alternative method for irregular copy work when proper artificial lighting is not available. Using natural light does, however, avoid some of the problems encountered by the inexperienced and occasional slide producer who is not familiar with how to use appropriate color filters and artificial lighting to insure maximum color fidelity.

In photography the range of color accuracy or error is based upon the relationship of the primary and complimentary colors. For example, in order to correct for an image having a red cast, a cyan filter is used, for green, a magenta filter, and for blue, a yellow filter. The cyan filter is actually absorbing the red and this is referred to as additive color mixture. The reverse also applies—if an image has a cyan cast, a red filter is used, for magenta, a green filter, and for yellow, a blue filter. The latter process is called substractive color mixture.

Additive Color Mixture	Substractive Color Mixture
red ◄——— cyan	red ———► cyan
green ◄— magenta	green ——► magenta
blue ◄——— yellow	blue ———► yellow

There are different filter intensities that can be used depending upon the intensity of the color error. Combinations of different filters can also be used for color correction, e.g., for a magneta cast, a yellow plus cyan filter, for yellow, a cyan plus magenta filter, and for cyan, a magenta plus yellow filter. This is a highly simplified explanation of the actual photographic changes occurring but the reader needs to recognize this color range to understand a basic explanation of color correction.

When examining color photographs or reproductions from books, the following questions should be asked:

1. **Is the image in focus or are the edges of objects fuzzy?**
2. **Do whites or skin tones appear to be unnatural?**
3. **Does the entire image have a red, green, blue, cyan, magenta or yellow cast? If so, is this in keeping with the fidelity of the original image or is it a distortion of the image?** This question can be particularly problematic with regard to contemporary art as the likeness of the image to reality is no longer a valid criterion for color accuracy. Instead, the image must be judged in terms of the artist's style and general use of colors. The same may apply to geological or scientific studies where comparisons with the original image are not possible so that the quality of the image must be judged as it appears and not based upon preconceptions.
4. **If the reproduction is in a book, do all the plates exhibit the same color cast? If so, are all the plates by the same artist or of the same object? Or, are all the plates of different objects or works of art?** If all the reproduced works in a book or magazine are of different art objects, images, or scenes, then they should not have the same color cast. If it is still impossible to judge the quality of a plate, a teacher or individual should be consulted having experience with the subject matter illustrated.
5. **What is the general quality of the publication? Is poor quality paper used, e.g., paper having the quality of newsprint? Does the quality of paper vary for color plates as compared with text pages?** It is not always necessary to print the text and plates on different types of paper if, for example, plates make up the major content of the publication and very little text is reproduced or if quality paper is used throughout. Under these circumstances, it is rare to find different types of paper due to the added expense. Sierra Club publications have excellent quality nature studies and frequently utilize only one paper type which is highly conducive to quality plate production. Magazines such as *Apollo*, *National Geographic*, and *Scientific American* use the same paper throughout while maintaining high reproduction standards. Art publications by the Abrams Company and scientific publications by C. V. Mosby and Freeman also provide excellent slide copy. Abrams, Mosby, and Freeman frequently use different paper types for text and plate material. Museum issued publications also provide sources for quality slides as most museums are prepared to produce high quality photographic copies of their holdings under controlled conditions because they can make original photographs directly from the objects themselves. Each field has its quality publishers and a slide librarian should become familiar with these to insure maximum copy standards for slides added to the collection using this method.

Numbers 1, 2, and 3 may also be used to judge the quality of commercially produced color slides. Whether color or black and white slides are being made from reproductions or photographs, some loss in quality from the original is to be expected as part of the duplication process resulting in increased contrast, a loss in sharpness, and changes in color value. If precautions are taken as outlined, quality loss should be minimized.

EQUIPMENT FOR SLIDE PRODUCTION

Basically, there are four different methods by which slides can be institutionally produced.

1. Purchase the necessary equipment and supplies and hire a part- or full-time photographer.
2. Purchase the necessary equipment and supplies and have the slide library staff shoot and process the slides or send the film to a commercial film processor.
3. Hire a professional photographer who already has the equipment and can purchase supplies and pay him by the slide or by the hour.
4. Have the institutional audiovisual center or museum photography division make the slides and pay the center by the slide or by the hour whichever is customary in that institution.

Any of these approaches will vary greatly in cost with any of the three systems being capable of ranges from less than $100 to more than $1,000 for supplies and equipment purchases, or for labor costs. If the decision is made not to purchase supplies and equipment for institutional slide production, a Polaroid set-up for quick slide copy or equipment for slide duplication may be desirable to have in the slide library.

Each institution will have budget and production schedules which will form the parameters for experimentation and acquisition of slide copying and duplicating equipment. Unless the slide librarian has had previous photographic experience, the nomenclature alone will prevent her or him from making valid equipment choices for this aspect of slide production. It is true in this area as in others that a little background can hinder selection more than none at all. The individual with limited background frequently will purchase equipment thinking that he knows all that is necessary while the individual without any previous experience will consult a specialist in photography or photographic equipment. In either case, consultation with a specialist should be mandatory before costly and irreversible errors are made. Those institutions having media centers or museums having photographic facilities should have built-in sources of information on this topic. If an institution has a photography department, the staff or faculty should be consulted about copying set-ups. A good overview of the equipment and facilities necessary for copy work is provided in the *Encyclopedia of Photography* under the heading "Copying and Close-up Photography" (1965, vol. 6, pp. 964-982). If a particular institution does not offer the various possibilities for information cited, then those which do should be consulted.

How do other schools handle slide production? Yale University has slides made through the audiovisual center on campus and pays for the cost of materials only while labor costs are absorbed by the center. Other schools like Cornell University, History of Art Department, hire a professional photographer to use university equipment to make slides. Equipment includes a Reprovit Copy Stand (made by Leitz) and a 35mm Leica single-lens reflex camera illustrated in Photograph 1.

Photograph 1. Reprovit copy stand (made by E. Leitz, Inc.) with 35mm Leica single-lens reflex camera. Department of Art History. Cornell University.

The University of California at Santa Cruz is primarily involved in slide purchasing at the present time but does have a Recordak Micro-File Film Unit in their slide library for institutional production when necessary. The University of Chicago allows for a professional photographer in their slide budget who is paid by the slide at the rate of $1.50 each for which he provides all his own equipment and supplies. Harvard University also engages a professional photographer at the rate of $0.30 per slide. The range in costs for slide production will depend upon the conditions of employment for the photographer, e.g., part-time, full-time, professional, non-professional, supplies and equipment furnished or not, and whether the slides are bound or unbound. Lower per slide costs for professional work usually indicate that supplies and possibly a photography facility for copy work are furnished by the institution. These figures should not be construed as absolutes but only as indicative of the possible ranges in cost from one institution to another depending upon how the slides are made. Other schools, including the University of Illinois at Chicago Circle and Indiana University, have their own complete photographic facility and hire photographers—frequently students—who are paid an hourly rate to shoot black and white and color slides. Vassar College utilizes a Polaroid MP-3 Multi-Purpose Industrial View Land Camera for slide production and employs a professional photographer on a part-time basis. At the present time, more than 55% of academic collections employ a photographer on a part-time basis to make their slides. By comparison, only 15% of the collections surveyed utilize the services of a full-time photographer or of the audiovisual services on their campuses.

Until October 1973, black and white slides could be processed without making negatives by using either a Kodak Panchromatic Direct-Positive Film or Panatomic-X Film. The latter film has now been removed from the market by Kodak. Panchromatic Direct-Positive is a faster film allowing for a higher speed when shooting slides. A cable release for camera stability would no longer be required as it is possible to shoot at 1/60 of a second. Although few slide libraries keep a negative file, Panatomic-X did allow for this option while direct-positive developing kits need to be used with Panchromatic Direct-Positive Film which is only available in 50 and 100 ft. rolls. A different processing technique can be used with this film to produce negatives but the process is quite complicated. Another alternative is available to institutions desiring negatives. Ektachrome film may be used to make black and white slides by using filters which prevent a blue cast typical of this film type. Local processing with developing kits which can be purchased for Ektachrome or color processing by commercial labs is also possible. In addition, Ektachrome film can be purchased in 100 ft. rolls for bulk loading which greatly decreases film cost. Color slides made from Kodachrome II Professional Film, Type A, will have to be mailed or delivered to a dealer for processing. Kodachrome is not available for bulk loading. Kodachrome does provide high quality color slides, however, and is commonly used by most academic institutions which make their own slides. For further information on producing slides from Kodak films—either black and white or color—the reader should examine the most recent "Kodak Audiovisual Data Book" on this topic (*Producing Slides and Filmstrips*, 1970).

The *PMI Products and Services Directory* (n.d.) includes a listing of "Still Color Lab Services and Filmstrip Services" in their annual publication. This listing also gives sources which make slides "From Color Negatives" and "From Artwork." The *Professional Photographic Catalog* (1971) issued by Standard Photo Supply in

Chicago includes guides to different film types from motion picture films to 35mm films. Both of these directories should be readily available to the slide library.

For copy photography from books, special supplies are required to compensate for the distortion of the image caused by book bindings. Merely opening the book and placing it on a stand without flattening the pages is insufficient preparation for shooting book plates. There are several solutions to this problem—many of which are not satisfactory. For example, weighted boards could be placed across the book providing for an awkward and time-consuming process. The least expensive, yet relatively practical solution is the use of a piece of optically treated glass which will both flatten the pages and prevent distortion of the image. Optimally, a Leitz framing box which handles books up to 11½" by 14" should be used because it provides greater pressure than a sheet of glass and is more efficient to use. For books larger than this size, however, the optical glass will be necessary. An added benefit provided by the framing box is that by placing the surface of a page perpendicular to the image cone of the camera lens and that by proper arrangement of the lighting, a reduction in glare from shiny pages is minimized, i.e., the light is polarized. If polarization is a problem, several publications are available which explain this concept and how to manipulate it. In its pamphlet "Kodak Pola-Lights," Kodak explains the use of polarizing screens and lights (1964). The *Encyclopedia of Photography* has a thorough explanation of polarization under the heading "Polarized Light in Photography" (1965, vol. 16, pp. 2926-2932).

Various set-ups are possible for slide production and the literature does include discussions of some of these systems. Articles such as the one by William Siddall, Chairman, Division of Geography, Kansas State University, on "Making Slides from Printed Materials" is one of the more detailed discussions available in the periodical literature. Mr. Siddall explains how he has set up this type of facility at Middlebury College and at Kansas State University for less than $300 in each case (1969). Or, you can build your own copy stand and purchase a camera separately. The "Kodak Audiovisual Data Book S-8" includes complete diagrams on "How to Make a Copying Stand" (*Producing Slides and Filmstrips*, 1970, pp. 22-25). Equipment for slide duplication, i.e., duplicating slides rather than making slides from reproductions, has also been discussed in the literature (Wiesinger, 1964). The Kodak Etagraphic Visualmaker includes a camera, stand, and accessories for slightly over $100 (*Producing Slides and Filmstrips*, 1970, pp. 39-41). Specifically written to explain the problems confronted by museums preparing slides for sale to educational institutions, an article by Brian N. Rushton (1968), Manager of the Publication Department of the Tate Gallery in London, provides a description of the costs, equipment, facilities and procedures used at the Tate Gallery.

Another aspect of production is slide duplication. The question of copyright must, of course, be considered, but for slides where copyright does not apply, duplication is a convenient process for having multiple copies of slides readily available for teaching. In fact, Carlton Erickson, Director of the Audiovisual Center and Professor of Education, the University of Connecticut, has said that drawer filing of slides is becoming a phenomenon of the past and that once a teacher's use patterns are established, the slides should be copied and placed in magazines for that teacher's use (1968, p. 319). Certainly, there is a valid argument for this set-up in school systems but Erickson is assuming the validity of the "canned" lecture. It is not the function of this work to debate such uses of slides but if this method is used, slide duplication equipment should be available. The teacher constantly changing or updating lecture materials would also find immediate access to slide duplicators conducive to such teaching methods.

A specific type of film is made for slide duplication. In general, duplicate film does not last as long as Kodachrome. Life expectancy of film will vary greatly depending upon humidity, temperature and storage conditions, but some films are not as stable as others and therefore more prone to deviations in quality before others. In addition, the color quality of duplicate film tends to be more harsh and not as rich in color range as that of Kodachrome or Ektachrome. Processing and varying film brands occasionally may affect the overall quality of duplicates so that ultimate judgments regarding the purchase and production of slide duplicates will be dependent upon each slide librarian's experience. For example, a wide range of duplicate slide quality is possible among the numerous European distributors and producers from one country to the next because of local film usage and processing methods.

Various set-ups are available for this process. Examples include the Bowens Illumitran made by the Bogen Photo Corporation which includes a camera and stand for approximately $1,000, the Repronar by Honeywell, Inc., for less than $450 (for additional cost, a kit for making and duplicating filmstrips can also be purchased), and duplicating equipment by Sickles which include apparatus for making slides from regular plate copy, reducing slides to filmstrips, making transparencies as large as 8" x 10", color correction, and other possibilities with a range from $2,000 to approximately $9,000.

For further information the reader should refer to the bibliography on production methods, equipment directory and to the *Audio-Visual Equipment Directory* (1972), *Audiovisual Marketplace* (1972), the PMI directory, and the Standard Photo Supply catalogs. In order to keep abreast of equipment changes and new products, these directories should be regularly consulted along with media specialists. Periodicals such as *Audiovisual Instruction*, *Arts and Activities*, *Educational Product Report*, *AV Guide* (formerly *Educational Screen and AV Guide*), *Nation's Schools*, and *Previews* are also useful sources of information on new equipment and media production methods.

BUYING SLIDES FROM COMMERCIAL SOURCES

Whether slides are being institutionally produced or commercially purchased, high quality levels should still prevail. As frequently as possible, slides should be purchased on approval so that after careful examination, they can be returned to the source if unsatisfactory. If, out of a purchase of 50 slides, fewer than five are unsatisfactory, it may not be worth the effort and added expense to return so few slides; but, if 20% or more of a single order does not meet satisfactory quality standards as outlined in this chapter, the slides should be returned. Many academic institutions try not to purchase from those companies which do not allow for preview of orders. This policy favors those companies which base their reputation on quality slides and who can therefore allow such preview conditions.

Another factor to check when buying slides commercially is whether the slides being offered are originals or duplicates. Original slides are slides taken directly at the site or location in large quantities. Duplicates can be of various types. Many museums such as the Philadelphia Museum of Art, which has a large purchase-order program for slides, keep a master file of high quality slides from which they directly make their duplicates for sale purposes. Such duplicates frequently maintain standards as high as the originals because of the quality controls on the master file and duplicating procedures. Slides taken from a master file of negatives should be considered originals. A slide made from a duplicate which may or may not have been taken from the original slide is another type of duplicate. The very process of reproducing photographic images from other photographic images usually yields some loss in quality so that slides produced directly from the "original" or from the objects or sites should be better quality images than slides produced from duplicates. Many commercial distributors or producers will indicate the source of their slides through the use of these terms. It is up to the purchaser to request a definition of these terms if one is not adequately indicated in the catalogs.

Commercial slides range in price from $0.25 to $3.00 per slide depending upon the source and whether or not the slides come pre-bound and labelled, and if they are duplicates or originals. Most producers and distributors will provide slides in cardboard mounts with the producer's catalog number on the slide plus descriptive information or with a brief description printed or written directly on the mount or a paper label. Slides purchased with only the cardboard mount and minimal pre-cataloging data are usually less expensive than those supplied fully glass-mounted with a completed label. Unless the collection's cataloging system differs radically from the supplier's, many of these slides are ready to be filed upon receipt after a quality check is made. Frequently, however, such pre-labelled slides do require changes in cataloging data if only to rearrange the information in terms of a given collection's entry format and filing order. If a notation system is used, this information will also have to be added to the label.

Original slides are usually more expensive than duplicates because the producer's costs are greater. He must travel to the original site or location of an art object in order to maintain his selection of slides while duplicates can be made quite simply at a relatively low cost for equipment and supplies. At the same time, a purchaser is, of course, also paying for the producer's overhead, equipment, staff, and supplies. Similar costs for an institution producing its own slides must be compared to commercial costs before accurate estimates can be made regarding the efficiency and cost advantages of commercial versus institutional production of slides. For example, a cost study made at Indiana University revealed the following breakdown for producing slides but does not include overhead:

Sample of Per Slide Production Costs

Labor	$0.22½
Equipment	0.23
Processing	0.14½
Total	$0.60

Labor includes the photographer's, binder's, and typing and cataloging time. Equipment includes the cost of the film, slide label, and slide mount. Processing includes the cost for physically processing the film. These costs were found to be quite close for both color and black and white slides because of the decreased costs of bulk processing. Costs can also be cut by not having color slides which are commercially processed placed in readymounts. These costs will of course vary from one institution to another depending upon local price and wage variances.

Many times, however, it is necessary to purchase slides because the information is not available in any other convenient format. For example, many European producers offer slides of art objects which are not reproduced in publications or if they are, the reproductions are so poor that slides cannot be made from them. This same problem will also occur in other disciplines so that a highly diversified and comprehensive slide library will have to rely upon slide distributors and producers to provide material not available elsewhere. A choice between commercial and institutional slide production is a difficult one to make and in most instances, should not be made at all. Instead a coordination between commercial and institutional slide production should be considered. Usually, a new collection does not have slide production facilities and relies heavily upon commercial suppliers. As the collection expands and as its budget increases, the addition of production facilities should be studied.

COPYRIGHT CONSIDERATIONS

The matter of copyright protection is posed in making slides from book plates in the same manner as it is in reproducing pages of books with copying machines. When reviewing the question of "fair use," the issues of partial copying which does not interfere with the commercial value of the original item and copying for nonprofit purposes have been important criteria for determining whether use is indeed "fair" (Siebert, 1964, pp. 26-27). In addition, whether or not the copying of an item interferes with the demand for that item also is a factor in "fair use" interpretation. If one plate from a book is copied, it might be argued that the one slide made from that plate does not distract from the value of the original book in the way that one printed page copied once for nonprofit purposes may not be considered a copyright infringement unless that one page or one plate represents a significant portion of the book. Does copying every slide in a book enhance the demand for that book or decrease it? If a slide collection is used only for teaching purposes and students are encouraged by the use of visuals to supplement their visual lecture material through books having those visual representations, demand for the books may be encouraged by the students' temporary visual access to the slides in the classroom situation. If, on the other hand, the slides are used directly by the students as a total substitute for book reproductions and plates from which they may have been taken, then, in fact, the demand for the book has been decreased. Even though slides are used for nonprofit educational purposes, an infringement of "fair use" may apply based upon the other criteria cited.

In the case of duplicating commercial slides, not a single page or sentence is being removed from the original item but instead the total item itself is being plagarized. Whether the educational intent is pure or not in this situation, a case for copyright infringement has been made. Many commercial distributors and producers have been indicating copyright protection on each slide or in their catalogs. Discretion should be exercised against indiscriminate copying of commercially produced slides particularly if copyright is indicated. As a courtesy to the commercial producer and in order to avoid conflicts with copyright restrictions, consultation with the producer is advised. The issue of copyright protection for educational copying purposes is in question at the present time and with the wide-spread use of duplicating processes may continue unresolved for an indefinite period of time. Slides are classified under 17:USCA§202.11 of the *United States Code Annotated*. For further information, see the references on copyright in the bibliography.

SUMMARY

One of the primary advantages of institutionally producing slides is that they can be more quickly available for classroom use than commercially produced slides. If Polaroid copy facilities are available, a slide can be ready for use within a matter of minutes. If black and white or color slides are needed, the shooting and process-ing may be completed within one day. If commercial processing is required for color slides, several days might be needed before the slides can be ready for use. Frequently, institutional expense per slide may be lower than that for commercial slides. At the same time, however, ordering commercial slides in bulk orders often lowers their cost to a rate commensurate with institutional production.

A department or library may not have to purchase its own copying facilities if an audiovisual center is available. Museums usually have a photographic set-up which may include copying equipment. Commercial slides which are labelled, cataloged and mounted offer advantages to slide libraries, particularly those with a small or inadequate staff. The precise method of collection building is an institu-tional prerogative based upon the needs and demands of each school or museum.

Unfortunately, many still approach slide production rather lightly assuming that the size of the object is in direct proportion to its importance and acquisition requirements. In the past, the mere absence of a title page relegated a great deal of material to discard piles—and in some cases, it still does. The fact that it is extraordinarily easy to produce or purchase slides at a relatively low per item cost should not overshadow the necessity for adequate funds for cataloging, classifying, record keeping, and staffing. A total program for slide production and processing should be realized from the outset of collection building.

REFERENCES

Artwork Size Standards for Projected Visuals. Rochester, New York: Eastman Kodak Company, 1968. (Kodak Pamphlet No. S-12).

The Audio-Visual Equipment Directory. 18th ed. Virginia: National Audio-Visual Association, 1972.

Audiovisual Marketplace. A Multimedia Guide. 1972-1973 ed. New York: R. R. Bowker, 1972. Biennial publication as of the fourth edition.

The Encyclopedia of Photography. New York: Greystone Press, 1965.

ERICKSON, Carlton W. H. *Administering Instructional Media Programs*. New York: The Macmillan Company, 1968.

GRUBER, M. T. "Make Your Own Slide Show." *Arts and Activities*, 65:38-39 (March 1969).

HOLLAND, Ben F., HARTSELL, Horace C., and DAVIDSON, Raymond L. *Audio-Visual Materials and Devices.* Lubbock, Texas: Rodgers Litho, 1958.

Kodak Pola-Lights When and How to Use Them. Rochester, New York: Eastman Kodak Company, 1964. (Kodak Pamphlet).

LEWIS, John N. C., and SMITH, Edwin. *The Graphic Reproduction and Photography of Works of Art.* London: W. S. Cowell Ltd., 1969.

MEES, C. E. K. *From Dry Plates to Ektachrome: A Film Story of Photographic Research.* New York: Ziff-Davis, 1961.

MOODY, G. J. "Impressions Projected on Acetate Slides." *Arts and Activities,* 59:28-30 (March 1966).

PMI Photo Methods for Industry Catalog and Directory of Products and Services. New York: Gellert Publishing Corporation, n.d. Published annually.

Producing Slides and Filmstrips. 5th ed. Rochester, New York: Eastman Kodak Company, 1970. (Kodak Publication No. S-8).

Professional Photographic Catalog. Chicago: Standard Photo Supply, 1971.

RITCHIE, Andrew C. *The Visual Arts in Higher Education.* New York: College Art Association, 1966.

RUSHTON, Brian N. "Producing and Selling a Quality Service to Education Slides." *Museum News,* 46:27-32 (January 1968).

SIDDALL, William R. "Making Slides from Printed Materials." *Journal of Geography,* 68:430-432 (October 1969).

SIEBERT, Fred S. *Copyrights, Clearances, and Rights of Teachers in the New Educational Media.* Washington, D.C.: American Council on Education, 1964.

WIESINGER, Robert. "Instant 35mm Slides." *Educational Screen and AV Guide,* 43:88 (February 1964).

6–STORAGE AND ACCESS SYSTEMS

INTRODUCTION

Storage for any type of information whether it is in book, microfiche, microfilm, magnetic tape, or slide format is constantly changing depending upon the technology available. In the future, it is possible that traditional book libraries as they exist today may only be rare book archives or in history museums because the common information medium may be microfiche combined with audio systems, or computer data banks accessible by on-line consoles in homes, offices, or educational institutions. Many of these changes are occurring at the present time. Ultimately, visual data may be electronically stored and retrievable through display consoles in each classroom so that teacher and student would never become involved in the physical removal of slides from a drawer or file. At the present time, there are automated carrels on the market which offer the student unlimited possibilities for independent learning situations combining audio-tape, filmstrip, 16mm projectors, and slide systems. However, until the complete storage and retrieval of visual data is a standard procedure, manual slide storage and access systems will prevail for lack of a better solution.

HOW TO SELECT A STORAGE FACILITY

In order to select a suitable facility for filing slides, both the storage and the accessibility function of that facility should be considered. Ten questions should be asked and answered in a satisfactory manner to determine which type of facility will be best suited to institutional needs.

1. **How are the slides to be used?** This question is one of the most critical asked to determine the type of housing needed. Slides filed and used by set or individually should have a storage system that reflects this use pattern. Slide libraries based upon a set rather than an individual slide arrangement will also tend to have different acquisition, cataloging and classification systems. Slides used by set can be stored directly in the projector trays or magazines which can then be stored on open shelves, in cabinets, or in one of the multi-media units on the market designed to handle slides, filmstrips, tape, 16mm films and other media. If slides are used by set, any of the unitary image methods of storage would prove cumbersome and inconvenient while the opposite would apply to slides utilized individually. Groups of slides which are constantly needed for visual reference are inconvenient to the user if housed in drawers. Even tray or magazine storage may be undesirable if immediate visual study is necessary. Filing the slides on visual display racks or in plastic sleeves—holding 20 slides, 4 horizontally and 5 vertically—provides immediate visual access to the files without the aid of auxiliary equipment such as projectors.

2. **Who is to use the slides?** Different types of users will demand various storage systems. For teachers working in a given subject area who need immediate access to slides on a daily basis, slides filed together by sets will probably be most convenient. For individuals requiring a multi-disciplinary approach, it may be more

desirable to file slides individually by subject categories and allow each user maximum flexibility to integrate different areas. Whatever system is used, it should be relatively consistent throughout the collection. Too many methods of organization and storage within a single collection will tend to disperse materials and confuse the user. There is, of course, the possibility of duplicating or making multiple copies of slides so that a single image might be available in more than one place in the collection. Using multiple copies, a single image could be filed individually, by set, or in different subject categories at the same time.

3. **How frequently will the slides be used?** If users are constantly demanding the use of single slides which are normally kept in sets, it may be more efficient to begin a slide filing and storage system which is better suited to these requirements. Or, if users are continually frustrated by the individual filing system because they must always rearrange their slides by set for presentation purposes, a storage system should be adapted for this use pattern. If the collection is rarely used or is archival in nature, a storage system that provides maximum protection from handling, humidity, and temperature fluctuations should be selected.

4. **How many individuals will the collection serve?** If a great many users are served by the collection, congestion may occur at the files if the slides have not been stored to allow access by more than one user at a time. Single vertical cabinets having a capacity of 7,000 to 8,000 slides may be undesirable because only one user at a time can have access to the files. Because drawers in large capacity cabinets are usually quite large and heavy, they are usually awkward to remove for consultation. Some vertical cabinets, however, can be designed with removable trays that fit inside the drawers. There are also small cabinets available for housing about 2,500 mounted slides or fewer which have easily removable drawers and can be stacked or placed on table tops throughout the slide library. In selecting proper storage equipment it is important to know the number of people who use the files at one time. Photographs illustrating various housing types in this chapter will assist in decision-making on this subject.

5. **What type of expansion schedule will the collection have?** Some storage systems are not conducive to rapid expansion rates while others are. If the slides are filed by set within trays or magazines, acquisition will not affect those slides already filed, but if constant interfiling of new slides is required for visual display rack cabinets, moving and readjusting slides on these racks can be quite time-consuming and impractical with this housing system. It is most convenient when entire drawers or trays of slides can be moved in groups to allow for expansion which is possible in most standard drawer-type cabinets.

6. **How will the collection be filed?** A collection of slide sets would not have the same access demands as an individually filed collection. Even in a predominantly unitary image collection, there may be a select number of slide sets for standard lectures. Flexibility and user requirements should dictate multiple types of storage when necessary. The effects of filing on storage will be discussed with the various types of storage systems.

7. **How will the collection be circulated?** If it is to be circulated in sets, then it should be housed and possibly filed in sets if at all feasible. A collection which is not circulated and used only for visual access will demand a storage system conducive to visual examination without necessarily involving the removal of slides from their housing. For example, visual display rack or plastic sleeve filing in loose-leaf notebooks may be practical in this case. Or, the core or basic collection

may never circulate because duplicates are automatically made for lecture purposes and for research use of slides.

8. **How much time can be allowed for slide presentation preparation?** In some instances, faculty or lecturers may prefer not to rummage through drawers locating slides individually for slide presentations, but would rather have access to slides by tray, magazine or set so that the entire slide show is ready as soon as the set or tray is removed from the shelf or cabinet in the slide library. This method of storage, however, is neither recommended nor advisable for all institutions or individuals utilizing slides. Visual display housing may aid in the convenient and more rapid selection of slides depending upon the user's needs. In other instances, drawer housing may prove adequate.

9. **How much care should be taken to prevent handling of individual slides?** In the past, adequate slide mounts have not been readily available or economically feasible for many collections. With the advent of plastic and aluminum slide mounts, the problems previously associated with handling are not as critical as they have been. Staff time and expense for mounting slides and for protecting them properly from damage may still be prohibitive for some collections, although many of the new mounts—particularly the plastic ones—require a minimal amount of time for binding. Such mounts are reusable. If the slides are kept in cardboard mounts without the protection of glass, they should be handled as little as possible to avoid marring the film, fingerprints, scratches and dirt. The visual display rack method of storage is more viable for slides not protected by glass mounts than a drawer system because the user is less likely to handle or remove the slides from the cabinet unless he intends to use them. Visual display storage allows study and examination of slides with minimal slide handling because the slides do not have to be removed from their housing for viewing.

10. **What are the budget limitations for the collection?** Storage systems will range in cost from less than $10.00 for a box, tray or magazine, to over $500 for a wooden or metal cabinet. Some cabinets may be as high as $1,000 depending upon whether they are wood or metal, have custom-made drawer interiors, or visual display racks. The most expensive cabinet is not necessarily the most efficient or best solution for slide housing in a given institution. If all the factors of use and collection building do not influence cabinet choice, an extremely costly and unfortunate error may result.

TYPES OF STORAGE

There are four basic types of slide storage:

1. Filing drawer cabinets for individual slides or slide sets. Slides must be removed from the drawers for viewing.
2. Visual display rack cabinets. Slides are filed on metal frames which pull out for immediate visual access.
3. Tray or magazine storage. Trays designed for projector viewing and boxed slide sets are placed in boxes which can be stacked or shelved.
4. Plastic sleeve storage. Slides inserted into plastic sleeves held in loose-leaf binders are easily accessible for viewing.

Filing Drawer Cabinets—The majority of academic collections in the United States utilize a metal filing drawer cabinet allowing for individual slide filing. This method of storage is indicative of the use, cataloging, circulation, and filing patterns used in most academic institutions. These collections have relatively heavy use patterns and need a system whereby large quantities of individual slides may be frequently removed from the drawers. Each slide is individually filed, cataloged, and circulated as a single unit rather than as part of a predetermined subject set. Moreover, most of these collections exhibit extensive expansion patterns so that storage must be readily adaptable to continual interfiling of new slides.

Within the range of filing drawer cabinets, there are various cabinet types. Cabinets may be either metal or wood, have a fixed filing slot for each slide or for a group of slides, or have an expansive system using some form of backstop to keep the slides in an upright position. Some cabinets can be supplied with either fixed single slide or group filing inserts—often supplied with the cabinets—so that variable filing arrangements are possible. Neumade and the Luxor slide cabinets can accommodate either group or single slide filing systems (see Photograph 2).

Photograph 2. Neumade 2" x 2" slide cabinet shown with drawers for single
slide filing and for group filing (bottom). (Photograph
courtesy of Neumade Products Corporation.)

One of the most common group filing systems is a standard wooden card catalog modified as a slide cabinet. This type of cabinet is a stock item made by the Library Bureau Division of Sperry Remington (formerly Remington Rand) and is referred to as a 2" x 2" file cabinet (Photographs 4, 5, 6). An added feature of these cabinets is the availability of sliding reference shelves such as those used with standard library card cabinets which provide flat workspace at the file. Each drawer has a fixed wooden panel placed down the center which has slots that correspond to those on wooden panels placed down the sides of each drawer. Within these slots either cardboard or fibreboard cards may be inserted to hold the slides in an upright position. The height of the insert cards is the same height—or slightly higher—as the height of the wooden drawer panels which correspond to the interior height of the drawer. Diagrams 4 and 5 illustrate how these different interiors appear in perspective and provide overhead views of a single row. Drawers may vary from two to seven or more rows. The filing slots for either single or group slide filing may be the same height as the top of the drawers or as close as ½" above the drawer bottom. The panels placed inside card catalog drawers for slide storage conversion may be designed for single or group filing of slides. Backstops similar to those used in standard card catalog cabinets may be used for slides.

User preferences play an important role in drawer selection. Some may consider it an inconvenience to have to remove each slide individually as would be the case with fixed single slide filing slots. In this case group filing is preferred. The backstop drawer also allows for more flexibility within each filing row because new groups of slides may be added to the row without moving slides from one fixed group or single unit location to another. A drawer designed for group filing will usually accommodate twice as many slides as one for single filing because of the amount of space required to section the interior of the drawer for single slide filing slots. Slides in cardboard mounts require about half the filing space of those with plastic, metal or glass mounts. Some slide drawers are designed to hold only cardboard mounted slides—this is only true of drawers for fixed slot single slide filing. Regular mounted slides can be filed eight per inch; cardboard mounted slides can be filed 16 per inch. Cardboard or fibreboard inserts spaced every inch support eight slides. Seven of the eight slides can be removed without having the remaining slides fall to the bottom of the drawer. With any group or sequence filing system, the slides should be grouped so that a user may withdraw most of the slides from a single group without having the remaining slides dependent upon the removed slides for their support within the drawer—this is the function of the fibreboard insert.

Another factor affecting cabinet choice is the user preference for cabinets having easily removable and relatively lightweight individual drawers. For example, the small lightweight metal Neumade, the wooden Nega-File, and the Library Bureau wooden slide cabinets have drawers which can be removed from the cabinets and used throughout the slide library (see Photographs 2, 3, 5). Such stacking units are usually a convenient size, have lightweight drawers, and have either single or group filing slots for slides. The large single unit metal filing cabinet will hold up to 11,500 slides and requires less space than the stacking units for an equivalent number of slides. Because of the size of individual drawers, and their storage capacity which may be as high as 1,000 slides per drawer, these drawers are too bulky and heavy for removal for daily use by patrons. The drawers are usually the width and depth of standard metal filing cabinets, while the height of

Photograph 3. Nega-File slide cabinets, custom-made light tables in foreground and Library Bureau 3¼" x 4" cabinets in rear. Department of Art and Archaeology. Princeton University.

Photograph 4. Library Bureau 2" x 2" wooden slide cabinets with custom-made illuminators. Chicago Art Institute.

Photograph 5. Library Bureau 2" x 2" wooden slide cabinets with custom-made illuminators and work areas in foreground. Graduate School of Fine Arts. The University of Pennsylvania.

Photograph 6.   Library Bureau wooden slide cabinets and carrels for slide viewing (adapted from Model No. 65901 made by Herman Miller, New York). The Metropolitan Museum of Art. (Photograph courtesy of the Metropolitan Museum of Art.)

Diagram 4—Wooden panels that change card catalog drawers into slide
files—perspective view

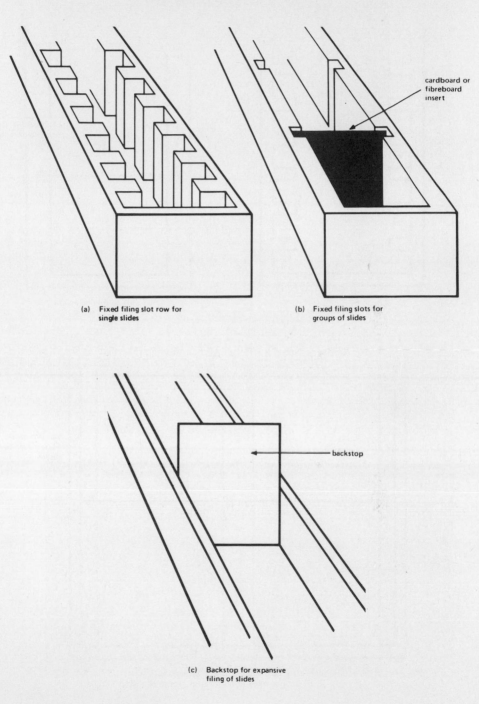

(a) Fixed filing slot row for single slides

(b) Fixed filing slots for groups of slides

cardboard or fibreboard insert

backstop

(c) Backstop for expansive filing of slides

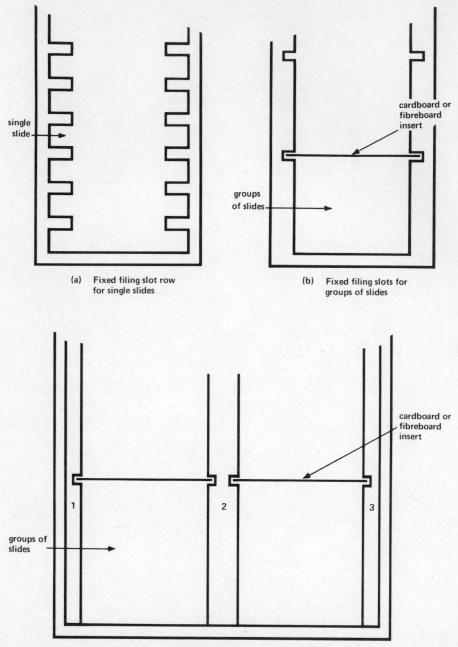

Diagram 5—Wooden panels that change card catalog drawers into slide files—overhead view

single slide

cardboard or fibreboard insert

groups of slides

(a) Fixed filing slot row for single slides

(b) Fixed filing slots for groups of slides

cardboard or fibreboard insert

1   2   3

groups of slides

(c) Converted card catalog drawer with panel inserts (1, 2, 3) with fixed filing slots for groups of slides the cabinet may vary from four to five feet or more depending upon the type of base used. Photographs 7 and 8 include views of vertical metal slide cabinets utilized at Harvard University and Indiana University. In order to allow the patron to remove sections of a drawer conveniently, it is possible to have removable trays built for the drawers of metal files as has been done at the University of Illinois at Chicago Circle. The cabinets used are ten-drawer Steelcase metal files identical to those in Photograph 7. Diagrams 6 and 7 illustrate how such trays may be designed and placed in the drawers.

Diagram 6—One of eight trays designed to be placed in a Steelcase metal filing cabinet

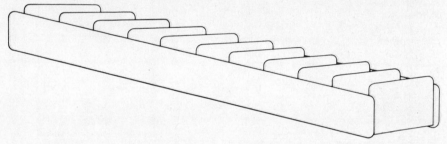

Diagram 7—Overhead view showing eight trays per drawer

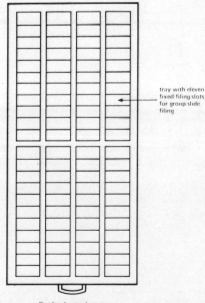

tray with eleven fixed filing slots for group slide filing

Overhead view showing eight trays per drawer

Photograph 7. Steelcase slide filing cabinets for 2" x 2" slides, Library Bureau wooden 3¼" x 4" slide cabinets in rear, Telescreen (table-top rear projection screen made by Hudson Photographic Industries, Inc.) on top of Steelcase files and custom-made light tables (right). Fogg Art Museum. Harvard University.

Photograph 8. Library Bureau metal 2" x 2" slide cabinets with Library Bureau 3¼" x 4" wooden cabinets placed on top of the metal files. Custom-made sloped illuminators are placed on standard 3' x 5' library table. Fine Arts Department. Indiana University.

The metal cabinets illustrated thus far have been designed for slides although interior alterations may have been made. The Philadelphia College of Art, Photograph 9, demonstrates how an imaginative conversion of a filing system can be made to adapt to slide storage. A custom-made tray has been designed to fit on the six levels of a metal horizontal filing cabinet. There are eight trays per level: each cabinet holds 48 trays for a total slide capacity of about 6,500 slides. Each tray holds two rows of slides without the use of fixed filing slots or a backstop. The trays may be removed and set on top the cabinets for slide examination. These cabinets can be stacked if they are bolted together and then fastened to the wall.

Photograph 9. Conserva Files (made by Supreme Steel Equipment Corporation) with custom-made illuminators for slide preparation and viewing in foreground. The Conserva File is a waist-high cabinet with pull-out racks for which custom-made trays have been made which are shelved 8 per rack, a 48-tray capacity per cabinet. Each cabinet holds from 6,000 to 7,000 slides. Philadelphia College of Art.

If it is necessary to take precautions against the indiscriminate or accidental removal of guide or shelflist cards from the drawers, rods may be installed in either metal filing cabinets such as those by Library Bureau or in the wooden filing cabinets (see Diagram 1, Chapter 4). In cabinets designed for metal rods, the rod may not have been set low enough for this particular function but the amount of tipping may be so slight that it may not present a problem depending upon the height of the rod from the dropped portion of the drawer. At Indiana University, a rod system of this type which comes as standard equipment with the Library Bureau cabinets is being used for the shelflist and guide cards. (Photograph 10—drawer interior.) If the cabinets do not come equipped with rods, standard metal slide files such as those by Steelcase or General Fireproofing could be altered to hold rods. (Photograph 11—drawer interior of General Fireproofing cabinet.)

Photograph 10. Library Bureau metal 2" x 2" slide drawer. Interior view showing Mylar shelflist cards placed in front of slides. Fine Arts Department. Indiana University. (Photograph courtesy of Suzette Baker.)

Photograph 11. Drawer of General Fireproofing 2″ x 2″ metal slide cabinet (four-drawer legal file modified for slide storage showing CBD insert to house cards 2″ x 2″). (Photograph courtesy of General Fireproofing Company.)

A small number of collections have custom-made cabinets which campus or private workshops build to their specifications. Others have purchased standard filing cabinets which are fitted with trays designed and built within the institution. Commercially available cabinets vary in price from less than $50 per unit to more than $500 per unit. If custom-made trays are used, the additional cost may be $200 or more depending upon the size of the cabinet and the number of trays needed. Whether a great deal of money is saved by custom-designing the entire cabinet is questionable. The efficiency of custom-made systems varies from one institution to another. Before embarking upon the task of custom-designing cabinet storage systems, those available commercially should be studied and examined.

Portable slide storage cases could be used as temporary housing for slides (see Chapter 9), but are not recommended as permanent storage. They are not designed to stack or to be shelved vertically. The primary function of these cases is for carrying slides and not for storing them.

Visual Display Rack Cabinets—The second type of storage system uses display racks which support slides on metal frames. This system allows slides to be examined without removing them from the cabinet (see Photographs 12 and 13). Visual display rack storage is particularly well suited to laboratory or studio use where comparison and examination of slides is desirable. However, a supplementary index to the slides stored in display racks is necessary. It is not possible to include guide cards on the racks unless they are the exact dimensions of the slide—2" x 2" or 3" x 4"—including surface and density dimensions. The cost of guides equivalent in size to slides would be prohibitive and the additional space required for them would substantially decrease the filing capacity of the cabinet. Frequently, these cabinets are supplied with an indexing card which allows for the listing of slides by rack and frame. Because of the large amount of time required to rearrange and refile slides in display racks, this type of storage system is not well suited to rapidly expanding collections or those with extensive acquisition programs. If, however, slides are arranged by accession order, or if the growth pattern is low, these cabinets may provide adequate storage for slides.

An interfiled shelflist for slides stored in display racks is most difficult to implement although a separate shelflist is quite functional. If a circulation system is necessary, charge-sheets or cards arranged by call number, accession number, or the name of the user are the most viable systems.

A single slide rack may hold up to 100 or more slides depending upon the type of cabinet. As is shown in Photograph 12, these cabinets usually come equipped with their own viewing equipment such as a lightbox built-in behind the racks to illuminate the slides for convenient viewing. The storage system can affect the way in which a collection may be utilized and organized. Visual display rack cabinets adapt best to situations which demand immediate visual access, avoid complicated interfiling arrangements, file slides by accession order or which closely limit expansion within the main body of the collection.

Tray or Magazine Storage—For detailed storage, formal presentations on a single subject or topic, slides can be stored in trays or magazines for immediate classroom use. Both the teacher and the students can enjoy the convenience of slides

Photograph 12. ABODIA 5000-Visual slide storage cabinet (made by Elden Enterprises, Inc.). The slides can be locked behind plexiglas doors with access to each rack possible from the top of the cabinet. Fifty metal racks hold 100 slides each. The racks pull out from both sides of the cabinet. Each base drawer can hold up to 3,250 cardboard mounted slides. (Photograph courtesy of Elden Enterprises, Inc.)

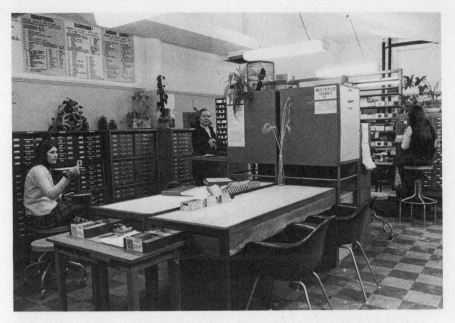

Photograph 13. Neumade 2" x 2" stacking slide cabinets against wall at left. Custom-made light tables in foreground. Multiplex 2" x 2" cabinet at rear center. Student working at authority file at right. Syracuse University. (Photograph courtesy of Ramona Roters, Slide Librarian.)

previously selected and arranged for them on a specific topic. A large number of companies have slide sets available (see Directory of Slide Sources) and such sets should be kept together if they are consistently used as sets. The boxes in which commercially produced slide sets are sold can be used as permanent storage. These boxes, however, will tend to vary greatly in durability and general quality so that they may not be satisfactory for long-term storage. For heavily used sets, storage directly in projector trays is recommended. Trays or magazines of the circular or rectangular box type vary in size and capacity depending upon the projector for which they are designed. The use of this type of storage is based on the following prerequisites: (1) the institution is using automatic slide-changing projectors or projectors equipped with slide-changing trays; (2) only 2" x 2" slides are purchased and used; (3) the institution has an adequate indexing system to insure maximum utility of slides; (4) as the slides will receive no handling or at least, minimal handling, they will probably not require heavy-duty mounts (glass, plastic, or metal binders with glass) to protect them. Slide mounts, however, do serve more functions than merely protection from handling and these will be discussed in Chapter 9.

Circulation is relatively simple as each box rather than each individual slide can be charged out by call number or accession number. Magazines or trays are usually supplied with cardboard or plastic boxes which provide the permanent housing for the slide trays. The filing arrangement of the slides within magazines or trays is predetermined by the slide distributor or manufacturer, or by the individual who developed the sets. These boxes of magazines or trays can be shelved on standard library shelves, in cabinets or on projection stands. Using this system, the slides may be satisfactorily intershelved with the book collection. Both the trays or magazines and the boxes are relatively inexpensive, usually costing less than $10.

Plastic Sleeve Storage—The fourth type of storage system files groups or sets of slides in plastic or vinyl holders. Each sleeve contains 20 pockets for slides. The holders can be purchased in standard sheet size, 8½" x 11" to fit in loose-leaf binders. This system also allows for immediate visual access and has the same limitations and advantages as the visual display rack cabinets. These holders are designed for cardboard mounted slides only. Each vinyl sleeve costs less than $0.50 and are stocked by most photography stores. Whether this method of storage is advisable for a large collection of slide sets is questionable unless the slides are rarely removed for projector viewing and are only used in the holders either for direct visual examination or with overhead projectors.

7–PLANNING FOR PHYSICAL FACILITIES

INTRODUCTION

Of the limited number of publications on slides and slide libraries, none have provided recommendations on spatial requirements for slide library facilities. Certainly, there is a multitude of general media facility literature but slide facilities are only considered as a small part of such planning, if at all. Many of the books on media center planning do include sections on space and building requirements, but they do not satisfy the needs of a comprehensive slide library facility.

The following are typical observations made after a direct study of more than 25 slide libraries which were evaluated on the basis of functional layout, planning and space allocations:

spacious but not well planned–office and work areas have inadequate space allocations;

entire facility crowded–no space for expansion or proper space allocations;

moderately allocated space in terms of collection needs but too diffused for efficient administration and staffing;

spacious new facility with inadequate lighting, storage and work spaces;

work area large though poorly planned; inconvenient for staff.

More often than not, even if the slide library had been allocated an area large enough for efficient operation, improper internal allocations or layout of areas negated the benefits derived by the amount of space acquired. This chapter will examine the requirements of a total slide library facility with any facet capable of integration into a general media facility.

FUNCTIONS DEFINED

In order to determine the spatial requirements of a slide library, the functions which it performs must be outlined and defined. The following represent the major functional spaces with their respective requirements indicated:

1. Storage
    slide housing
    user catalogs

2. Viewing
    tables with sloped wooden or metal illuminators and/or
    carrels with built-in illumination and/or
    light tables
    previewers providing magnification and/or
    rear screen projection viewer
    front screen projection (room or space)

3. Circulation and Reference
   desk for charging out slides
   area for slide return
   reference desk

4. Administration and Operation
   slide librarian's office
   general operation or work area
      typing spaces for a specified number of supportive staff
      cataloging desk(s)
      filing cabinet(s) for correspondence and commercial catalogs
      cabinets for authority, shelflist and source files (if applicable)
      tables for slide mounting and wall shelving for supplies
      storage cabinets for projectors, office and slide supplies, and extra previewers, miscellaneous equipment
      book cases for internal library and for books from which slides are made and booktruck (optional)
      slide sorting table(s) for preparing slides for refiling
      sink

5. Storage for Slides Prepared for Classroom Use
   tables for slide cases, trays or magazines and/or
   wall or free-standing shelving to hold cases, trays or magazines

6. Photography and Processing (optional)
   copystand and camera
   slide duplicator
   storage for photography supplies

Storage—The storage area should encompass the slide housing and catalogs such as author, artist, title, and/or subject. This space will vary in total dimensions based upon the type of cabinet selected. Space for opening drawers, for the user standing in front of an opened drawer, and for aisles or traffic patterns should be included.

Diagram 8—Space requirements for cabinets

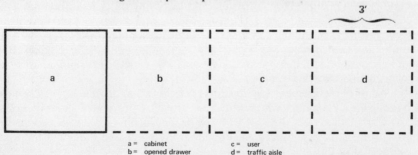

a = cabinet
b = opened drawer
c = user
d = traffic aisle

Total dimensions for each cabinet space would be a + b + c + d. Depending upon the location of the cabinet, space for traffic aisles on either side of the cabinet may be necessary. This combination of spaces would also apply to user catalogs. Space "a" is equivalent to "b" varying according to the depth of the cabinet and corresponding depth of each drawer. The amount of space for the user, "c," and traffic aisle, "d" (average aisle width is three feet), will vary according to whether or not the slides are examined only at the cabinets or have drawers or trays which may be easily removed for use at tables. Keyes Metcalf, a nationally recognized authority on library buildings, recommends space allocations for card catalogs which are also useful for determining slide storage space (1965, pp. 335-340).

A metal vertical slide cabinet such as those made by General Fireproofing, Library Bureau and Steelcase will house from 7,000 to 11,000 slides. These cabinets range in size from 4' to 5' high, approximately 13" wide by 28" deep and contain eight to ten drawers. Card catalog cabinets modified for slide storage are usually five drawers wide (approximately 33"), nine drawers high (approximately 5") and are approximately 18" deep. Each cabinet is usually composed of three 15-drawer stacking units with a total slide capacity of about 6,500 slides. Although a modified card catalog cabinet has a smaller capacity than a vertical slide cabinet, a modified cabinet requires nearly one-half square foot more floor space than a vertical cabinet. The slide capacity of the modified cabinet can be made equal to that of the vertical cabinet by the addition of a fourth 15-drawer unit. However, this added height may make the cabinets inconvenient for the user. For a comparison of cabinet heights see Photographs 4, 5, and 6 (Chicago Art Institute, Univ. of Pennsylvania, and the Metropolitan Museum of Art). The height of the drawer units plus the base determine the total base height of the cabinets. Obviously, bases from 1' to 1½' high, will allow more units to be stacked resulting in larger filing capacity. Vertical cabinets having a large capacity can usually be purchased with low bases for more convenient access. File drawers placed 1½' to 2' above the floor are functional if low seating is supplied for the users. However, a base lower than 18" is not recommended.

Viewing—The slide viewing areas are frequently one of the most inadequately allocated areas in the slide library. Although the size of slides may be relatively small in comparison to books or other media, in order to view and to arrange them for presentation purposes, a *minimal* space of 2' x 3' per regular user should be allocated with 3' x 4' allocated if possible. There are various types and sizes of illuminators available for slide examination. The Metropolitan Museum of Art has a combination of sloped table-top illuminators (Photograph 14), illuminators built-in to custom-made carrels (Photograph 6), and rear-screen projection viewers (Photograph 14). While the carrel or light table has a predefined space, the table-top illuminators may be placed on 3' x 5' desk tops or grouped on large tables. In order to determine spatial requirements for viewing, the variety, size, and quantity of viewing devices must be resolved.

Another requirement for viewing is the allocation of an area, ideally a room, adjoining the slide library which allows for projector preview of slides by users and staff. This area provides the staff with the proper facilities for evaluating the quality of institutionally produced and commercially purchased slides and the teacher an opportunity to simulate classroom presentation.

Electrical fixtures and outlets for viewers, light tables, illuminators or projectors must be planned for the viewing area. Viewing equipment is not always placed directly against walls so that adequate outlets located throughout the viewing area may be necessary. Consultation with electrical and building planning specialists should be sought.

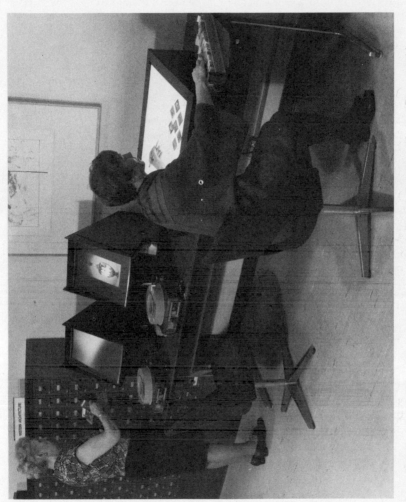

Photograph 14. Kodak Carousel projectors used with two Caritels (made by Hudson-Photographic Industries, Inc.) and a sloped illuminator (made by the Stacor Corporation). The Metropolitan Museum of Art. (Photograph courtesy of the Metropolitan Museum of Art.)

The viewing area may surround the slide housing, be placed centrally to the slide housing, or be integrated with storage. If slide cabinets and facilities are completely separated from one another, use of the slide collection may be impaired. Ideally, space should be allotted within the slide storage sections for limited and multiple viewing areas. Viewing facilities should be easily accessible from the slide files. Examples of viewing areas placed centrally to the slide housing are shown in Photographs 5, 13, and 15 (University of Pennsylvania, Syracuse University, and the University of Illinois at Chicago Circle), integrated storage and viewing in Photographs 4 and 6 (Chicago Art Institute and the Metropolitan Museum of Art), and of the viewing area on the perimeters of the storage space in Photograph 7 (Harvard University).

Photograph 15. Steelcase 2" x 2" slide cabinets, custom-made light tables, circulation table against wall (left) and reference library in rear. College of Architecture and Art. University of Illinois at Chicago Circle.

Circulation and Reference—A specified space is necessary for the charging and discharging or return of slides whether a simple charge-card, sheet, or microfilming set-up such as the Recordak system is used. Proper storage facilities are necessary to hold returned slides in an upright rather than flat position. This decreases the possibility of damage or breakage and makes sorting easier if the slides are kept in an orderly arrangement when returned. In some institutions, the individual returning slides places them in pre-sorting trays by historical topic, medium or subject. Consequently, these items are immediately accessible on a limited basis without having to shuffle through a large quantity of randomly grouped slides. This particular type of pre-sorting device is only feasible with unitary image collections. Slide collections arranged in sets may handle the returned slides in the same manner as books or other media.

Slide drawers may be used as pre-sorting or slide return trays; custom-made wooden boxes may be designed using the basic format of a slide drawer. The width and length of the return tray may vary depending upon the use of the collection. Wooden trays may be stacked inside a shell made for this purpose (see Diagram 9).

Diagram 9—A wooden portable stacking tray for returned slides

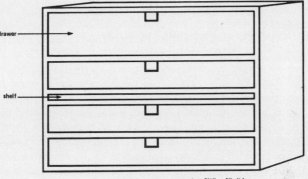

Top drawer is larger to accommodate 3¼″ x 4″ slides

(a) Stacking box

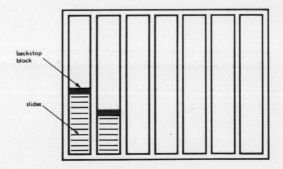

(b) Drawer interior

The bottom of each drawer may be of metal or have a metal insert so that a magnetic backstop block device may be used. The custom-made circulation desk at the Metropolitan Museum of Art has slide return boxes designed to accommodate magnetic backstops. A 3' x 5' desk or table would represent a minimal space allocation for slide charging and return. Again, the amount of space necessary for this function will vary depending upon how many users the collection serves.

Administration and Operation—The supervisor of the slide library, a slide librarian, should have adequate space for staff and user consultation without disturbing the other operations of the collection. A separate office is recommended. If the slide collection is part of a general media collection, the media specialist supervising these collections should have an area allocated for administrative functions. Visiting guests, dealers and manufacturers should have an opportunity to speak with the slide librarian or media specialist without disturbing the users and staff. A preview room should also be available for this purpose.

Whether the library handles books, records, photographs, slides or any other media, the generous allocation of space to the operational or work areas is critical for the efficient preparation of materials for the user. Acquisition includes those procedures related to the purchasing, ordering and preparation of slides apart from the actual filming and processing. This area would include files for catalogs of dealers, equipment manufacturers, and commercial sources for slides, typing facilities and desks for label preparation, cataloging and classification, correspondence, and order preparation. In addition, tables for the mounting and repair of slides allowing approximately 3' x 4' per worker are necessary. Space is required for cataloging aids which includes a small reference library, shelflist and authority files. Adequate wall shelving and portable book shelving, e.g., booktrucks, should be provided for the reference materials, books being held in the library for slide production, and for slide binding supplies.

The work area should also include a large sorting table—a minimum of 3' x 5'—for the slide filing or refiling process. If the slides are kept as sets, then minimal space will be required for this procedure. Within academic slide libraries having over 100,000 slides, as many as 2,000 or more may be circulated and refiled in a single week. Appropriate spaces will vary according to the arrangement and use of the collection. A table or desk-top having a white or off-white surface is recommended. If a great deal of slide masking is done, an illuminator such as the one made by the Stacor Corporation (Photograph 14) will be needed. Several illuminators should also be available for staff use within the work area. Adequate electrical wiring and outlets to accommodate this equipment should also be included in the work area.

Storage for Slides Prepared for Classroom Use—Depending upon the circulation procedures of each institution, a large number of slides which are ready for classroom presentation may need storage space in the slide library. For example, many institutions require that slides only be removed from the library when they are in actual classroom use. Consequently, an area must be allocated within the slide library to accommodate cases or trays of slides previously selected and arranged for presentation. At the University of Michigan, vertical wall shelving along a wall in the cataloging and work room, approximately 12' long and five shelves high, serves this function. It holds cases, boxes or trays of slides. When a teacher or user is preparing a slide presentation over a period of time, he may prefer to keep his slides in the library. By leaving slides in the library until they are to be used for presentation purposes, other users and staff may have access to the slides. The location of a shelving unit may be in the storage, circulation or work areas depending upon where the least user inconvenience occurs.

Photography and Processing—A room large enough to accommodate a copystand, duplicator, processing facilities (tanks, sinks and so forth) plus refrigerated storage for film and other photographic supplies should be provided. Approximately 75 square feet should be allocated but this will vary depending upon the number of functions actually performed by the slide library. If the slide library purchases slides only and does not produce them for the collection, this area will be unnecessary. Space for a duplicator could be allowed within the work or operational area.

PREPARING A BUILDING PROGRAM

Planning for a slide library should begin with the preparation of a building program. Even though a new building *per se* is not being planned, a building program represents a systematic approach to outlining functions and their corresponding functional spaces and for determining the dimensions required for given areas. If a building is being planned, the building program is the guide used by the architect to prepare the building plans. For comprehensive information on building programs, user requirements, office and general work space, and other areas of library planning, see Metcalf's *Planning Academic and Research Library Buildings* (1965).

In order to illustrate how a building program would be written for a slide library, a sample program is included. This particular program has been excerpted from an art library building program prepared for a combined museum and library building to be constructed at Indiana University (Irvine, 1973). When preparing a building program, spatial requirements must be based upon projections of the size of a given collection. Both present and ultimate size is included in the program. Such projections can be determined by current growth rates and by the desired length of time which the new facility should provide for adequate housing and use of the library. Although the sample program provides for the needs of a rather sizeable slide library, the figures and types of calculations given may be extrapolated for either larger or smaller collections. Dimensions for aisles, users, and staff are based upon standard allocations provided in Metcalf's book.

Four basic elements of a building program are given: statement of general objectives and requirements; functional areas with square footage allocations; summary of space estimates; and a diagram showing the spatial relationships of the staff and public areas.

* * *

BUILDING PROGRAM FOR A SLIDE LIBRARY
AT INDIANA UNIVERSITY

Note: Sections I and V have been specially prepared by the author while the remaining sections are excerpted from the "Fine Arts Pavilion Library. Preliminary Building Program." Indiana University (ibid.). The information in Sections I and V is incorporated into the general material about the total library facility in the original building program.

I.   GENERAL OBJECTIVES AND REQUIREMENTS

Enhancing and facilitating the study and teaching of art history and the fine and applied arts at Indiana University is the primary objective of the planned Slide Library. The general design of the Slide Library should be conducive to sustained periods of user preparation of lecture material. The slide collection is primarily a teaching collection utilized for classroom instruction; consequently, use is limited to faculty and staff with only occasional student access for the preparation of special or seminar reports. The Slide Library should be readily accessible to all users. Proximity to faculty offices and to the art library is desirable.

II.   SLIDE STORAGE/VIEWING

a. Present collection: 180,000 slides (includes 5,000 3" x 4½" slides)
b. Ultimate collection: 350,000 slides, 35mm
c. Storage: 1 file unit 13" w x 28" d x 46.5" h holds 7,000 35mm slides = ± 8 sq. ft. per cabinet. **Note:** Dimensions are for a metal Library Bureau slide file. Eight square foot per cabinet was derived from the following: ± 2 sq. ft. per cabinet plus ± 2 sq. ft. for opening drawer plus 4 sq. ft. for aisle = 8 sq. ft. per cabinet.

   1 file unit 33" w x 17" d x 55" h holds 555 3" x 4½" slides = ± 18 sq. ft. per cabinet. **Note:** Dimensions are for a wooden Library Bureau lantern slide file. Eighteen square foot per cabinet was derived from the following: ± 4.5 sq. ft. per cabinet plus ± 4.5 sq. ft. for opening drawer plus 9 sq. ft. for aisle = 18 sq. ft. per cabinet.

   350,000 35mm slides = 50 units = 400 sq. ft.
   5,000 3" x 4½" slides = 10 units = 180 sq. ft.

d. Viewing area: in storage space; should allow for 20 people working concurrently @ 25 sq. ft. ea. or 500 sq. ft.
e. Circulation desk: 50 sq. ft.
f. Storage for lecture slides: 120 linear ft. of 12" deep shelving, 3 shelves high or 40 sq. ft.
g. Space for slide sorting desk: 50 sq. ft. or 2 workers @ 25 sq. ft. ea.
h. Space for slide viewing by projector equipped with a screen: 100 sq. ft. (small room without windows).

Special Requirements

a. Viewing tables: flat, with a vertical or sloped translucent backlighted viewing surface at rear.
b. Size of viewing surface: arranged for standard flourescent 4 ft. long tube size.
c. Table size: 3' deep x 5' long tables if tables are used. **Alternative:** adjoining carrels with built-in viewing facilities.

III.   SLIDE WORK SPACE

Location: contiguous to slide storage and viewing area.

Work Space for Staff:

1 slide librarian's office .... 150 sq. ft.
2 non-professionals (@ 100 sq. ft. ea.)............................. 200 sq. ft.
General work space: 10 student assistants (6 working concurrently @
   50 sq. ft. ea.).. 300 sq. ft.
                                                     650 sq. ft.

Growth allowance........ 150 sq. ft.

Total .... 800 sq. ft.

Special Requirements

a. Sink
b. General electric service for slide mounting equipment, and viewing equipment.
c. Office and workspace shelving for books, slides and photographs.

General Comments

The following functions will be performed in the slide workroom: cataloguing of all slide orders (+ 300 per week); typing of all slide labels and file guidecards; preparation for filing of slides daily (+ 500 to 1,000); maintenance of source and authority files; preparation of all commercial orders and maintenance of dealer catalogs; development and typing of interfiled shelflist; preparation of all orders of commercial equipment and materials; receipt of all equipment and materials; maintenance and storage of charge-out equipment which includes + 15 projectors and several vertical portable viewing screens, and opaque projector, etc., and preparation of general office and correspondence records.

IV.   SUMMARY OF SPACE ESTIMATES

Storage..580 sq. ft.
Viewing area..................................500
Circulation 50
Storage/lecture slides 40
Slide sorting area 50
Viewing room.................................100
Work space:
     Slide librarian's office 150
     Non-professional staff.......................200
     General work space 300
Growth allowance.............................150

Total .... 2,120 sq. ft.

Diagram 10. V. Spatial Relationships of Staff and Public Areas

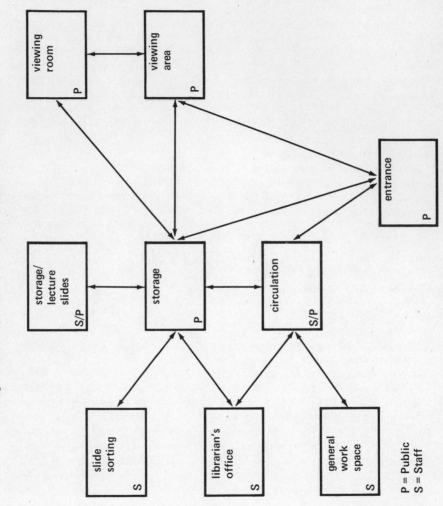

P = Public
S = Staff

* * *

FLOOR PLANS

Few slide librarians will assert that their facilities are exemplary models of design and planning. Depending upon use, the size of the collection, number of staff and functions to be performed within the library envelope, each slide library will exhibit overall layout characteristics which have been adapted to suit institutional demands and requirements. In order to appreciate and understand some of the approaches used for slide library planning, a select number of floor plans are included. The plans illustrated are of slide libraries in relatively new buildings or in newly designed facilities. The Metropolitan Museum of Art facility was designed in 1968, Indiana University in 1972. [For further information on the Metropolitan Museum of Art Slide Library, see an essay by Margaret P. Nolan, Chief Librarian, the Metropolitan Museum of Art—Slide Library, in *Planning the Special Library* (1972, pp. 101-103).] New buildings were constructed at the following institutions: Syracuse University, Ernest Stevenson Bird Library, 1972; University of Pennsylvania, Graduate School of Fine Arts, 1968; and the University of Wisconsin, Elvehjem Art Center, 1970.

With the exception of the Metropolitan Museum of Art, each plan represents a slide library designed for limited use restricted to faculty and staff only. Most academic institutions, however, do allow for student preparation of special or seminar reports using slides. As is readily apparent from a comparison of the Metropolitan plan with that of the academic institutions, general circulation and viewing areas require a great deal of space when public access to a collection must be accommodated. As slide libraries become generally available to faculty throughout an entire campus, rather than to only those within a single department, careful planning will be required to allow ample space for the selection and viewing of slides. At the present time, most academic slide libraries limit use of the collection to the faculty within the department or school in which the collection originated.

Unfortunately, the slide librarian is rarely consulted about the design of the spaces which will house and provide use of the collection. As a consequence, many facilities are ill-equipped to meet the variety of demands placed upon them. Such lack of consultation typifies the planning for new buildings although the slide librarian is usually free to make decisions about how predetermined spaces will be used once the facility is built. The plans illustrated conform to this pattern with one exception—the Metropolitan Museum of Art Slide Library. In terms of circulation, storage, viewing, and general office and work areas, the Metropolitan has a model slide library. The staff of the Slide Library played a major role in the design of this facility. While studying the Metropolitan plan, the reader should keep in mind the size of the collection and its functional requirements to one of the largest museum curatorial staffs in the United States, and to the general public of a metropolis. As a general rule for the design and planning of any slide library facility, the slide librarian should be required to prepare a building program, and to offer assistance for the design of special facilities (e.g., work space for mounting slides, slide preview rooms), needed in a slide library. Both the staff and the users will enjoy the benefits of a properly planned facility.

Diagram 11—The Metropolitan Museum of Art (150,000 lantern slides, 121,000 35mm slides).
(Photograph courtesy of the Metropolitan Museum of Art.)

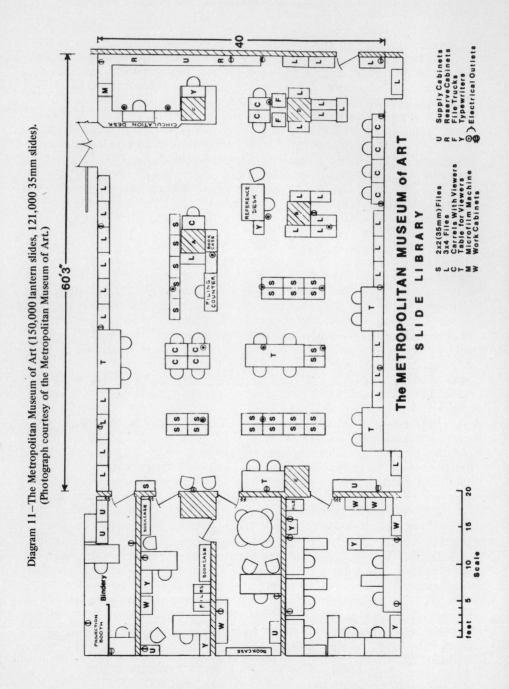

The METROPOLITAN MUSEUM of ART

SLIDE LIBRARY

S   2x2(35mm) Files
L   3x4 Files
C   Carrels With Viewers
T   Table for Viewers
M   Microfilm Machine
W   Work Cabinets

U   Supply Cabinets
R   Reserve Cabinets
F   File Trucks
Y   Typewriters
⊙⊃ Electrical Outlets

feet   5   10   15   20
              Scale

Diagram 12–Indiana University (5,000 lantern slides, 185,000 35mm slides)

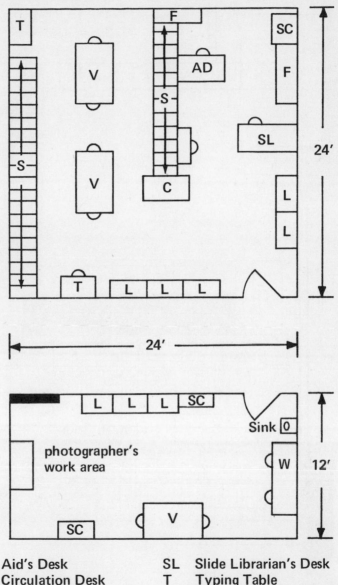

AD Aid's Desk
C   Circulation Desk
F   Filing Cabinet
L   Lantern Slide Cabinets
S   2'' x 2'' Slide Cabinets
SC Supply Cabinets

SL Slide Librarian's Desk
T   Typing Table
V   Viewing Tables with Sloped
    Illuminators
W   Work Table for Slide
    Preparation

Scale: 1/8'' = 1'

Diagram 13—Syracuse University (90,000 slides—includes lantern and 35mm slides)

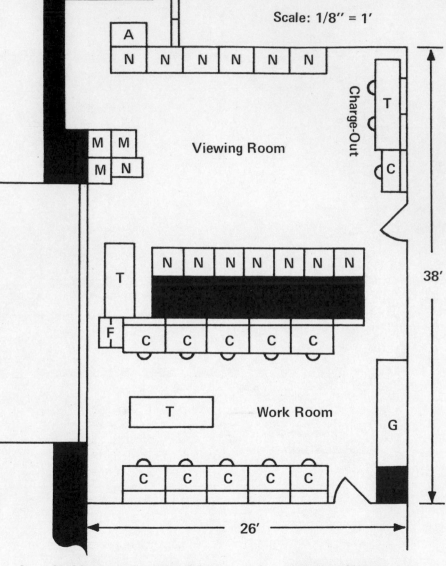

Scale: 1/8″ = 1′

Viewing Room

Charge-Out

38′

Work Room

26′

A	Architecture Lantern Slides	L	Lantern Slides
C	Hanging Carrels with Shelves and Tables	M	Multiplex Slide Cabinets
		N	Neumade Slide Cabinets
F	File Cabinets (ten-drawer)	T	Light Tables
G	General Supplies Cabinets		

Diagram 14 – University of Pennsylvania (114,000 35mm slides)

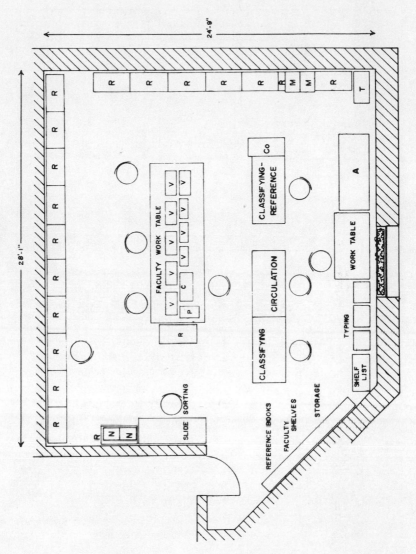

DRAWN BY C.A. EVERS

Diagram 15—University of Wisconsin (64,600 lantern slides, 73,000 35mm slides)

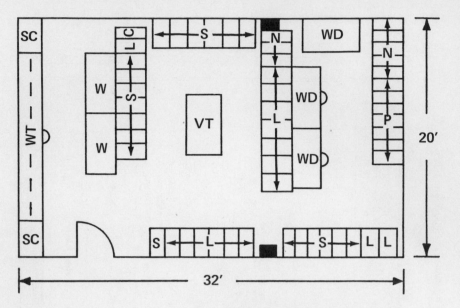

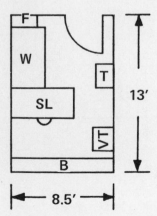

B	Bookshelves (built-in)
C	Card File
F	Filing Cabinet
L	Lantern Slide Cabinets
N	Filing Cabinets for Negatives
P	Filing Cabinets for Photographs
S	2″ x 2″ Slide Cabinets
SC	Supply Cabinets (built-in)
SL	Slide Librarian's Desk
T	Typing Table
VT	Viewing Table
W	Work Table
WD	Work Table for Drymount Press
WT	Work-top with Sink and Overhead Supply Cabinets

Scale 1/8″ = 1′

REFERENCES

IRVINE, Betty Jo. "Fine Arts Pavilion Library. Preliminary Building Program."
Rev. Bloomington, Indiana: Indiana University, September 1973.
(Mimeographed).

METCALF, Keyes D. *Planning Academic and Research Library Buildings.* New
York: McGraw-Hill Book Company, 1965.

NOLAN, Margaret P. "The Metropolitan Museum of Art–Slide Library." *Planning
the Special Library*. Edited by Ellis Mount. New York: Special Libraries
Association, 1972.

8–PROJECTION SYSTEMS

INTRODUCTION

Projectors, stands, screens, and general facilities for the use of this equipment have received a great deal of attention in the past ten years in both the book and periodical literature. As a consequence of the ready availability of information on this topic—certainly not a common phenomenon for slides—it is unnecessary to dwell at length on this subject. Instead, a bibliography dealing with projection systems is appended. A directory of manufacturers and distributors of equipment is also provided in the Appendix. Therefore, this chapter functions only as an outline of the kinds of information available. When relevant, of course, suggestions and recommendations are offered regarding problem areas in which conflicting ideas may prevail.

TYPES OF PROJECTORS

Projectors have changed in some respects while in others, they have remained similar to the seventeenth century "magic lantern." Today, the basic manual prototype of the magic lantern such as the lantern slide projector or 3¼" x 4" and the 2" x 2" or miniature slide projector, are still used although the 3¼" x 4" is not as common as the miniature projector which can be equipped with adapters for filmstrips. Recent innovations include the development of automatic slide changing and remote control or self-focusing miniature projectors—projectors having these capabilities are made by Argus, Inc., the DuKane Corporation, the Eastman Kodak Company, Honeywell, Inc., E. Leitz, Inc., and others. A development which has become available within the past five years is the sound-slide system made by the Kalart Victor Corporation, which incorporates a slide and tape into a single cassette. With this system as each slide is projected, a coordinated audio presentation is also made.

At the present time, most coordinated sound-slide systems depend upon the use of a programming unit that connects to both an automatic slide-changing projector and to a tape recorder. Random access projectors are available from companies which include Decision Systems, Inc. and Spindler and Sauppe, Inc. Random access means that the projector has the capability of allowing for access to individual slides out of their established sequence in a tray or magazine. Random access eliminates unwanted projection of or viewing of an illuminated screen which has no projected image upon it. These programming units and projector systems are illustrated and annotated in *The Audio-Visual Equipment Directory* (1972). Another new projector concept developed by the Fordham Equipment Co. is a miniature projector complete with adapters for microfiche, aperture cards, filmstrips and slides. The *Photo Methods for Industry Catalog* (PMI, n.d.) and the *Professional Photographic Catalog* (1971) issued by Standard Photo Supply are both annual publications which provide information on types of projection equipment with illustrations, and prices.

132

The overhead slide projector such as the one made by the Buhl Projector Co., Inc. offers the same advantages as an overhead transparency machine, however, it can be used only for short-throw projections. This projector can also be used with slides stored in plastic sleeve holders. Descriptions of this projector can be found in Eboch and Cochern's book on audio-visual equipment (1968, p. 41), and in Erickson's *Fundamentals of Teaching with Audiovisual Technology* (1965, p. 334). Projectors can be equipped to handle not only standard visual images but also microscope slides. Projection of microscope slides with 2" x 2" projectors requires the use of lens adapters such as those produced by the Leitz Company. Microscopic projections are particularly useful in chemistry and biology classes (ibid., pp. 64-68; Wittich, 1973, pp. 414-415). Projectors especially designed for microscopic projection are listed in *The Audio-Visual Equipment Directory* as "Micro-projectors" and are available from several companies including Bausch and Lomb, Inc., and Ken-A-Vision Manufacturing Co., Inc.

Although most standard 2" x 2" slide projectors do come with adapters for filmstrips and slides, "A Plea for TWO Projectors" was made in a recent *Audiovisual Instruction* article pointing out the inconvenience of constantly switching back and forth from filmstrip to slide projection in the same machine and to the obvious advantages of having separate automatic slide and automatic filmstrip projectors (Ruark, 1968). Certainly, each institution should study the use pattern of its equipment and should allow for adequate varieties of projectors for each type of teaching situation.

For complete discussions on the use and care of projectors, the following chapters or sections of various books are recommended: Brown, Lewis and Harcleroad, "Projection-equipment Principles" (1973, pp. 478-479), and "2-by 2-inch Slide Projectors" (ibid., pp. 482-485); Davidson, "Slide Projectors" (1969, pp. 22-49); De Kieffer, "Slides and Slide Projectors" (1962, pp. 116-124); Eboch and Cochern, "Still-Picture Projection" (1968, Chapter III, pp. 35-48); Erickson, "The Filmstrip and 2-Inch by 2-Inch Slide Projector" (1965, pp. 325-330); and Pula, "Still Projection Equipment" (1968, Chapter IV, pp. 49-64). With the present rate of technology, the reader is urged to keep abreast of innovations through the various publications available on the market including those already mentioned and the following periodicals: *Audiovisual Instruction*; *Consumer Bulletin*; *Consumer Reports*; *Educational Product Report*; *AV Guide* (formerly *Educational Screen and AV Guide*); *Indiana Arts and Vocational Education*; *The Nation's Schools*; and *Previews*. Part of the slide librarian's responsibilities is to keep informed of equipment innovations and changes. This can be accomplished by monthly sessions in an academic or comprehensive public library audiovisual collection or by consulting media specialists.

PROJECTION BOOTHS AND STANDS

Deciding upon the proper projector and then placing it in the classroom or lecture hall are frequently considered two separate procedures having little relationship to one another. At least this appears to be the case upon examining a number of academic classroom projection set-ups although lecture halls or auditoriums also have had surprisingly little planning for projection booth facilities. Ignorance of alternatives and solutions has contributed to this unfortunate situation. Media specialists and the literature should not be overlooked when an institution is planning a new or remodeled facility.

There are basically four set-ups for accommodating projectors:

1. Tables or any other flat-surfaced furniture, e.g., a desk.
2. Mobile metal projection tables or stands equipped with wheels.
3. Fixed, partially enclosed sound-proofed booths.
4. Enclosed sound-proofed projection booths built into a classroom or auditorium having remote control facilities.

Tables and Flat-Surfaced Furniture—The first set-up relies upon the use of whatever surfaces may be available and is rarely satisfactory. If the projector table is too low, some people have to move out of the way of the projected image, or the projector has to be radically tilted (above a 9 degree angle) which may cause a keystoning effect (Culclasure, 1969, pp. 39-40). Standard projection tables or stands can be purchased for less than $50 thereby denying the validity of inadequate set-ups for economic reasons alone. If, however, the table has been specifically designed to accommodate a given viewing room and allows for proper projection height and convenient use, a table may adequately serve its function. The projector table is an integral part of the viewing room and functions in conjunction with the other furniture and equipment in the room—chairs, speakers, and projectors—to perform a specific function in a specific location. This latter utilization of furniture and equipment is not commensurate to the haphazard selection of any available table-top for slide projection.

Mobile Projection Stands—If one or two projectors are regularly used throughout a building in different classrooms, the second type of projection facility would probably be the most convenient for transporting and using projectors. Metal projection tables or stands usually equipped with wheels are expressly designed for holding a variety of projection equipment and are recommended for teaching situations that do not demand daily use of projectors for a given classroom. The primary advantage of these stands is their mobility and height which easily adjust to various locations. In situations requiring daily use of projectors within a given classroom or group of classrooms as is necessary for the teaching of art history on the academic level, a mobile stand which is not equipped with acoustical controls or remote controls is inadequate. A disturbance is created by the noise of the projectors—two or more are usually used for comparative purposes in the majority of academic institutions teaching art history—and by the need to signal the projectionist every time a slide should be changed. Companies making these stands include the Jack C. Coffey Co., Inc., Neumade Products Corp., and Wallach and Associates, Inc. An entire section in *The Audio-Visual Equipment Directory* is devoted to "Projection Tables and Stands."

Partially Enclosed Sound-Proofed Booths—An example of the third type of facility is illustrated in Diagram 16. This particular booth was designed specifically for classroom use in the Indiana University Fine Arts Department. Booths of this type vary greatly from one institution to another because of custom-made modifications.

Diagram 16–Partially enclosed projection booth. Fine Arts
Department. Indiana University.

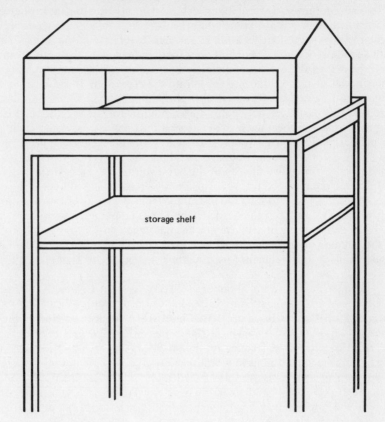

storage shelf

Partially enclosed booths of this type may appear to be more trouble than they are
worth in terms of design and cost but in the majority of academic departments
which regularly use projectors, at least two if not four (two 2" x 2" projectors and
two 3¼" x 4" projectors) are used in every classroom for the teaching of art history. If nothing is done to eliminate some of the noise created by the projector
motors and slide changers, a high level of distraction can be created. The booth
in Diagram 16 represents an attempt by one school to relieve some of this distraction but by no means all of it. Many institutions studied made no attempts at
all to control the noise and distraction caused by the projectors even though the
problem was recognized.

  Of the 100 institutions reporting on the use of dual projection set-ups (two
2" x 2" and/or 3¼" x 4" projectors), 45% stated the present use of a multiple
projection facility (2" x 2" and 3¼" x 4" projectors) and 50% were using combinations of automatic and manual projectors. The use of either manual projectors or
combinations of manual and automatic projectors requires the assistance of a projectionist to change the slides. As soon as more than one projector is to be consistently utilized in a single classroom, some arrangements should be made to
decrease or minimize the noise and distraction caused by such equipment. The

booth designed at Indiana University is not ideal and should not be viewed as a model but it does provide some means of coping with multiple projectors in the classroom. Moreover, its limitations yield design modifications for other projection booths. Although it is not attached to the floor, it is bulky enough to prevent regular removal from one location to another. It is lined on the inside of the hood with sound-proofing tiles, but this only partially decreases the noise from the projectors: the rear of the hood is completely open allowing the sound to bounce off the smooth wall surface behind the booth into the classroom. If a curtain or other sound-proofing surface were applied to the wall, the noise would be appreciably reduced. This particular booth also does not allow for the varying heights of 2" x 2" projectors used together such as automatic Kodak Carousel and manual Viewlex projectors. Each projector must be at a proper height for alignment through the opening in front of the booth. A stand for the projectionist must also be provided to raise him above the top of the hood so that he can hear slide-changing instructions given by the teacher. This booth also does not allow for the use of remote control projectors by the instructor from the front of the classroom. Unfortunately, far too many academic buildings constructed within the last ten years for the teaching of art have not been designed with projection booths as part of the building plan. Rather, at some later date after completion of the building, a custom-made and frequently inadequate booth, table, or stand is acquired to serve this need.

In an article by Wendell Simons (1965), Assistant University Librarian at the University of California at Santa Cruz, on "Choosing Audio-Visual Equipment," he comments that enclosed projection booths are unnecessary and an inconvenience until used in a room having a 200 or more than 300 person capacity (ibid., p. 513). However, quite frequently, the problem of noise and distraction is the most critical in small rooms in which several projectors are in use. If there are 30 students in a small classroom (25 student capacity) and the noise from the projectors is noticeably audible in the back two to three rows, then one-third or more of the students may be affected by the noise levels of the projectors. Mr. Simons was also referring to the classroom in which projectors are moved in and out on a daily or weekly basis for use throughout a building or a system. Where projectors are used on a daily basis for lectures within a given classroom, any facility not having a partially or completely enclosed booth should not be considered conducive to a satisfactory teaching and learning environment.

Enclosed Sound-Proofed Booths—The fourth facility is based upon a completely enclosed projection booth such as the one designed for the Department of Art History at Cornell University for a 200-student lecture hall. Photograph 16 shows the front exterior of the booth and Photograph 17 illustrates the interior and the multiple projection systems. This booth houses six projectors, two for automatic projection (Kodak Carousels) and four for manual projection (two Leitz Prado 500 and two Beseler Slide King 3¼" x 4" projectors). Although this booth is free-standing, it is permanently fixed to the floor. More common is the projection room for auditorium or large lecture halls which are built as an integral part of the auditorium. In contrast to the limited internal space of the booth at Cornell, full-scale projection rooms may be quite large providing space for several people to

Photograph 16. Projection booth. Exterior. History of Art Department. Cornell University.

Photograph 17. Projection booth. Interior showing two Kodak Carousel, two Leitz Prado 500 and two Beseler Slide King 3¼" x 4" projectors. Speaker at right for slide projectionist to hear instructions for slide changing. History of Art Department. Cornell University.

work simultaneously under acoustically controlled conditions. Such facilities should allow for remote control access of the projectors by the speaker at the front of the lecture room.

A great deal of attention is directed in the literature toward the development of multi-media rooms or centers including those at the following institutions: Colgate University (Morgan, 1963); Ithaca College Instructional Resources Center ("College Core," 1969); Kent State University Audiovisual Center (Mitchell, 1967); Pennsylvania State University Instructional Learning Systems and Research Center (Carpenter, 1965); State University of New York four-year campuses ("SUNY...," 1970); University of Texas at Austin Undergraduate Library (Colbert, 1961); and the University of Wisconsin Multimedia Instructional Laboratory ("AV Practices ...," 1964). "Designing Multimedia Rooms for Teaching or, The Instructor as the Forgotten User!" is a useful article on this subject by David S. Haviland (1970), Director of the Center for Architectural Research, Rensselaer Polytechnic Institute, Troy, New York. Mr. Haviland also helped to develop the latest edition of the AECT/NEA publication, *Educational Facilities with New Media* (Green, 1966). The wealth of information on this subject makes the development of inadequate facilities unnecessary.

PROJECTION SCREENS AND OTHER VIEWING ROOM FACILITIES

In addition to the consideration of various projector models and their housing, acoustical control, lighting, ventilation, the location and number of electrical outlets, and viewing surfaces such as screens or walls should receive the attention of the individual maintaining, planning, or involved in the use of classrooms for slide presentations. If the slide librarian is not directly responsible for the viewing rooms, it may never be necessary for him to be concerned with this area. However, it is not uncommon for this responsibility to fall within the jurisdiction of the slide library.

Of the 101 collections surveyed, less than 20% indicated that the slide librarian was not responsible for the classrooms' projection equipment. As is frequently the case, if an individual is responsible for even a single aspect of the classroom projection facility, it is quite possible that he will be called upon for advice regarding stands, booths, screens, pointers and any other problem related to furnishing a classroom with viewing equipment. Such responsibility, however, should not necessarily be demanded of the slide librarian. When it is feasible, the proper source for providing this service should be the institutional audiovisual or media center. In institutions where slide collections are located within the immediate jurisdiction of a media facility, this function is integral to the media center or program facility. If the slide librarian is called upon for advice in this area, unless he has had a thorough training and background, a media specialist should be consulted. The information presented in this chapter only provides a skeletal structure from which a slide librarian may pose questions and seek further guidance from media specialists, technicians, and the literature.

Projection screens are of four types: aluminum-painted or aluminized; glass beaded; matte white; and silver lenticular. Each of these have different levels of light reflection, angles or reflection or diffusion properties, and distances of reflection. The amount of light reflected is judged according to the amount of light reflected along the projection axis which is the center line perpendicular from the projector to the midpoint of the screen.

Diagram 17—Projection axis

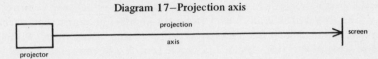

Light diffusion varies among screens because each has different angles of reflection. For example, with many of the daylight screens, the audience must be in direct alignment along the projection axis or only slightly to either side of it, otherwise the projected image will not be visible. Daylight screens do not have the capacity to diffuse the light at radical enough angles to allow viewers on the edges of a room to see the projected image. Diagram 18 illustrates how the angle of reflection or diffusion principle works.

Diagram 18—Angle of reflection

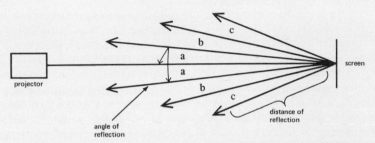

The distance between letters a, b, and c represent angles of reflection off the screen. If a screen has a small angle of reflection as in "a," viewers sitting in the range of "b" or "c" would be unable to see the projected image satisfactorily. David James and George Nichols (1967; 1968) of Texas A&M University have written two excellent articles describing their testing of the four screen types and how each compared in their angles and distance of reflection. In the course of their research, they found that the aluminum-painted screen has the greatest distance and least wide angle of reflection and that the matte screen has the greatest angle of reflection and the least amount of distance for reflection—compare "a" and "c", respectively, in Diagram 18 for an analogous example of how the screens differ in their reflection patterns.

The matte screen has the greatest angle for diffused light or reflection but it does not permit the same intense level of brilliance of light reflection for as long a distance as does the aluminum-painted screen. The matte white screen is most conducive to a room that is wide but not very deep while the aluminum-painted screen is best suited to a long narrow room. The silver lenticular and glass beaded screens, respectively, fall between the ranges of the matte white and aluminum-painted screens.

A new concept in screens is the black screen which is distributed in the United States by International Audio Visual, Inc. Like the daylight screens, the black screen can be viewed under normal light conditions without darkening a room; but it reflects light equally over a wide viewing angle which cannot be achieved with most daylight screens. This screen is supposed to provide a greater brilliance and clarity of image than most screens. Certainly, the reader should take note of this projection screen innovation, read the literature regarding its use, and consult a media specialist for further information.

The *Audiovisual Equipment Directory* includes an entire section on "Projection Screens" which covers both front and rear projection screens. With rear projection screens, the projectors are placed behind the screen rather than in front of it. Simons (1965, p. 512), briefly comments on the widespread use of rear projection screens. A critical examination of these facilities is made in an article in *Audiovisual Instruction* which enumerates the specifications for equipment and the complexities involved in the efficient utilization of rear projection systems (Wyman, 1966). Institutions using a rear-screen facility include the following: Indiana State University, Terre Haute; Ithaca High School, New York ("New Buildings . . .," 1966); Kent State University (Mitchell, 1967); North Division of Niles Township Community High Schools, Skokie, Illinois (Cress and Stowe, 1967); Pennsylvania State University (Carpenter, 1965); University of Miami (Simons, 1965); and the University of Texas at Austin (Colbert, 1961).

As indicated earlier, acoustical control plays an important role in classroom or auditorium environment. Wall and floor surfaces in addition to the type of projection stand or booth should be considered as integral parts of media room planning based upon each institution's use patterns. When rooms without windows are designed for projection, careful attention should be given to the development of an adequate ventilation system and to proper lighting controls such as dimmer switches. A classroom designed for students who will be taking notes while viewing slides should have controlled lighting to allow for different light levels which compensate for satisfactory viewing of the projected image and for note-taking. The teacher should also have control of the lighting both at the back and at the front of the classroom so that he can make adjustments without distracting the class. He should also have a suitable pointer for use with front and rear-screen projections. Ednalite, Spindler and Sauppe and other companies listed in the Appendix supply pointers for every need and budget. In a small classroom, the teacher may not consider such a device necessary but for auditorium or large-screen projections, it is essential if he is to clearly indicate details of the visual image. A simple wooden pointer may suffice in the average classroom but an illuminated pointer which projects a beam of light onto the screen satisfies the demands of lecture hall or auditorium presentations.

For more thorough discussions on the development of media rooms, the following publications are recommended: Cable, *Audio-Visual Handbook* (1970); Culclasure, "Film and Filmstrip Media" (1969, pp. 35-51); De Bernardis, *Planning Schools for New Media* (1961); Erickson, "The Physical Environment for Media Utilization" (1968, Chapter 6, pp. 175-225); Lewis, "What to Watch When You Select Projection Screens" (1967); Patrie, "How Does It Look from Where You Sit?" (1966); and Pula, "Supporting Equipment for Audiovisual Use" (1968, Chapter XI, pp. 277-290).

REFERENCES

The Audio-Visual Equipment Directory. 18th ed. Virginia: National Audio-Visual Association, 1972.

"AV Practices Among Colleges and Universities." *American School and University,* 36:26 (July 1964).

BROWN, James W., LEWIS, Richard, and HARCLEROAD, Fred F. *A-V Instruction: Technology, Media, and Methods.* 4th ed. New York: McGraw-Hill, 1973.

CABLE, Ralph. *Audio-Visual Handbook.* 3d. ed. London: University of London Press Ltd., 1970.

CARPENTER, C. Ray. "The Pennsylvania State University: The Instructional Learning Systems and Research Center." *Audiovisual Instruction,* 10:134-135 (February 1965).

COLBERT, Charles R. "Researching an Auditorium-Teaching Centre." *American School and University,* 1961:H1-H6.

"College Core; Ithaca's Instructional Resources Center Includes a Dial-Access-Information-Retrieval-System for Students." *College Management,* 4:23-26 (November 1969).

CRESS, Hal J., and STOWE, Richard. "We Designed and Constructed a Remote Control Classroom." *Audiovisual Instruction,* 12:830-835 (October 1967).

CULCLASURE, David. *Effective Use of Audiovisual Media.* Englewood Cliffs, New Jersey: Successful School Administration Series, Prentice-Hall, 1969.

DAVIDSON, Raymond L. *Audiovisual Machines.* 2d ed. Scranton, Pennsylvania: International Textbook Company, 1969.

De BERNARDIS, Amo, DOHERTY, Victor W., HUMMEL, Errett, BRUBAKER, Charles William. *Planning Schools for New Media.* Washington, D.C.: Office of Education, U.S. Department of Health, Education and Welfare, 1961.

De KIEFFER, R. E., and COCHRAN, Lee. *Manual of Audiovisual Techniques.* 2d. ed. Englewood Cliffs, New Jersey: Prentice-Hall, 1962.

EBOCH, Sidney, and COCHERN, George W. *Operating Audio-Visual Equipment.* 2d ed. San Francisco, California: Chandler Publishing Company, 1968.

ERICKSON, Carlton W. H. *Administering Instructional Media Programs.* New York: Macmillan, 1968.

ERICKSON, Carlton W. H. *Fundamentals of Teaching with Audiovisual Technology.* New York: Macmillan, 1965.

GREEN, Alan C., ed. *Educational Facilities with New Media.* Washington, D.C.: Department of Audiovisual Instruction, National Education Association, 1966. (Stock No. 071-02302).

HAVILAND, David S. "Designing Multimedia Rooms for Teaching or, The Instructor as the Forgotton User!" *Audiovisual Instruction,* 15:78-81 (October 1970).

JAMES, David A., and NICHOLS, George V. "Adequate Slide Projection." *Indiana Arts and Vocational Education,* 57:90, 92, 94, 96, 98 (March 1968).

JAMES, David A., and NICHOLS, George V. "Experimental Comparison of Projection Screens." *Indiana Arts and Vocational Education,* 56:44-46 (November 1967).

LEWIS, P. "What to Watch When You Select Projection Screens." *Nation's Schools,* 79:88, 90, 92 (January 1967).

MITCHELL, John W. "Viewing Wall Contains Complete Audiovisual System." *Nation's Schools*, 79:70 (May 1967).

MORGAN, Kenneth W. "When Amateurs Make an Audiovisual Room." *Audiovisual Instruction*, 8:220-221 (April 1963).

"New Buildings Designed for A-V Use." *American School and University*, 38:39-41 (April 1966).

PATRIE, M. "How Does It Look from Where You Sit?" *Audiovisual Instruction*, 11:186-187 (March 1966).

PMI Photo Methods for Industry Catalog and Directory of Products and Services. New York: Gellert Publishing Corporation, n.d. Published annually.

Professional Photographic Catalog. Chicago: Standard Photo Supply, 1971.

PULA, Fred John. *Application and Operation of Audiovisual Equipment in Education.* New York: John Wiley and Sons, Inc., 1968.

RUARK, Gerald L. "A Plea for Two Projectors; Utilizing Filmstrips and Slides." *Audiovisual Instruction*, 13:500 (May 1968).

SIMONS, W. W. "Choosing Audio-Visual Equipment." *Library Trends*, 13:503-516 (April 1965).

"SUNY Learning Resources Focus on Multimedia Rooms." *College and University Business*, 48:68 (January 1970).

WITTICH, Walter Arno, and SCHULLER, Charles F. *Instructional Technology: Its Nature and Use.* 5th ed. New York: Harper and Row, 1973.

WYMAN, Raymond. "A Critical Look at Multimedia Rear-Screen Presentation Halls." *Audiovisual Instruction*, 11:373-374 (May 1966).

9–MISCELLANEOUS EQUIPMENT AND SUPPLIES

INTRODUCTION

A great deal of specialized equipment and supplies are necessary for the efficient operation of a slide library. Slide mounting materials, portable viewers, light tables, magnifiers, slide sorters, carrying cases, slide catalog filing cards, and typewriters with small type and variable line spacing will be described and discussed. In the Appendix the Directory of Distributors and Manufacturers of Equipment and Supplies lists sources for all items cited in this chapter.

MOUNTING MATERIALS

Mounting materials include slide mounts, masks, film cleaners, and labels. Optional equipment dependent upon the type of slide mount used and the budget of the slide library include automatic film cutters and slide mounting machines. Both the *Professional Photographic Catalog* and the *Photo Methods for Industry Catalog* are useful aids listing and illustrating all types of mounting materials.

The type of slide mount selected depends upon the following factors:

1. How frequently will the slides be used?
2. Who will use the slides? How many individuals?
3. How will slides be stored?
4. What types of projectors will be used?
5. What will be the average projection time per slide?
6. How much expense can be absorbed for mounting materials and for binding time?

If the slides will receive only occasional use, heavy-duty mounts may not be necessary, but if they are subjected to constant use and subsequently are handled frequently by a great many users, then to provide maximum film life, a mount giving adequate film protection both from smudging and from heat should be used. If slides are stored in trays or magazines as sets without being handled each time they are used, a less substantial mount possibly without glass may be adequate. Slides that are stored in cabinets from which they will be manually removed, do need protection to prevent fingerprints and scratches on the film surface. In addition, a cardbound mount may not provide the durability desired for constant handling and use of slides. Slides that are projected for long periods of time—over five minutes per slide—should also have the protection that glass and heavy-duty mounts provide.

A heavy-duty mount is a slide mount with glass covering both sides of the film. The glass should have been treated to retard or prevent Newton rings. These rings are created by the diffraction of light which occurs when moisture is present as the slide comes in contact with glass. Anti-Newton ring glass is uneven on one side and this side is placed against the non-emulsion or smooth side of the film, thereby preventing a flat contact between the film and the glass. The emulsion side is uneven from the outset so that the glass resting against this side of the film need not be treated. Both light and heat reduces the lifetime of a slide; the added

143

protection provided by glass is necessary to prolong the life of the film if subjected to rigorous classroom use.

The Kodak Customer Service Pamphlet, *Storage and Care of KODAK Color Films* (1965), is an eight-page brochure which gives useful advice on prolonging film life and on cleaning film. According to this booklet, "A relative humidity of 25 to 50 percent and a temperature of 70 deg. F or less are best" (ibid., p. 6). Obviously, when projected, slides should be used in projectors having an adequate cooling and ventilation system. The exact bulb wattage required for use in various projectors should also be closely observed as the cooling and ventilation have usually been adjusted to compensate for the heat levels generated by the wattage recommended for a given projector.

Slide mounts may be classified by the following categories:

1. Cardboard or fibreboard
2. Glass
3. Plastic—with or without glass
4. Aluminum or metal—with or without glass

The different types of slide mounts vary in cost and in binding time. The least expensive is a cardbound mount without glass while the metal mount with Anti-Newton ring glass usually requires the highest expenditure per mount. With the exception of the cardboard or ready-mount slide binding, all other categories are considered heavy-duty if they fulfill the qualifications defining this type of mount.

Cardboard or Fibreboard Mounts—The term "cardboard mount" refers to the type of mount used to bind slides that are commercially processed. Slides can be ordered in roll format. These are not pre-cut or mounted in cardboard which usually decreases commercial processing costs. Cardboard mounts can also be purchased separately by institutions making and processing their own slides. If slides are not handled regularly and are not used for prolonged periods of time, these mounts may suffice as permanent bindings. Slide protectors (sealed-edge sleeves), made of acetate can be purchased to provide temporary protection during projection. A frequent use of cardboard mounts is as masks between two cover glasses (2" x 2"), which are bound with a narrow plastic, paper, self-adhesive or electrical tape. Tapes of this type are available from stationary, hardware or photography shops. Scotch electrical, Leitz, or 3M tapes are common tapes used for this purpose.

The fibreboard mount made by Esco includes glass, a fibreboard frame, and a paper adhesive mask which adheres to the frame. The paper mask comes in a variety of colors which are used for coding of different subject areas. Any mount dependent upon adhesive paper which requires moisture to make it adhere can present problems. Too much moisture may damage the film. Tapes used for binding or masking slides which are not self-adhesive and require added moisture also have the same disadvantage. Cardboard mounts can be quickly bound and cost relatively little—less than $0.05 per slide—while fibreboard mounts may be double the cost of cardboard mounts and will require more binding time. As more parts are required for binding—glass, masks, mounts and tapes—the binding time will increase in direct proportion to the complexity of the mount and the time required for masking film.

Glass Mounts—Glass mounts are composed of a mask 2" x 2" (or 2¼" x 2¼" or 3¼" x 4") glass, and binding tape. The mask in this instance holds the film between the glass. Brands of masks include the Kodak Ready-Mount, the Emde Readymount Binder, the Emde aluminum mask, the Leitz mask, or the Kodak mask. The Kodak Ready-Mount and the Emde Readymount Binder are equivalent to standard cardboard mounts and therefore can provide two functions as either a slide mount or a slide mask which is part of a slide mount. The Leitz and Kodak masks are intended to be used with glass and not alone because they are too thin to provide support to the film for projection. Frequently, when cardboard mounts are used between two pieces of glass, the bound slide is too thick for projection in many of the automatic projectors. The slots in the trays or magazines of some projectors are not wide enough to hold bound slides. Consequently, the type of projectors utilized should affect the type of mount selected by the slide librarian.

Masking a slide can refer to the process of placing it in a holder or to placing tape along the edges of an image to block out an undesirable or distracting background or object. If the image has been masked while being photographed, then taped masking is not usually necessary. In this case a standard metal, paper, or cardboard mask is adequate. If additional masking is necessary, the tape is applied directly to the film. Standard masks or frames and tapes are also used to cover the sprocket holes along the top and bottom of the film. Supplementary masking may be required for any slide mount depending upon the image and whether it needs masking in addition to that provided by the standard masks or frames. The following diagrams show a standard 2" x 2" slide mask—paper or metal—with a 35mm frame inserted into the mask. This type of mask is usually made with press-out flaps that hold the film in place while it is being bound. The film is inserted into section "a" of the mask and "b" is folded over as shown in Diagram 19. Another type of mask has only one section. Masks are also available to fit different film sizes. If additional masking is required, the tape may be applied directly to the film overlapping the mask as shown in Diagram 21. Masking tape is available in different colors but black is most commonly used. All masking tape is opaque.

The mask and the readymount or cardboard mount are quite similar although the cardboard is thicker than the material used for a mask. Glass used with masks or cardbound mounts can be purchased with or without Anti-Newton ring treatment. Anti-Newton ring glass will be slightly more expensive than plain binding glass but the long-term benefits should make the small additional expenditure worthwhile.

Plastic Mounts—Plastic mounts may be purchased with or without glass with the option for either plain or Anti-Newton ring glass. Usually, they are white plastic on one side with either blue or grey plastic on the other, e.g., Titania, Gepe, Agfacolor and Kindermann mounts. The Lindia slide mount is grey plastic on both sides and Kaiser mounts are white. Some mounts may be purchased without glass, e.g., Gepe and Kaiser. The reason for mounting slides in plastic mounts without glass is to prevent jamming in automatic projectors (possible from the frayed edges of cardboard mounts) and to provide a means of handling the slides without touching the film. Companies such as Kaiser, Seary and Sickles also manufacture equipment that will automatically mount different types of plastic slides. Automatic mounting equipment ranges in price from about $150 to over $1,000 per machine.

Diagram 19—Sample 35mm slide mask

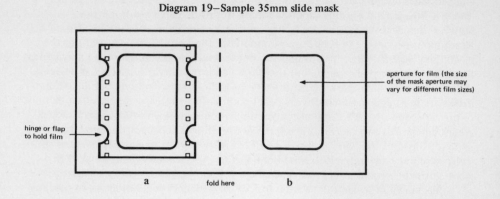

hinge or flap
to hold film

aperture for film (the size
of the mask aperture may
vary for different film sizes)

a

fold here

b

Diagram 20—Slide mask closed with film in place

Diagram 21—Slide mask with additional masking tape

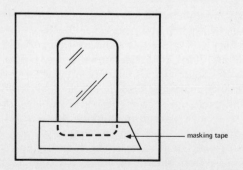

masking tape

Plastic mounts are available with pre-inserted glass (Agfacolor and Kindermann), with glass that is inserted separately during the binding process (Titania and Lindia), and as a single-hinged unit with pre-inserted glass (Kindermann). They also come in a variety of widths to fit automatic and manual projectors. For the extremely thin plastic mounts, additional masking of the film with tape may not be possible because the added bulk of the tape may prevent the closing of the two sides of the plastic mount. This will vary depending upon the density of the mount and the tape used. Manufacturers or distributors will send samples upon request in most cases. It is recommended that various types of mounts be examined first-hand in order to evaluate and select the mount best suited to a given institutional need.

Plastic mounts may be slightly more expensive than glass mounts but with the purchase of Anti-Newton ring glass for both mounts, tapes, and masks for glass mounts, the price may vary only slightly if at all. The plastic mount, however, will usually require less binding time because a fewer number of operations is necessary than with the glass mount. For slides purchased commercially which usually come pre-bound in cardboard mounts, a glass mount may be more convenient because the film is already masked and supported.

Plastic and metal mounts are a relatively new innovation. Glass mounts are the oldest and most commonly used mount because the early lantern slides were glass slides which readily adapted to the use of an additional glass plate for protection of the emulsion side of the image. Many academic institutions still depend upon glass mounts for protecting their slides, e.g., Chicago Art Institute, Columbia University, the Massachusetts Institute of Technology, Harpur College of the State University of New York at Binghamton, and the University of Chicago. Plastic mounts are used by Indiana University, Northern Illinois University, the University of Pennsylvania, and Yale University with metal mounts used at Cornell University (History of Art Department), the Henry Francis du Pont Winterthur Museum, and the Metropolitan Museum of Art.

The primary difficulty encountered with using plastic mounts is the tendency for the plastic to melt after prolonged use or for it to warp from excessive heat. The white side of the mount usually will reflect enough heat to retard this process but mounts having a dark color on one side may be particularly susceptible to heat absorption. Depending upon each institution's use patterns, this characteristic may or may not be a problem.

Aluminum or Metal Mounts—Aluminum mounts include Perrotcolor and Emde mounts. These mounts come equipped with either Anti-Newton ring or plain glass. Some metal mounts also come without glass, e.g., Emde, and can be used to protect cardboard mounts. Metal mounts with Anti-Newton ring glass cannot break or snap apart, come in the proper width to fit automatic projectors, and will withstand the heat and heavy use to which they may be subjected over long periods of time. Metal and plastic mounts which have the same type of glass are usually close in price although metal mounts may be slightly higher in some instances. The cost will also vary depending upon how much bulk ordering can be done by a given institution.

Film Cleaners and Labels—Additional mounting materials include film cleaners and labels. Before the film is bound in a closed mount such as plastic, metal or glass, the film should be free of smudges and lint. This can be accomplished by using a camel's hair brush such as those made by Kodak or a Staticmaster brush made by Nuclear Products. As many of the glass and metal mounts cannot be easily taken apart for film cleaning without destroying part of the mount, the film should be cleaned before it is mounted. A small speck of lint may not seem of consequence during the mounting process but once the slide is projected, it will present an annoying distraction to the viewers. Edwal Scientific Products makes cleaning fluids for films that will prevent the growth of fungus and make the film resistant to scratches, static, and color fading. Accidental smudging of the film surface can usually be corrected by use of this type of film cleaning fluid. An alcohol and water solution may be used to clean the glass before it is placed against the film. Or, any standard glass cleaner may be used for this purpose. It is important that both the film and glass are clean before the slide is permanently mounted.

Labels that adhere to glass, paper, plastic or metal mounts and which do not curl up on the corners after long-term exposure to heat are necessary for permanent identification of each slide. Avery, Erskine, the American Library Color Slide Company, and the Professional Tape Company make or distribute labels for slides. Slide labels may be gummed, require moisture to be applied, or may come in press-apply format. They also can be purchased in rolls or in sheets. Or, a self-adhesive paper or standard file folder label may be cut to fit a slide mount. This latter process, however, requires a prohibitive amount of staff time and the resultant labels may not adhere as well as those specifically designed to be applied to glass, metal or plastic surfaces.

Self-adhesive or press-apply marking dots which indicate how the slide is to be placed in the projector can be part of the label or purchased separately and applied directly to the label or to the mount. Most stationary and photography shops will have a variety of dots available. Alternatives to separate dots include the use of "magic markers" to indicate the projection or thumbmark on each slide. The eraser tip of a pencil, inking it on a stamp pad, can be used to print a dot on the slide label. This dot is sometimes referred to as a thumbmark because the projectionist holds the slide with his thumb over the dot when placing it into the projector with his right hand. Whatever type of dot is used, it should be one that adheres readily and permanently to the slide mount or label. If the dot falls off the label or mount, slides may be placed in the projector incorrectly.

If the image is horizontal, the dot should be placed in the lower left-hand corner of the front of the slide and if it is vertical, in the left-hand corner at the bottom of the image. When the slide is placed in the projector correctly, it is upside down and backwards, i.e., the slide is upside down and facing the projectionist rather than the screen. Labels can also be purchased with pre-printed dots or an institution may have them custom-designed with dots or thumbmarks of various colors which also indicate different subject areas, e.g., a red dot for geology, blue for architecture, and so forth. Color coding of this type can decrease the amount of time required for slide sorting before refiling.

Whatever thumbmark system is utilized, it should be consistently applied throughout the collection so that it is clear to the projectionist how the slide is to be placed correctly into the projector, the tray or magazine. Although a seemingly minor aspect of slide mounting, many users are discouraged from using slides

Diagram 22—Slide with dot or "thumbmark"

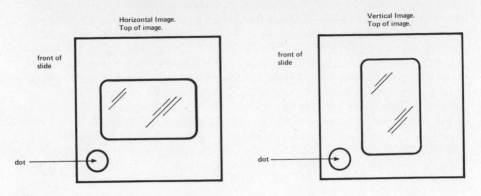

because of the frequency of upside down projections which create a disturbance in the classroom and a break in the continuity of a lecture. Distraction of this type is unnecessary if the slides are mounted and labelled correctly.

A particularly useful publication on mounting slides has been written by Norman Rothschild and George Wright (1961), authors of numerous articles on photography. This book and the dealers and manufacturers listed in the Appendix are recommended for further information on this subject.

FILE GUIDES AND CARDS

A filing and storage system which is not based upon fixed tray or magazine housing and which does not use a visual display rack cabinet will need guide cards within the drawers to divide and subdivide slide categories. If durable guide cards or guides are not used, constant replacement is necessary involving additional staff time and expense for materials. Moreover, sturdy and legible guides make the collection easier to use. Unfortunately, an efficient and economical solution has not been provided for most unitary image slide libraries.

The most common method for making slide guide cards is to cut them from bristol board, approximately 2" x 2½". The identifying information is either typed across the top of the card or on adhesive papers or labels which can easily be inserted into the typewriter, moistened—if not self-adhesive—and attached to the top of the guide card. Fibreboard or lightweight cardboard can also be cut and used in a similar manner.

Another solution is to use fibreboard which has been cut to the correct size and attach a clear plastic tab to the top of the fibreboard. Plastic tabs are readily available in most stationery shops. This type of guide has the advantage of having a clear plastic tab through which paper labels may be inserted—those available in stationery shops come with pre-cut paper on which the identifying information can be typed. A guide prepared in this way is illustrated in Diagram 23. Clear plastic tabs of this type are commonly used as notebook guides. A modification of the fibreboard and plastic tab guide is used at the Boston Museum of Fine Arts, the Metropolitan Museum of Art and Yale University, and can be custom-ordered

Diagram 23—Guide card with clear plastic tab

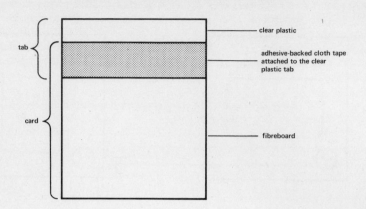

from the Koller and Smith Co. The fibreboard is pre-cut by this company along with a clear plastic tab insert as shown in Diagram 24.

Diagram 24—Modified guide card with clear plastic tab

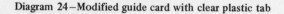
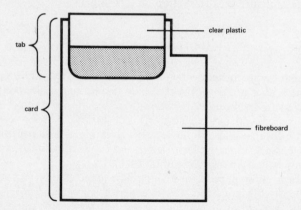

In both cases, a paper insert can be placed behind the clear plastic tab so that the typed information is protected from smearing and fading from handling. The primary advantages of this type of tab is that it is reusable, has a variable holder or tab into which a label may be inserted allowing for at least three typed lines of information, and is relatively durable. With a collection that is heavily used, continual thumbing through the files will cause most bristol or cardboard guides to become dog-eared and bent within a year. Some institutions staple together two pieces of bristol board or cover the top edge with Scotch Magic Tape to make them wear longer. Even this practice is questionable as a means of providing heavy-duty guide cards and may consume an unnecessary amount of staff time.

In addition to the use of bristol board and fibreboard, standard library guides may be cut to fit slide drawers. At the University of California at Santa Cruz, 3" x 5" full-cut Demco Golden Guides are trimmed to the proper size for use as slide guide cards. These guides are made of a durable plastic, are thinner than fibreboard guides, and have a clear plastic tab for inserting paper labels. Diagram 25 shows the original size guide cut to the correct size for slides as indicated by the dotted lines.

Diagram 25—Demco Golden Guide card modified
for slide files

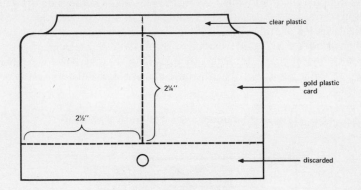

As is immediately apparent from the diagram, relatively little waste in materials occurs with only a small fraction of the card being discarded but staff time is still necessary in order to cut the cards. Using the above principle and the same plastic, Demco designed a slide guide card (with or without holes for rods) but has not marketed them as a standard item (see Diagram 26).

Diagram 26—Demco Golden Guide card designed for slide files

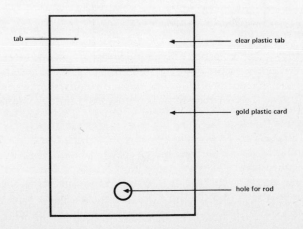

These guides can, however, be custom-ordered from Demco.

In both diagrams illustrating modifications of a Demco Golden Guide, a clear plastic tab is available at the top of the card for paper label inserts. These cards are constructed as single sheets of plastic rather than as two separate types of material adhered to one another as in the case of the fibreboard and plastic tab guide.

Another plastic file guide made of Mylar may be custom-ordered from Demco or Library Bureau and is used by the slide library at Indiana University. The Mylar slide file guides are 2¼" x 2½", and are made so that a lightweight paper or bristol board measuring approximately 2¼" x 2" may be inserted into the guide. It has the same advantages as other plastic guides including durability, flexibility (it may be designed with or without holes and bends easily as the user thumbs through the files), and minimal thickness which demands little space in the slide drawers in comparison to fibreboard or cardboard guides. Unlike the other guides, however, this particular guide provides 75% of its surface for cataloging or classification information in addition to guide headings. This latter advantage is, of course, available with bristol board or cardboard guides but they may not wear as well as the plastic or Mylar guide. Cardboard guides are also difficult to insert in a typewriter carriage.

Diagram 27—Custom-ordered Mylar slide file guides

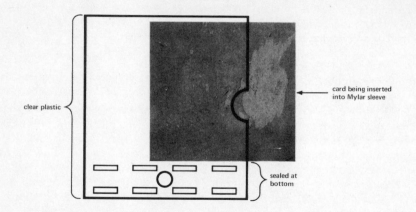

The custom-ordered plastic or Mylar guides are usually more expensive than fibreboard or cardboard guides but they are more durable and have more space for typed information. As more slide libraries demand quality supplies and equipment for their collections, the cost necessitated by custom-ordering materials will hopefully decrease.

TYPEWRITERS

In order to provide adequate cataloging and classification data on each slide label and guide card, typewriters with small or "micro" print sizes are required. Companies supplying small type sizes include IBM, Olivetti, and Royal. Although such typewriters may appear to be a luxury item, they most certainly are not. If the slide library does not have small print typewriters available, it is frequently forced to omit or abbreviate information to the degree that the label may be barely readable to anyone except the cataloging staff.

In addition to small type, some typewriters can be purchased with variable line spacers so that as many as four lines per 3/8" label may be typed (the average slide label is 3/8" x 1-7/8"). Caution should be exercised to avoid typing the lines too close together. Labels for 3¼" x 4" slides readily adapt to either pica or elite type.

Frequently, a new ribbon will cause smearing of the label, but if the label is handled carefully when removed from the typewriter and allowed to set for a few minutes, the problem should be somewhat alleviated. Carbon ribbons may also be used to prevent smearing, although most institutions do not find it necessary to take precautions of this type. Different label surfaces will also be affected by a new ribbon more readily than others, e.g., a coated or slick-surfaced paper will smear more easily than a flat-surfaced paper. If the problem is considered serious, either the ribbon or paper type should be changed. Another solution is to spray the labels immediately after typing with a clear plastic fixative or non-smear spray available in most shops handling art supplies. Unless the slide library is well ventilated, however, this procedure may be uncomfortable for both the staff and users. More commonly used is a mixture of water and white glue, e.g., Elmer's Glue, which is brushed over the labels immediately after typing. Smeared labels are difficult to read by both users and the staff and time wasted by retyping procedures are unnecessary if adequate precautions are taken in advance.

LIGHT TABLES, VIEWERS, AND MAGNIFIERS

A viewing medium for preview, lecture preparation and slide examination is necessary for every collection of slides. That medium may be part of the storage system as with visual display rack cabinets, a plastic or metal hand or table-top viewer, an illuminator, a table-top light table that may or may not be an integrated part of the table, a portable rear projection screen used with a standard projector, or a standard screen used with a projector. Any medium having a light source which illuminates slides may be called an illuminator, although a distinction in terminology is usually made based upon the size of the illuminated surface. A viewer or previewer has an illuminated surface ranging in size from slightly larger than the slide to about 6" x 6". A viewer is small enough to be hand-held during use in most instances. In contrast, a light table gives the viewer an illuminated surface 2' square to 3' x 4' or larger. Screen projection varies greatly in size but again the illuminating device—the projector—is not intended to be held while used. The term "illuminator" is normally used to refer to vertical or sloped surface illumination ranging in size from 12" x 18" to 2' x 3' or larger. There are modifications of these various types but a consistent application of the terms is desirable for explanatory purposes.

Hand or table-top viewers are commonly purchased by individuals and institutions using slides because they are easy to handle and operate, require minimal space, provide illumination, may be battery or electrically powered, and satisfy most demands for magnification of miniature slides. Photograph 18 shows a Kindermann metal previewer used in conjunction with sloped illuminators which

Photograph 18. Custom-made illuminators with Kindermann
metal previewers placed on table-top in front
of illuminators. Yale University.

are custom-made. GAF, Argus, Standard, Arequipt, Bro-Dart and other companies manufacture viewers of this type. Although made for miniature slides, not all of these viewers will accept slides bound in glass, metal, or plastic mounts. When selecting viewers for purchase, the brochures or distributor's guides should be carefully read to be sure that the viewer fulfills the qualifications required by a specific collection.

A light table is a table having a built-in surface for illumination. The entire surface of the table may be capable of illumination or only a section of it. Photographs 7, 3, 13, and 15 include light tables which have been custom-designed having the entire surface of the table illuminated (Harvard University, Princeton University, Syracuse University, and the University of Illinois at Chicago Circle). Glass, plastic or plexiglass may be used for the illuminating surface. In the pamphlet *Audiovisual Planning Equipment*, Kodak recommends the use of cool white flourescent lamps for slide illumination (1969, p. 5). The problem frequently encountered with this type of light table is the amount of glare which occurs when an entire surface of a table is capable of illumination. The tables used at the University of Illinois at Chicago Circle, although having a relatively small surface area, approximately 2' x 3', still present this problem. Some light tables have only a section of the table surface designed for illumination. Consequently, they do not create as much glare as an entirely illuminated surface might. Hamilton Manufacturing makes tracing tables which have glass working surfaces with flourescent lighting that can also be used for viewing slides. This type of product is listed as a "Transparency Illuminator" in the *Professional Photographic Catalog.*

More commonly used than a light table is the vertical or sloped metal or wood illuminator. The small illuminators which have only fixtures for light bulbs are called "slide sorters." Slide sorters usually have a viewing surface that is about 12" x 16".

In the Kodak pamphlet *Audiovisual Planning Equipment* (1969), the production of a wooden slide-sequence illuminator is explained. Placing slides in a specific viewing sequence often prompts the usage of the term "sequence" with various illuminators. Many academic institutions have custom-made and designed variations of the type specified in the Kodak pamphlet including the Chicago Art Institute, Princeton University, the University of Pennsylvania, and Yale University. As is apparent in Photographs 4, 5, and 18, all of these illuminators are quite similar. Princeton's, however, are particularly distinctive because they are built with wooden flaps which can be placed above the miniature slides to prevent glare and lifted for viewing larger or 3¼" x 4" slides. One of the most convenient aspects of the Kodak designed unit is the relative ease in changing bulbs which can be accomplished by sliding out the vertical plastic viewing panel. Many of the custom-made versions require the removal and placement of bulbs from underneath or back of the illuminator necessitating the movement of the illuminator. Moving such an illuminator can be quite cumbersome, inconvenient, and create a disturbance in the slide library.

Photograph 19 illustrates the use of an upright illuminator called Ednalite Sequential Editor/Transviewer made by the Ednalite Corporation. This illuminator is especially made for viewing slides, transparencies, x-rays, and other transparent or translucent film materials. The illumination surface is made of plexiglass and has eleven removable and adjustable metal channels for different size materials. This unit is also supplied with a magnifier made by Ednalite.

Many slide libraries provide several types of viewing devices to allow for individual viewing preferences and variations in viewing requirements. In Photograph 14, two types of illuminators used at the Metropolitan Museum of Art are shown. The gently sloped metal table-top illuminator is made by the Stacor Corporation and the upright rear-projection screen cabinet called a Caritel, is made by Hudson-Photographic Industries and distributed by Bro-Dart and other library suppliers. The Metropolitan also provides custom-made carrels by Herman Miller of New York for slide study and viewing by their curatorial staff and the general public. Media carrels readily available on the market which include facilities for front and rear projection screens for slides and filmstrips are illustrated in *The Audio-Visual Equipment Directory*. Articles on the design of media carrels have also appeared in the literature.

Similar to the Caritel are other preview set-ups for rear screen projection such as the portable LenScreen by Polacoat, models by Lester A. Dine, Radiant Sales, and others which can be found in *The Audio-Visual Equipment Directory*. The Telescreen distributed by Bro-Dart is shown in Photograph 7 of the Harvard collection placed on top of the vertical slide filing cabinets. The projector is placed to the side of the screen and can be used in daylight conditions as is typical of most rear screen projections. Screens of this type can be placed on carrels because they require a relatively small amount of space for use.

As noted earlier, a magnifier is supplied with the Ednalite illuminator but it may also be purchased separately. Agfa, Bausch and Lomb and other companies make hand magnifiers which are listed in the *Professional Photographic Catalog*.

Photograph 19. Ednalite Sequential Editor/Transviewer with Ednalite
magnifinder. (Photograph courtesy of the Ednalite
Corporation.)

Hand magnifiers are useful for rapid examination of slides for visual details and for preview of commercially purchased slides when other methods of viewing are not available or are inconvenient. Although it is desirable to have a preview room near the slide library for use by the staff and patrons of the slide library, this is not always feasible so that other types of magnified illumination should be available for this function. The Dazor Manufacturing Corporation makes a variety of Floating-Arm Magnifiers which combine magnification with incandescent or flourescent lighting. These magnifiers may be attached to a table top or be purchased in free-standing pedestal models having iron bases and are similar in principle to the standard floating arm desk lamp.

CARRYING CASES

Whether a collection of slides is being circulated throughout an entire city or within a given institution, it is necessary to have adequate cases or trays available for the transport of slides which will keep them in presentation order and prevent their being broken or damaged. R. K. Jones Company specializes in custom-made wooden carrying cases for miniature slides to 3¼" x 4". Smith-Victor, Nega-File, and Keystone Ferrule handle ready-made metal or plastic cases for 2" x 2" up to 2-3/4" x 2-3/4" slides. Other companies are listed in the Appendix. Projectors which have their own trays or magazines may be used to transport slides as long as the magazines are to be used in projectors which they fit. Carrying cases of this type are usually available in photography stores and are frequently described as "storage cases." They may be used by hobbyists or other individuals for slide housing but are not recommended as institutional storage.

REFERENCES

Audiovisual Planning Equipment. Rochester, New York: Eastman Kodak Company, 1969. (Kodak Pamphlet No. S-11.)
ROTHSCHILD, Norman, and WRIGHT, George B. *Mounting, Projecting and Storing Slides.* 2d ed. rev. New York: Universal Photo Books, 1961.
Storage and Care of Kodak Color Films. Rochester, New York: Eastman Kodak Company, 1965. (Kodak Pamphlet No. E-30.)

SELECTED BIBLIOGRAPHY

Each citation in the following bibliography has been selected based upon its relevance to the management of slide libraries. The majority of all works cited provide either direct references to slides, equipment such as projectors, or to general principles involved in handling audiovisual materials which also apply to slides.

In order to facilitate use of the bibliography which includes approximately 400 citations, the following outline of the classified headings is provided.

I. GENERAL WORKS

American Art Directory. 45th ed. New York: R. R. Bowker, 1974.
Art Bibliographies Modern. Santa Barbara, Calif.: American Bibliographical Center, 1969– . Semi-annual.
> An indexing and abstracting service providing abstracts of articles, books and exhibition catalogs relating to nineteenth and twentieth century art; of special note are sections entitled "Theoretical Bibliography and Art Librarianship" and "Librarianship" which include citations on bibliography, picture and slide collections. Prior to Volume 4, 1973, it was issued annually.

Ash, Lee. *Subject Collections.* 4th ed. New York: R. R. Bowker (in preparation).
Bennett, Edna. *Pictures Unlimited: Sources of Pictorial Illustrations.* New York: Photographic Trade News Corporation, 1968.
The Encyclopedia of Photography. New York: Greystone Press, 1965.
The Focal Encyclopedia of Photography. London: Focal Press, 1965.
Frankenberg, Celestine G., ed. *Picture Sources.* 2d ed. New York: Special Libraries Association, 1964.
> Lists collections of pictures and includes slides.

Kruzas, Anthony T. *Directory of Special Libraries and Information Centers.* 3d ed. Detroit: Gale Research, 1974.
Mees, C. E. K. *From Dry Plates to Ektachrome: A Film Story of Photographic Research.* New York: Ziff-Davis, 1961.
Photo-Lab-Index. 31st ed. New York: Morgan and Morgan, January 1973.
> See sections entitled "Transparencies and Slides" and "Copying."

Ritchie, Andrew C. *The Visual Arts in Higher Education.* New York: College Art Association, 1966.
Shaw, Renata V. *Picture Searching: Techniques and Tools.* New York: Special Libraries Association, 1973.
> A bibliography listing 500 printed sources that aid in the identification or location of pictures.

II. GENERAL WORKS–AUDIOVISUAL

American Association of School Librarians and the Department of Audiovisual Instruction of the National Education Association. *Standards for School Media Programs.* Chicago and Washington, D.C.: American Library Association and the National Education Association, 1969.
Audiovisual Marketplace. A Multimedia Guide. 1972-1973 ed. New York: R. R. Bowker, 1972.
> Biennial publication as of the fourth edition.

Brown, James W., Lewis, Richard, and Harcleroad, Fred F. *AV Instruction: Technology, Media, and Methods.* 4th ed. New York: McGraw-Hill, 1973.
Cable, Ralph. *Audio-Visual Handbook.* 3d ed. London: University of London Press, 1970.
Cuadra, Carlos A. "Libraries and Technological Forces Affecting Them." *A.L.A. Bulletin,* 63:759-768 (June 1969).
De Kieffer, Robert E. *Audiovisual Instruction.* New York: The Center for Applied Research in Education, 1965.
Gould, Geraldine N., and Wolfe, Ithmer C. *How to Organize and Maintain the Library Picture/Pamphlet File.* Dobbs Ferry, N.Y.: Oceana, 1968.

Grove, P. S., and Totten, H. L. "Bibliographic Control of Media: The Librarian's
Excedrin Headache." *Wilson Library Bulletin*, 44:299-311 (November 1969).
Hicks, Warren B., and Tillin, Alma. *Developing Multi-Media Libraries*. New York:
R. R. Bowker, 1970.
Kemp, Jerrold E. *Planning and Producing Audiovisual Materials*. 2d ed. Scranton,
Pa.: Chandler Publishing, 1968.
Kujoth, Jean Spealman, ed. *Readings in Nonbook Librarianship*. Metuchen,
N.J.: Scarecrow Press, 1968.
Lewis, Stanley T. "Experimentation with an Image Library." *Special Libraries*,
56:35-38 (January 1965).
McClusky, F. Dean. *The A-V Bibliography*. Dubuque, Iowa: William C. Brown
Co., 1950.
Mason, Donald. *A Primer of Non-Book Materials in Libraries*. London: Association
of Assistant Librarians, 1958.
Miller, Shirley. *The Vertical File and Its Satellites: A Handbook of Acquisition,
Processing and Organization*. Littleton, Colo.: Libraries Unlimited, 1971.
Previews. New York: R. R. Bowker, 1972– . Monthly (September through May).
News and reviews of non-print media and hardware.
Rufsvold, Margaret I. *Audio-Visual School Library Service: A Handbook for
Librarians*. Chicago: American Library Association, 1949.
Saettler, Paul. *A History of Instructional Technology*. New York: McGraw-Hill,
1968.
Shores, Louis. *Instructional Materials*. New York: Ronald Press, 1960.
Wittich, Walter Arno, and Schuller, Charles F. *Instructional Technology: Its
Nature and Use*. 5th ed. New York: Harper and Row, 1973.

Administration and Staffing of Media Programs

"AAJC-ACRL Guidelines for Two-Year College Library Learning Resource Cen-
ters." *College and Research Libraries News*. No. 9:265-278 (October 1971).
Association for Educational Communications and Technology. *Jobs in Instruc-
tional Media*. Washington: Association for Educational Communications and
Technology, 1970.
Case, Robert N. "School Library Manpower Project Defines: Who Should Do What
in the Media Center." *Wilson Library Bulletin*, 45:852-855 (May 1971).
De Kieffer, Robert E., and De Kieffer, Melissa H. *Media Milestones in Teacher
Training*. Washington: Educational Media Council, 1970.
"Education of the Media Specialist: What Do the New Media Standards Say about
Staffing; a Symposium." *Library Journal*, 94:1719-1737 (April 1969).
Erickson, Carlton W. H. *Administering Instructional Media Programs*. New York:
Macmillan, 1968.
Goldstein, Harold. "The Importance of Newer Media in Library Training and the
Education of Professional Personnel." *Library Trends*, 16:259-265 (October
1967).
Hubbard, R. D. "AV and Library: Complement or Merge." *Audiovisual Instruction*,
11:442-3 (June 1966).
Lowrie, J. E. "Personnel Requirements of the IMC." *Wisconsin Library Bulletin*,
62:354-6 (November 1966).
McGinnis, D. A. "Administrator and Librarian Work Together." *Wisconsin Library
Bulletin*, 62:211-13 (July 1966).

Peltier, E. J. "Toward Total Media Librarianship: The Expanding Role of the Film Librarian." *Film Library Quarterly*, 1:19-21 (Spring 1968).

School Library Manpower Project. American Association of School Librarians. *Occupational Definitions for School Library Media Personnel.* Chicago: American Library Association, 1971.

"The Subprofessional or Technical Assistant: A Statement of Definition." *A.L.A. Bulletin,* 62:387-397 (April 1968).

     Report developed by the Interdivisional Ad Hoc Committee of the Library Education Division and the Library Administration Division, approved at Midwinter A.L.A., January 1968.

Individual Media Programs

Christensen, R. M. "Junior College Library as an A-V Center." *College and Research Libraries*, 26:121-8 (March 1965).

"College Core: Ithaca's Instructional Resources Center Includes a Dial-Access-Information-Retrieval-System for Students." *College Management*, 4:23-6 (November 1969).

De Los Santos, A. "Role of the Multi-Media Center in Meeting the Educational Needs of the Junior College Community." *Illinois Libraries*, 51:490-7 (June 1969).

Fusaro, J. F. "Toward Library-College Media Centers: Proposal for the Nation's Community Colleges." *Junior College Journal.* 40:40-4 (April 1970).

Lenox, G. J. "Nonbook Materials, Recreational Reading and Faculty Reaction to Collections in the Center System Libraries." *Illinois Libraries*, 49:827-50 (November 1967).

Moore, Everett LeRoy, ed. *Junior College Libraries. Development, Needs and Perspectives.* Chicago: American Library Association, 1969. (ACRL Monograph No. 30.)

Stickney, Edith P., and Scherer, Henry. "Developing an AV Program in a Small College Library." *Library Journal*, 84:2457-2459 (September 1959).

Veihman, Robert A. "Media Departments and Junior Colleges." *Illinois Libraries*, 51:283-8 (April 1969).

III. GENERAL WORKS—SLIDES

Cummings, Frederick. "Art Reference Library." *College and Research Libraries*, 27:201-206 (May 1966).

Ellis, Shirley. "Thousand Words about the Slide." *A.L.A. Bulletin*, 53:529-532 (June 1959).

Freitag, Wolfgang M. "Art Libraries and Collections." *Encyclopedia of Library and Information Science.* New York: Marcel Dekker, 1968. Volume 1.

Freudenthal, Juan R. "The Slide as a Communication Tool. A Selective Annotated Bibliography." Boston: School of Library Science, Simmons College, September 1973. (Mimeographed).

Guenther, Alfred. "Slides in Documentation." *UNESCO Bulletin for Libraries*, 17:157-162 (May/June 1963).

Irvine, Betty Jo. "Slide Classification: A Historical Survey." *College and Research Libraries*, 32:23-30 (January 1971).

Irvine, Betty Jo. "Slide Collections in Art Libraries." *College and Research Librar-ies*, 30:443-445 (September 1969).

Reinhardt, Phyllis A. "Photograph and Slide Collections in Art Libraries." *Special Libraries*, 50:97-102 (March 1959).

Rothschild, Norman, and Wright, George B. *Mounting, Projecting and Storing Slides.* 2d ed. rev. New York: Universal Photo Books, 1961.

Schuller, Nancy. "Slide Collections." *Texas Library Journal*, 47:208-10, 242 (September 1971).

Sleeper, H. R. "Library of Color Slides." *American Institute of Architects Journal*, 23:73-4 (February 1955).

Sloane, P. "Color Slides for Teaching Art History." *Art Journal*, 31:276-80 (Spring 1972).

Walker, Lester C., Jr. "Slide Filing and Control." *College Art Journal*, 16:325-329 (Summer 1957).

White, F. A., and Younger, J. "Slides and Filmstrips Add Service." *Wisconsin Library Bulletin*, 62:162-3 (May 1966).

College Art Association Programs

College Art Association. *Abstracts of Papers Delivered in Art History Sessions, Annual Meeting.* New York: College Art Association, January 24-27, 1973.
   See abstracts for papers delivered at the Slides and Photographs Session chaired by Margaret P. Nolan, Metropolitan Museum of Art.

"CAA Annual Meeting, Slide and Photograph Session." *Art Journal*, 32:422 (Summer 1973).

"CAA Slide and Photograph Session 1973." *Worldwide Art and Library News-letter*, 1:5 (December 1972).

CAA Slides and Photographs Newsletter. Published irregularly by a member of the Slides and Photographs Steering Committee, College Art Association, 1971— . (Mimeographed).

Collins, Eleanor. "Slide Librarians and the College Art Association of America." *Worldwide Art and Library Newsletter*, 1:1,3 (November 1972).

Irvine, Betty Jo. "Slides and Photographs Session." *Art Journal*, 30:306 (Spring 1971).

Keaveney, Sydney Starr. "Report of the Slides and Photographs Session, CAA Annual Meeting, January, 1973." *Worldwide Art and Library Newsletter*, 1:1, 2 (February 1973).

Maxwell, Barbara B. "Slides and Photographs." *Art Journal*, 31:320-21 (Spring 1972).

"Slide and Photograph Librarians Committees." *Art Journal*, 30:306 (Spring 1971).

Individual Slide Libraries

"American Artists Professional League Collection of Lantern Slides." *Art Digest*, 13:33 (December 1938).

"Chicago Public Library Lantern Slide Collection." *Illinois Libraries*, 17:108-9 (July 1935).

Conlon, J. E., and Kennedy, J. E. "An Afro-American Slide Project." *Art Journal*, 30:164-5 (Winter 1970-71).

Description of a project established at the University of South Alabama in 1969.

Curl, D. H. "University of Connecticut Slide Sets." *Audiovisual Instruction*, 12: 480 (May 1967).

Deal, Alice. "Slides and Catalogues at Virginia Commonwealth University School of the Arts Library." *Worldwide Art and Library Newsletter*, 1:1, 4 (April 1973).

Fennell, Yvonne. "Chester Photographic Survey." *Library Association Record*, 72:197-199 (May 1970).

Gardner, H. "The Lending Collection of Slides of the Ryerson Library Art Institute of Chicago." *Public Libraries*, 24:312-4 (1919).

"Lantern Slide File and Loan System in Use at the Cleveland Museum of Natural History." *Museum News*, 7:7-8 (May 1929).

"Lantern Slides and Stereographs in the Library." *A.L.A. Bulletin*, 23:366-67 (1929).
Chicago Public Library.

Moeller, P. L. "Slide and Photographic Services of the Museum of Modern Art." Special Libraries Association. *Proceedings of Forty-first Conference, Atlantic City, New Jersey.* New York: Special Libraries Association, 1950.

"New Thomas J. Watson Library at the Metropolitan Museum of Art." *Special Libraries*, 56:393-399 (July 1965).

Nolan, Margaret P. "Slides: History of Art (at the Metropolitan Museum of Art)." *Picturescope*, 15:37 (1967).

Swan, E. "Problems Involved in Establishing a Slide Collection in the School of Architecture, School of Melbourne." *Australian Library Journal*, 9:159-162 (July 1960).

IV. ACQUISITION AND SELECTION OF SLIDES

Asia Society. *A Guide to Films, Filmstrips, Maps and Globes and Records on Asia.* New York: The Asia Society, 1964.
Includes slides.

Davidson, Martha, and Pierson, William H., Jr., eds. *Arts of the United States. A Pictorial Survey.* New York: McGraw-Hill, 1960.
Introduction and text accompanying the slide survey of the arts of the United States sponsored by the Carnegie Foundation and distributed by the Sandak Company, New York.

Davidson, Martha, and Pierson, William H., Jr. "Carnegie Survey of American Art." *College Art Journal*, 17:171-180 (Winter 1958).

DeLavrier, Nancy. *Slide Buyer's Guide.* rev. ed. Published for The College Art Association of America. Kansas City: University of Missouri–Kansas City, 1974.

Educators Guide to Free Filmstrips. 1st ed.– . Randolph, Wisc.: Educators Progress Service, 1949– . Annual.
Includes slides.

"Fourteenth Annual Survey of Audiovisual Materials. Slides." *The Classical World*, 63:227-229 (March 1970).

Garrard, Mary D., comp. *Slides of Works by Women Artists: A Source Book.* New York: College Art Association Women's Caucus, January 1974.

Approximately 130 commercial and museum slide sources are identified. A directory of women artists is also included.

Hasbrouck, W. R. "Prairie School: The Domestic Architecture of Chicago." *Prairie School Review*, 8:24 (1971).

Index to Educational Slide Sets. 1st ed. Los Angeles: NICEM, University of Southern California, 1973.

Kocher, Sandra A. "2" x 2" Color Slides of Art." *Art Journal*, 23:42, 44 (Fall 1963).

Kusnerz, P. A. "Acquisition of Slides and Photographs: Results of a Survey of Colleges, Museums and Libraries." *Picturescope*, 20:66-77 (Summer 1972).

Lennox, Tom. "Slides Acquisitions: A Media Librarian's Problem." *Previews*, 1:5-11 (November 1972).

A basic listing of many esoteric slide sources, particularly cross-cultural and interdisciplinary.

Maslen, B. "Sources of Slides: Fine and Applied Arts." *ARLIS Newsletter (UK)*, No. 13:18-21 (December 1972).

Petrini, Sharon, and Bromberger, Troy-Jjohn. *A Handlist of Museum Sources for Slides and Photographs.* Santa Barbara, Calif.: The Slide Library, the Art Department, University of California at Santa Barbara, 1972.

Petrini, Sharon, and Bromberger, Troy-Jjohn. "Museums as Sources for Slides." *Worldwide Art and Library Newsletter*, 1:1, 4 (February 1973).

Robbins, E. S. "Slide Evaluation." *Art Journal*, 30:412 (Summer 1971).

Tom Lennox, Slide Librarian, California Institute of the Arts, has prepared a study evaluating lantern slides of art history subjects in collaboration with four other institutions in the Los Angeles area.

Rufsvold, Margaret I., and Guss, Carolyn. *Guides to Newer Educational Media.* 3d ed. Chicago: American Library Association, 1971.

Includes slides.

"Slide Project." *Art Journal*, 32:185 (Winter 1972-1973).

Report on "The Educational Lantern Slide Project" sponsored by the College Art Association to provide a source of inexpensive color slides.

Slides and Filmstrips on Art. Washington: National Art Education Association, May 1967.

"Some Sources of 2 x 2-Inch Color Slides." Rochester, N.Y.: Eastman Kodak, 1969. (Kodak Pamphlet No. S-2).

Sources of Slides. The History of Art. New York: The Slide Library, the Metropolitan Museum of Art, 1970.

"UNESCO World Art Series." *UNESCO Bulletin for Libraries*, 14:87-8 (March 1960).

"Where to Find Lantern Slides: A List of Distributors." *College Art Journal*, 5:137-139 (January 1946).

Urban Outlook: A Selected Bibliography of Films, Filmstrips, Slides, and Audio Tapes. Washington: U.S. Department of Housing and Urban Development, June 1969.

For sale by the Superintendent of Documents, U.S. Government Printing Office, Washington, D.C. 20402. A/MP-95.

Wasserman, Paul. *Museum Media: A Biennial Directory and Index of Publications and Audiovisuals Available from United States and Canadian Institutions.* Detroit: Gale Research, 1973.

V. CARE AND PRESERVATION OF FILMS AND SLIDES

"Color Slides Nibbled." *American Archivist*, 31:207 (April 1968).

Smidt, Donna C. "On Slide Binding." *ARLIS/NA Newsletter*, 1:16 (Summer 1973).

Farber, Paul. "Mount Your Slides in Plastic—A Fast and Inexpensive Way." *U.S. Camera*, 31:61 (April 1968).

Harrison, Howard. "Guide to Slide Mounts." *Camera 35*, 9:48-49, 62-63 (April/ May 1965).

Storage and Care of Kodak Color Films. Rochester, N.Y.: Eastman Kodak, 1965. (Kodak Pamphlet No. E-30.)

Storage of Microfilms, Sheet Films, and Prints. Rochester, N.Y.: Eastman Kodak, 1955. (Kodak Pamphlet No. F-11.)

VI. CATALOGING AND CLASSIFICATION—AUDIOVISUAL

American Institute of Architects. *The American Institute of Architects Filing System for Architectural Plates and Articles.* 2d ed., rev. Washington, 1956.

Association for Educational Communications and Technology. Cataloging Committee. *Standards for Cataloging Nonprint Materials*, rev. ed. Washington, AECT, 1971.

Badten, J., and Motomatzu, N. "Commercial Media Cataloging: What's Holding Us Up." *Library Journal*, 93:4352-3 (November 1968).

Brubaker, M. J. "A & P [Acquisition and Processing] of A.V. Materials." *Illinois Libraries*, 49:129-40 (February 1967).

Carson, Doris M. "Cataloging Nonbook Materials." *Wilson Library Bulletin*, 39: 562-64 (March 1965).

   An elaboration of the American Library Association and Library of Congress cataloging rules for maps, music, records, slides, etc.

Clarke, Virginia. *The Organization of Nonbook Materials in the Laboratory School Library*. Rev. ed. Denton, Texas: Laboratory School Library, 1969.

"Commercial Media Cataloging—What's Around?" "An SLJ [*School Library Journal*] survey of available services, their range of materials, cataloging policies, and marketing patterns." *Library Journal*, 93:4345-4351 (November 1968).

Cox, Carl T. "Cataloging of Nonbook Materials: Basic Guidelines." *Tennessee Librarian*, 21:155-8 (Summer 1969).

Daily, Jay E. "Selection, Processing and Storage of Non-Print Materials: A Critique of the Anglo-American Cataloging Rules as They Relate to Newer Media." *Library Trends*, 16:283-9 (October 1967).

Dunnington, D. B. "Integrating Media Services." *RQ*, 9:116-18 (Winter 1969).

Foster, Donald L. *The Classification of Nonbook Materials in Academic Libraries: A Commentary and Bibliography.* Illinois: University of Illinois Graduate School of Library Science, September 1972. (Occasional Papers No. 104.)

Gambee, Budd L. *Non-Book Materials as Library Resources.* Chapel Hill: The Student Stores, University of North Carolina, 1967. (Bibliographies for Chapters 1, 2, 4, and 5 were revised June 1970.)

Geller, E. "Commercial Media Cataloging: What's Around." *Library Journal*, 93:4345-51 (November 1968).

Harris, Evelyn J. *Instructional Materials Cataloging Guide.* Tucson, Ariz.: Bureau of Educational Research and Service, College of Education, the University of Arizona, 1968.

Hicks, Warren B., and Tillin, Alma B. *The Organization of Nonbook Materials in School Libraries.* Sacramento: California State Department of Education, 1967.

Holdridge, R. E. "Cataloging Nonbook Materials." *Audiovisual Instruction,* 12:358, 360 (April 1967).

Hopkinson, Shirley L. *The Descriptive Cataloging of Library Materials.* San Jose, Calif.: San Jose State College, Claremont House, 1963.

Johnson, Jean T., Franklin, Marietta G., McCotter, M. P., and Warner, Veronica B. *av cataloging and processing simplified.* Raleigh, N.C.: Audiovisual Catalogers, 1971.

McHenry, Nancy. *Subject Index.* Wilmette, Ill.: Encyclopaedia Britannica Films, 1965.
    Designed for a picture collection.

Newark Public Library. *The Picture Collection Subject Headings.* Hamden, Conn.: Shoe String Press, 1968.

Piercy, Esther J. *Commonsense Cataloging.* New York: H. W. Wilson, 1965.

Strout, Ruth French. *Organization of Library Materials II.* Madison, Wisc.: University Extension Division, University of Wisconsin, 1966.

Thompson, Dixie. *Organization of Audio-Visual Materials.* Tempe: Curriculum Laboratory, Arizona State College, 1952.

Veihmann, Robert A. "Cataloging and Processing Non-Book Materials: A True Resources Center Concept." *Audiovisual Instruction,* 15:58-9 (December 1970).

Weihs, Jean Riddle, Lewis, Shirley, and MacDonald, Janet. In consultation with the CLA/ALA/AECT/EMAC/CAML Advisory Committee on the Cataloguing of Nonbook Materials. *Non-Book Materials: The Organization of Integrated Collections.* 1st ed. Ottawa, Canada: The Canadian Library Association, 1973.

Westhuis, Judith Loveys, and DeYoung, Julia M. *Cataloging Manual for Nonbook Materials in Learning Centers and School Libraries.* Rev. ed. Ann Arbor, Mich.: The Bureau of School Services, Association of School Librarians, The University of Michigan, 1967.

Computer and Data Processing Applications

Fleischer, Eugene B. "Uniterm Your A-V Library." *Audiovisual Instruction,* 14:76-8 (February 1969).

Dome, J. E. "Automation of Media Cataloging." *Audiovisual Instruction,* 11:446 (June 1966).

Liao, R. C., and Sleeman, P. J. "Inexpensive Computerized Cataloging of Educational Media: A Mini-System." *Audiovisual Instruction,* 16:12-14 (February 1971).

Motion Pictures, Filmstrips, and Pictorial Media Intended for Projections: A Marc Format. Draft—A Working Document. Prepared by Henriette D. Avram, Katharine W. Clugston, Leonre S. Maruyama, Lucia J. Rather, and Patrick J. Sheehan. Washington: Library of Congress, April 1970. (Typewritten).

"USC's Film Department Gets Grant for Automated Cataloging Project." *Library Journal*, 90:85 (January 1965).

Wasserman, M. N. "Computer-Prepared Book Catalog for Engineering Transparencies." *Special Libraries*, 57:111-13 (February 1966).
  The concept discussed could be applied to slides.

VII. CATALOGING AND CLASSIFICATION—SLIDES

Babbitt, Katherine M. *Indexing Art Slides. Term Paper.* New Paltz: School of Library Science, New York State University at New Paltz, January 1968.

Bachman, Barton. "Where's That Slide?" *U.S. Camera*, 22:78-79 (February 1959).

Bird, R. W. "Slides: The Cataloging, Classification and Indexing of a Collection of Slides." *Catalogue and Index*, 20:4 (October 1970).

Bogar, Candace W. *Annotated Bibliography of Published Literature on the Cataloging and Classification of Films, Pictures, and Slides in Architecture, City Planning, and Art.* Monticello, Ill.: Council of Planning Librarians, 1973. (Exchange Bibliographies No. 405.)

Chez, R. A., and Kubiak, R. J. "Organizing a Medical School's Slide Collection." *Audiovisual Instruction*, 14:121 (October 1969).

"Classification the Key to Slide Collection Vigor." *Library Journal*, 97:965-966 (March 1972).

Daughtry, Bessie. *Cataloging, Arrangement and Storage of Motion Pictures, Filmstrips, and 2" x 2" Slides.* M.A. Thesis. Tallahassee, Florida: Florida State University, 1948.

Davis, Barbara. *Control and Storage of a Slide File Collection.* Master's Thesis. Boston: School of Library Science. Simmons College, 1956.

Harvard-Williams, P., and Watson, S. "Slide Collection at Liverpool School of Architecture." *Journal of Documentation*, 16:11-14 (March 1960).

Kohn, L. E. "A Photograph and Lantern Slide Catalog in the Making." *Library Journal*, 57:941-945 (1932).

Lewis, Elizabeth M. "Control Without Cards: The Organization of Color Slide Collections Without Card Reference." *ARLIS/NA Newsletter*, 1:17 (Summer, 1973).

Lomer, G. R. "Lantern Slide Storing and Cataloging." *Canadian Library Association Bulletin*, 4:119-122 (March 1948).

Lucas, E. Louise. "The Classification and Care of Pictures and Slides." *A.L.A. Bulletin*, 24:382-385 (1930).

McCord, Carey P., and Cook, Warren A. "A Classification System for Lantern Slides and Other Visual Aids in Occupational Health." *Industrial Medicine and Surgery*, 27:46-49 (January 1958).

Miller, Ralph "Skipper." "Where's That Slide?" *Camera 35*, 7:48-49, 54-55 (April/May 1963).

Perusse, L. F. "Classifying and Cataloging Lantern Slides." *Journal of Cataloging and Classification*, 10:77-83 (April 1954).

"Photograph and Slide Library." New York: Slide Library, the Metropolitan Museum of Art, May 1968.
  Outline of the slide classification system used by the Metropolitan Museum of Art.

Rice, Mary Lois. *A System of Classification and Subject Headings for a Slide Collection in Architecture.* Master's Thesis. Denver: University of Denver, February 1949.

Roberts, M. "Slide Collections: Some Retrieval Problems." *CIIG Bulletin*, 1:5-12 (October 1970). [CIIG: Construction Industry Information Group].

Selected Materials in Classification—A Bibliography. New York: Special Libraries Association, 1968.

> Bibliography of the classification systems and subject headings lists at the Bibliographic Systems Center, Case Western Reserve University. Includes coverage of slide classification systems.

Skoog, A. C., and Evans, G. "Slide Collection Classification." *Pennsylvania Library Association*, 24:15-22 (January 1969).

Tselos, Dimitri. "A Simple Slide Classification System." *College Art Journal*, 18:344-349 (Summer 1959).

White, Brenda. *Slide Collections. A Survey of Their Organisation in Libraries in the Fields of Architecture, Building, and Planning.* Edinburgh, 21 Morningside Gardens. November 1967.

> Available from Ms. White.

Computer and Data Processing Applications

Bogar, Candace W. "Computer Application to the Classification of Slides." *Librarian*, (The University of Michigan), 4:8-9 (May 1973).

Davis, L. R. "Locate Your Slides and Negatives with This Punch Card File System." *U.S. Camera*, 16:68-69 (September 1953).

Diamond, Robert M. *The Development of a Retrieval System for 35mm Slides Utilized in Art and Humanities Instruction.* Washington: Bureau of Research, Office of Education, U.S. Department of Health, Education, and Welfare, 1969. (Final Report, Project No. 8-B-080.)

Diamond, Robert M. "A Retireval System for 35mm Slides Utilized in Art and Humanities Instruction." *Bibliographic Control of Nonprint Media.* Edited by Pearce S. Grove and Evelyn G. Clement. Chicago: American Library Association, 1972.

Kuvshinoff, B. W. "A Graphic Graphics Card Catalog and Computer Index." *American Documentation*, 18:3-9 (January 1967).

Lewis, Elizabeth M. "A Graphic Catalog Card Index." *American Documentation*, 20:238-246 (July 1969).

LoPresti, Maryellen. "An Automated Slide Classification System at Georgia Tech." *Special Libraries*, 64:509-513 (November 1973).

Motley, Drucilla. "How to Find Your Slides Fast!" *Educational Screen and AV Guide*, 49:18-20, 31 (May 1970).

Ohrn, Steven, and Siegmann, William. "An Indexing System for African Slides." Bloomington: African Studies Program, Indiana University, 1973. (Typewritten).

The Tansey Slide Classification System (formerly called the Santa Cruz System)

"Classification System for Slides." *Information Retrieval and Library Automation*, 3:9 (February 1968).

Simons, Wendell. "Development of a Universal Classification System for Two-by-Two Inch Slide Collections." *Bibliographic Control of Nonprint Media.* Edited by Pearce S. Grove and Evelyn G. Clement. Chicago: American Library Association, 1972.

Simons, Wendell W., and Tansey, Luraine C. "The Computer at Santa Cruz: Slide Classification with Automated Cross-Indexing." *Picturescope*, 18:64-75 (1970).

Simons, Wendell W., and Tansey, Luraine C. *A Slide Classification System for the Organization and Automatic Indexing of Interdisciplinary Collections of Slides and Pictures.* Santa Cruz, Calif.: University of California, 1970.

Simons, Wendell W., and Tansey, Luraine C. *A Universal Slide Classification System with Automatic Indexing.* Preliminary edition. Santa Cruz, Calif.: The University Library, University of California, 1969.

Tansey, Luraine C. *Slide Collection Index Application.* University of California at Santa Cruz. New York: International Business Machines Corporation, Data Processing Division, 1972(?). (GE20-0402-0).

VIII. EQUIPMENT

Audiovisual Instruction. Washington: Association of Educational Communications and Technology. 1955– . Monthly.
   "Guide to New Products" published annually.

Audiovisual Planning Equipment. Rochester, New York: Eastman Kodak, 1969. (Kodak Pamphlet No. S-11).
   Specifications for building a slide-sequence illuminator.

Balthaser, Kenneth James. *School of Education Audiovisual Programs in Institutions of Higher Education.* Ph.D. Dissertation. Bloomington, Ind.: Indiana University, 1967.

De Kieffer, R. E., and Cochran, Lee. *Manual of Audiovisual Techniques.* 2d ed. Englewood Cliffs, N.J.: Prentice-Hall, 1962.

Eboch, Sidney, and Cochran, George W. *Operating Audio-Visual Equipment.* 2d ed. San Francisco: Chandler Publishing, 1968.

Kaufman, Peter. *Guide to Basic and Miscellaneous Equipment Serving the Art Slide Curator or Librarian Including Annotated Bibliographies on Art Slide Librarianship.* Glendale, Calif.: Art Libraries Society/North America, 1973.

"NLM to Develop Prototype A-V Facility." *Library Journal*, 91:5916-5917 (December 1966).
   Description of an audiovisual carrel for screening films.

Pula, Fred John. *Application and Operation of Audiovisual Equipment in Education.* New York: John Wiley, 1968.

Simons, Wendell W. "Choosing Audio-Visual Equipment." *Library Trends*, 13:503-516 (April 1965).

Projectors and Projection Systems

"Automatic Focusing Slide Projectors." *U.S. Camera*, 30:50-53 (June 1967).

Culclasure, David. *Effective Use of Audiovisual Media.* Englewood Cliffs, N.J.: Prentice-Hall, 1969.

Designing for Projection. Rochester, N.Y.: Eastman Kodak, 1970. (V3-141).

"Developments in A-V Equipment." *Visual Education*, 47-63 (July 1970).

Edgerton, W. D. "Simplified Synchronizing." *Educational Screen and AV Guide*, 47:36 (September 1968).

Foldes, Joseph. "Slide Projectors." *U.S. Camera*, 25:58-61, 92-93 (November 1962).

Foss, H. A., and Pearce, G. L. "Liven Up Lab Learning with Synchronized 2 x 2 Sound Slides." *Audiovisual Instruction*, 13:288, 290 (March 1968).

Gregory, John R. "Synchronization—1. Why You Need It; 2. What It Can Do; 3. How to Achieve It; 4. Latest Directory of Equipment." *U.S. Camera*, 26:72-73 (October 1963).

"How to Make a Slide Show Click." *A.L.A. Journal*, 53:60 (April 1970). Reply: Risse, E. M. 54:76 (November 1970).

Keel, John A. "Answers to 25 Basic Questions About . . . Adding Sound to Slides and Movies." *U.S. Camera*, 26:70-71, 106 (October 1963).

McCarty, C., et al. "Multi-Projector Control Programmer." *Audiovisual Instruction*, 15:84-85 (September 1970).

Mannheim, L. A. "Audio-Visual Automation—The Dynamic Still." *Camera*, 50:43-44, 48, 50-51 (July, August 1971).
    Lists new equipment.

Mannheim, L. A. "AV Projector with Integral Pointer." *Camera*, 48:47 (August 1969).

Miller, Ralph "Skipper." "Cue-Tips for Sound-Slide Shows." *U.S. Camera*, 25:44, 65, 77 (April 1962).
    How to add sound to slide shows.

Nelson, G. K. "Unconventional, But It Works: Overhead Projection in the Classroom." *Audiovisual Instruction*, 8:335 (May 1963).

Rothschild, Norman. "Slide Projectors: Where Do They Go from Here?" *Popular Photography*, 65:84-85, 132 (October 1969).

Ruark, Gerald L. "A Plea for Two Projectors: Utilizing Filmstrips and Slides." *Audiovisual Instruction*, 13:500 (May 1968).

Sleeman, Phillip J., and Adams, Sarah. "Planning and Producing a Tape-Slide Presentation." *School Activities*, 38:14-15, 19 (January 1967).

"Telelecture." *Journal of Health, Physical Education and Recreation*, 41:40 (May 1970).

Tierney, Lennox. "Double Image Slide Projection Technique." *Art Education*, 15:17-19, 27-28 (November 1962).

"U.S. Camera Tests 16 Automatic Slide Projectors." *U.S. Camera*, 24:46-49, 104 (November 1961).

Screens

"AV Practices Among Colleges and Universities." *American School and University*, 36:26 (July 1964).

Freed, C. W. "Make Your Own Rear-Projection Screen." *School Shop*, 27:54-56 (May 1968).

James, David A., and Nichols, George V. "Adequate Slide Projection." *Indiana Arts and Vocational Education*, 57:90, 92, 94, 96, 98 (March 1968).

James, D. A., and Nichols, G. V. "Experimental Comparison of Projection Screens." *Indiana Arts and Vocational Education*, 56:44-46 (November 1967).

Lewis, Phillip. "Slide and Film Projectors Let Tapes Do the Talking." *Nation's Schools*, 86:44, 46 (August 1970).

Lewis, P. "What to Watch When You Select Projection Screens." *Nation's Schools*, 79:88, 90, 92 (January 1967).

Mitchell, John W. "Viewing Wall Contains Complete Audiovisual System." *Nation's Schools*, 79:70 (May 1967).

Patrie, M. "How Does It Look from Where You Sit?" *Audiovisual Instruction*, 11:186-187 (March 1966).

Wyman, Raymond. "A Critical Look at Multimedia Rear-Screen Presentation Halls." *Audiovisual Instruction*, 11:373-374 (May 1966).

Selection Guides

Audio-Visual Equipment Directory. Fairfax, Virg.: National Audio-Visual Association. 1953– . Annual.

AV Guide (formerly *Educational Screen and AV Guide*). Chicago: Educational Screen, 1922– . Monthly.
> *Blue Book*, annual summer issue, is a comprehensive listing of the year's productions and directory of producers.

Educational Product Report. New York: Educational Products Information Exchange Institute. 1967– . Monthly (September-June).
> A service to members of the Educational Products Information Exchange Institute. A nonprofit cooperative conducting impartial studies of learning materials and systems.

PMI. Photo Methods for Industry. Catalog and Directory of Products and Services. New York: Gellert Publishing Corporation.
> Annual publication available from the Gellert Publishing Corporation, 33 West 60th Street, New York, New York 10023.

Professional Photographic Catalog. Chicago: Standard Photo Supply, 1971.

IX. PRODUCTION METHODS AND EQUIPMENT

Abrams, F. Russell. "Filmstrips Direct from Slides." *Audiovisual Instruction*, 15:95 (April 1970).

Ackerman, S. A. "Lightweight Lantern Slides." *Journal of Chemical Education*, 40:151 (March 1965).

Adler, Myles. "From Slide to B & W Print . . . Without a Negative." *U.S. Camera*, 26:26, 100 (October 1963).

Arnold, Rus. "The Nuisance of Newton Rings." *U.S. Camera*, 30:12, 76-77 (May 1967).
> How to compensate for this phenomenon.

Artwork Size Standards for Projected Visuals. Rochester, N.Y.: Eastman Kodak, 1968. (Kodak Pamphlet No. S-12.)

Bibler, Richard. "Make an Art Slide Library." *Design*, 56:105, 128 (January 1955).

Blatt, M. D. "Edges Rather than Corners: Eliminating Backward or Upside Down Images." *Audiovisual Instruction*, 15:83 (September 1970).

Campbell, Charles E., and Trooien, Carl. "An Easy Production Method for Filmstrips and 2 x 2 Slides." *Audiovisual Instruction*, 15:81-83 (January 1970).

Clark, J. "Making Sound Filmstrips from 2" x 2" Slides." *Audiovisual Instruction*, 10:402 (May 1965).

"How to Make a Slide Film." *U.S. Camera*, 24:56-57 (May 1961).

Lewis, Philip. "Latest Slide-Making Aids Break Usage Bottleneck." *Nation's Schools*, 82:80, 83, 85, 90 (November 1968).

"Local Production with 35mm Photography." *School Libraries*, 20:25-27 (Winter 1971).

Miller, Ralph "Skipper." "Slides to Prints." *U.S. Camera*, 26:50-51, 84 (August 1963).

Minor, Edward O., and Frye, Harvey R. *Techniques for Producing Instructional Media*. New York: McGraw-Hill, 1970.

Movies and Slides Without a Camera. Rochester, N.Y.: Eastman Kodak, Motion Picture and Educational Markets Division, n.d. (Kodak Publication No. S-47.)

Mulvehill, Larry. "B & W Slides from B & W Negatives." *U.S. Camera*, 29:26 (September 1966).

Patrie, M. I. "Make Your Own 2 x 2 Slides." *Educational Screen and AV Guide*, 40:597-598 (November 1961).

Planning and Producing Visual Aids. Rochester, N.Y.: Eastman Kodak, 1969. (Kodak Pamphlet No. S-13.)

Producing Slides and Filmstrips. 5th ed. Rochester, N.Y.: Eastman Kodak, 1970. (Kodak Publication No. S-8.)

Reynolds, G. William, and Ward, Roger W. "2-inch x 2-inch Slide Series: Make 'Em Yourself." *Physics Teacher*, 9:93-94 (February 1971).

Shaw, William H. R., and Aronson, John N. "The Preparation of Inexpensive Lantern Slides." *Journal of Chemical Education*, 40:483-484 (September 1963).

Siddall, William R. "Making Slides from Printed Materials." *Journal of Geography*, 68:430-432 (October 1969).
    Production.

Travel and Camera (formerly *U.S. Camera*). New York: U.S. Camera, 1938– . Bimonthly. Ceased publication 1971.
    From May 1958 to November 1965, a section entitled "Color Slides" by Ralph "Skipper" Miller appeared monthly or bimonthly in *U.S. Camera*, providing information on methods of production and equipment.

Walker, Lester C., Jr. "Low Cost Slide Production for Teaching Aids." *College Art Journal*, 13:39-41 (Fall 1953).

Color Film and Slides

Beam, P. C. "Color Slide Controversy." *College Art Journal*, 2:35-38 (January 1943).

Bridaham, L. B. "On Making Color Slides in Art Museums." *Art Journal*, 31:149 (Winter 1971-1972).

Bridaham, L. B., and Mitchell, C. B. "Duplicating Color Slides: Research in Color Photography at the Art Institute of Chicago." *Museum News*, 29:6-7 (December 1951).

Bridaham, L. B., and Mitchell, C. B. "Successful Duplication of Color Slides: Results of Research at the Chicago Art Institute." *College Art Journal*, 10:261-263 (Spring 1951).

Carpenter, J. M. "Limitations of Color Slides." *College Art Journal*, 2:38-40 (January 1943).

Cotes, Russell. "Coloured Lantern Slides." *Museum Bulletin*, 17:10 (March 1938).
"Directory of Color Films." *U.S. Camera*, 30:52-53, 72 (September 1967).
E-4 Processing Errors with Kodak Ektachrome Film. Rochester, N.Y.: Eastman
    Kodak, 1966. (Kodak Pamphlet No. E-62.)
Edelson, Mike. "The Kodachromes and Ektachromes." *U.S. Camera*, 30:40-43,
    64-65 (August 1967).
Jasienski, S. "Colour Corrections to Transparencies Subsequent to Processing."
    Camera, 44:37-38 (October 1965).
Marx, W. R. "How to Reduce Your Cost of Colored Slides." *Art Journal*,
    31:424, 427 (Summer 1972).
        Importance of purchasing a bulk loader and purchasing 100' rolls of
    film.
Perrenoud, F. "Copy Colour Slides." *Camera*, 40:48 (April 1961).
Rushton, Brian N. "Producing and Selling a Quality Service to Education SLIDES."
    Museum News, 46:27-32 (January 1968).
        Problems faced by museums.
Spialter, Leonard, and Smith, Jonathan S., II. "Dye Solutions for the Preparation
    of Colored Slides." *Journal of Chemical Education*, 38:473 (September
    1961).
"U.S. Camera Tests—Kodachrome II." *U.S. Camera*, 24:58-61, 76 (May 1961).

Copy Stands and Duplicators

"A Cool Copy Cat." *U.S. Camera*, 31:20, 88 (July 1968).
        How to use the Duplivar slide duplication unit for 35mm SLR cameras;
    adaptor unit.
"Duplicate Your Slides." *U.S. Camera*, 24:72-73 (September 1961).
"How to Make a Slide Copier." *U.S. Camera*, 24:92-93 (November 1961).
Kodak Pola-Lights. When and How to Use Them. Rochester, N.Y.: Eastman
    Kodak, 1964. (Kodak Pamphlet No. 160856).
MacLaren, Grant E. "A Method for Producing 35mm Slides of Teacher-Authored
    Textual Materials." *Audiovisual Instruction*, 15:101-103 (April 1970).
Seng, Mark W. "Color Slides and Filmstrips: An Easy Way." *Audiovisual Instruc-
    tion*, 14:84-85 (February 1969).
Smith, Darrell L. "Make Your Own Slide Duplicating Unit." *School Shop*,
    27:52-53 (September 1967).
Spears, C. J. "The Rapid Copy Stand." *U.S. Camera*, 31:50-51, 70 (January 1968).
        How to make a copy stand.
Wiesinger, Robert. "Instant 35mm Slides." *Educational Screen and AV Guide*,
    43:88 (February 1964).

Slides Made Without Film

Allcott, J. "Hand-Drawn Slides for Use with Photographic Slides." *College Art
    Journal*, 18:155-156 (Winter 1959).
Eben, L. E. "Do-It-Yourself Slides." *Grade Teacher*, 87:96-97 (April 1970).
Gruber, M. T. "Make Your Own Slide Show." *Arts and Activities*, 65:38-39
    (March 1969).
Harper, G. "Making Transparent Slides." *Instructor*, 76:115 (January 1967).

Holland, Ben F., Hartsell, Horace C., Davidson, Raymond L. *Audio-Visual Materials and Devices*. Lubbock, Tex.: Rodgers Litho, 1958.
Moody, G. J. "Impressions Projected on Acetate Slides." *Arts and Activities*, 59:28-30 (March 1966).
Wolf, Frank E. "Drosophila Holder and Multi-Purpose Chambered Slide." *The Science Teacher*, 31:47 (September 1964).

Titling Slides

Cress, H. J., and Stowe, R. A. "Slide Captions Made Easier." *Audiovisual Instruction*, 12:51-54 (January 1967).
    Using clamped-on letters for captions.
Nye, R. Glenn. "Titling Your Slides." *U.S. Camera*, 22:82-83 (November 1959).
Wilhelm, R. Dwight. "High Quality Superimposed Titles Inexpensively Produced." *Audiovisual Instruction*, 11:758, 760, 762 (November 1966).

X. PHOTOGRAPHY OF ART AND ARCHITECTURE

Gernsheim, Helmut. *Focus on Architecture and Sculpture: An Original Approach to the Photography of Architecture and Sculpture*. London: The Fountain Press, 1949.
Lewis, John N. C., and Smith, Edwin. *The Graphic Reproduction and Photography of Works of Art*. London: W. S. Cowell, 1969.
Lewis, John N. C., and Smith, Edwin. *Reproducing Art: The Photography, Graphic Reproduction and Printing of Works of Art*. New York: Praeger, 1969.
Mathews, Sydney K. *Photography in Archaeology and Art*. New York: Humanities Press, 1968.
Nolan, Margaret P. "The Release of Photographic Reproductions of Art Objects." *Special Libraries*, 56:42-46 (January 1965).
Shulman, Julius. *Photographing Architecture and Interiors*. New York: Whitney Library of Design, 1962.
Shaw, Leslie. *Architectural Photography*. London: George Newnes, 1949.

XI. COPYRIGHT

Bender, Ivan. "Copyright: Chaos or Compromise?" *Reviews*, 2:3-5 (November 1973).
    Brief overview of history and current status of copyright legislation and its relationship to the duplication of educational materials.
Clapp, Verner. *Copyright: A Librarian's View*. Washington: Washington Copyright Committee, Association of Research Libraries, 1968.
Kent, Allen, and Lancour, Harold. *Copyright. Current Viewpoints on History, Laws, and Legislation*. New York: R. R. Bowker, 1972.
Nicholson, Margaret. *A Manual of Copyright Practice for Writers, Publishers, and Agents*. 2d ed. with a New Preface, 1970. New York: Oxford University Press, 1956.
Pilpel, Harriet F., and Goldberg, Morton David. *A Copyright Guide*. 4th ed. New York: R. R. Bowker, 1969.
Siebert, Fred S. *Copyrights, Clearances, and Rights of Teachers in the New Educational Media*. Washington: American Council on Education, 1964.

[United States Code Annotated] , 17:U.S.C.A. § 101.
  Slides are classified under § 202.11 Photographs (Class J) of the United
  States Code Annotated.

XII. PLANNING PHYSICAL FACILITIES

American Library Association—Ad Hoc Committee on the Physical Facilities of
  Libraries. *Measurement and Comparison of Physical Facilities for Libraries.*
  Chicago: American Library Association, 1970.
Carpenter, C. Ray. "The Pennsylvania State University: The Instructional Learning
  Systems and Research Center." *Audiovisual Instruction*, 10:134-135
  (February 1965).
De Barnardis, Amo, Doherty, Victor W., Hummel, Errett, Brubaker, Charles
  William. *Planning Schools for New Media.* Washington: Office of Education,
  U.S. Department of Health, Education and Welfare, 1961.
Gilkey, R. "Designing Space for Use of Instructional Hardware." *The Clearing
  House*, 45:255-256 (December 1970).
Green, Alan C., ed. *Educational Facilities with New Media.* Washington: Depart-
  ment of Audiovisual Instruction, National Education Association, 1966.
  (Stock No. 071-02302.)
Irvine, Betty Jo. "Fine Arts Pavilion Library. Preliminary Building Program." rev.
  Bloomington: Indiana University, September 1973. (Mimeographed).
Metcalf, Keyes D. *Planning Academic and Research Library Buildings.* New York:
  McGraw-Hill, 1965.
Moriarty, J. H. "New Media Facilities." *Library Trends*, 16:251-258 (October
  1967).
"New Buildings Designed for A-V Use." *American School and University*, 38:39-41
  (April 1966).
*New Spaces for Learning—Designing College Facilities to Utilize Instructional Aids
  and Media.* New York: School of Architecture, Rensselaer Polytechnic
  Institute, 1961.
Nolan, Margaret P. "The Metropolitan Museum of Art—Slide Library." *Planning the
  Special Library.* Edited by Ellis Mount. New York: Special Libraries Associa-
  tion, 1972. (SLA Monograph No. 4.)
Stone, C. W. "Planning for Media Within University Library Buildings." *Library
  Trends*, 18:233-245 (October 1969).

Classroom Design

Colbert, Charles R. "Researching an Auditorium-Teaching Centre." *American
  School and University*, 1961:H1-H6.
Cress, Hal J., and Stowe, Richard. "We Designed and Constructed a Remote Con-
  trol Classroom." *Audiovisual Instruction*, 12:830-835 (October 1967).
Haviland, David S. "Designing Multimedia Rooms for Teaching or, the Instructor
  as the Forgotten User!" *Audiovisual Instruction*, 15:78-81 (October 1970).
McDougal, R., and Thompson, J. J. "Multi-Media Classroom: Planning and Opera-
  tion." *Audiovisual Instruction*, 12:826-829 (October 1967).
Morgan, Kenneth W. "When Amateurs Make an AV Room." *Audiovisual Instruction*, 8:220-221 (April 1963).

"SUNY Learning Resources Focus on Multimedia Rooms." *College and University Business*, 48:68 (January 1970).

Tanzman, J. "Media Starts with the Architect." *School Management*, 14:50 (May 1970).

XIII. USING SLIDES FOR INSTRUCTION

Carithers, P. "Color Slides that Show Teaching." *Michigan Education Journal*, 43:28-29 (May 1966).

Cook, R. I., and McElhiney, D. S. "A-V Term Report." *Audiovisual Instruction*, 12:696-698 (September 1967).

Cosgrove, L. "Use of Filmstrips and Slides." *Illinois Libraries*, 42:251-253 (April 1960).

Dennis, D. A. "Preproducction Planning: Key to Successful Slide Shows." *Audiovisual Instruction*, 10:401 (May 1965).

Edgerton, W. D. "Europe on One Roll of Film a Day: Photographic Suggestions for the Educator Traveling Abroad." *Audiovisual Instruction*, 15:99-101 (March 1970).

Foss, M. F. "Use Slides for Wood Identification." *Indiana Arts and Vocational Education*, 57:330 (October 1968).

Gaunt, J. H. "Developing Taped Narrations for Slide Presentations." *School Libraries*, 17:45-49 (Winter 1968).

Hollis, R. "Your Own Slides." *Catholic School Journal*, 70:30, 32 (March 1970).

"How Ten Top A-V Programs Compare." *Nation's Schools*, 82:74-78 (October 1968).

Jones, R. C. "Multicampus Instructional Resources Services: Three New Campuses in St. Louis." *Junior College Journal*, 36:11-13 (March 1966).

"OSU (Oklahoma State University) Library Will Loan Slides." *Kansas Library Bulletin*, 37:12-13 (Winter 1968).

Singer, Ira J. "Audio-Visual Dial Access Information Retrieval and the User." *Audio Visual Media. Moyens Audio Visuels*, 4:17-23 (1970).

Sister Gilmary. "Future Teachers Learn from Low Cost Methods." *Educational Screen and AV Guide*, 44:24-25 (September 1965).

Sleeman, Phillip J., and Adams, Sarah. "Research Report on the Development and Efflctiveness of Color Slides in Teaching and Learning." *School Activities*, 37:13-15 (December 1965).

"Slides and Slide-Lectures Offered by the Library." *Library Journal*, 94:1570 (April 1969).

Stanger, B. N. "Slide Presentation Contributes to Maximum Learning." *Agricultural Education Magazine*, 43:92 (October 1970).

"Teaching with Slides." *Classical World*, 63:153-154 (January 1970).

"Using Film, Slides and Transparencies to Expand Daily Learning." *American School and University*, 40:40-41, 61 (April 1968).

Wendt, P. R., and Butts, G. K. "A/V Materials: Filmstrips, Slides and Transparencies." *Review of Educational Research*, 32:144-146 (April 1962).

Art

Burden, E. "Slide Presentations [for Architects]." *Architectural Record*, 150:55-58 (July 1971).

Carleton, C. S. "Picasso=MC^2; Project CUE, An Experiment Designed to Integrate the Arts and Humanities Into the School Curriculum." *American Education*, 2:13-15 (March 1966).

Florian, V. L., and Novotny, D. F. "Enrich Art History with Sight and Sound." *Arts and Activities*, 58:38-41 (September 1965).

Hess, H. L., and James, D. "Presenting a Conventional Drawing Concept in 35mm Slides." *Indiana Arts and Vocational Education*, 56:51-53 (November 1967).

Hess, H. L., and Nystrom, D. C. "Using 35mm Slide Sets to Teach Pictorial Projection." *Indiana Arts and Vocational Education*, 57:46-47 (December 1968).

Hurwitz, A. "Turned-On Art." *American Education*, 6:14-17 (March 1970).

Geography

Miller, E. Willard. "Use of Color Slides as a Geographic Teaching Aid." *Journal of Geography*, 64:304-307 (October 1965).

Rafferty, M. D. "Field Techniques in the Classroom: The Use of Color Slides for Field Observations of Occupance Features." *Journal of Geography*, 69: 83-88 (February 1970).

White, Wayne R. "Slides: A Teaching Aid in Geography." *Audiovisual Instruction*, 11:352-354 (May 1966).

Language

"The Film, Slide, and Filmstrip Jungle." *Modern Language Journal*, 54:333-335 (May 1970).

"Gestaltungskriterien fur Diareihen in Fremdsprachenunterricht." (Criteria for the Preparation of Filmstrips and Slides for Use in Foreign Language Instruction). *Contact*, 13:19-22 (July 1969).

Walbruck, Harry A. "Films, Slides, or Tapes: German Instruction by Films." *NALLD Journal*, 5:19-27 (October 1970).

Library Orientation

Allen, K. W. "Use of Slides for Teaching Reference." *Journal of Education for Librarianship*, 6:137-139 (Fall 1965).

Biermann, J. "Library Orientation in Kodachrome." *Library Journal*, 8:2456-2457 (September 1958).

Bolvin, B. "Libraries of the Future: A Multimedia Presentation." *Library News Bulletin*, 34:286-288 (October 1967).

Donehue, B. K. "Sliding Toward Progress." *School Libraries*, 11:25-27, 57-58 (March 1962).

Evans, R. W. "Using Slides for Library Orientation." *Illinois Libraries*, 51:300-303 (April 1969).

Keller, C. W. "Monsanto Information Center's A-V Orientation Program." *Special Libraries*, 57:648-651 (November 1966).

Kent, N. "Sliding Into the High School Library." *Educational Screen and AV Guide*, 43:700 (December 1964).

Simons, Wendell W. "Slides Introduce the Library." *California Librarian*, 19:113 (April 1958).

Science

Bledsoe, J. C., et al. "Use of Film Slides in Introductory Microbiology." *Journal of Educational Research*, 63:86-93 (October 1969).

Kowles, R. "Camera in Teaching High School Biology." *American Biology Teacher*, 27:679-682 (November 1965).

"Visual Aids for Teaching Biochemical Pathways." *American Biology Teacher*, 31:83-85 (February 1969).

Zollinger, R. M., Howe, C. T. "The Illustration of Medical Lectures." *Medical and Biological Instruction*, 14:154-162 (July 1964).

DIRECTORY OF DISTRIBUTORS AND MANUFACTURERS OF EQUIPMENT AND SUPPLIES

"See also" references refer to the equipment and/or supplies listing under which the complete address of a distributor and/or manufacturer is provided.

GENERAL SOURCES

A.V.E. Corporation, 250 West 54th Street, New York, New York 10019 / Miniature slide projectors, projection screens, tables and stands, slide changers and controls.

The Advance Products Company, Box 2178, Wichita, Kansas 67214 / Pointers, projectors, screens, stands.

American Optical Corporation, 359 Beacham St., Chelsea, Massachusetts 02150 / Pointers, projectors, screens, slide mounting materials, stands, viewers.

Bro-Dart, Inc., 56 Earl St., Newark, New Jersey 07114 / Cabinets, cardboard slide mounts, projectors, screens, stands, viewers.

Demco Educational Corporation, Box 1488, Madison, Wisconsin 53701 / Card stock for slide file guides, pointers, projectors, screens, viewers.

NASCO, 901 Janesville Ave., Fort Atkinson, Wisconsin 53538 / Complete line of slide materials and equipment.

School Specialty Supply Company, Box 1327, Salina, Kansas 67401 / Complete line of slide materials and equipment.

Scott Education Division, 104 Lower Westfield Rd., Holyoke, Massachusetts 01040 / Pointers, projectors, screens, stands, viewers.

Standard Photo Supply, 43 East Chicago Ave., Chicago, Illinois 60611 / Complete line of slide materials and equipment.

CARRYING CASES

R. K. Jones Company, 72 Sedgwick St., Brooklyn, New York 11231 / Custom-made carrying cases.

Keystone Ferrule and Nut Company, 909 Milwaukee Ave., Burlington, Wisconsin 53105 / Metal carrying cases, slide files, slide sorter.

Nega-File, Inc. / Carrying cases. *See also* Filing and Storage Units.

Smith-Victor Corporation, Griffith, Indiana 46319 / Projection stands, slide cases, slide sorters (metal and plastic).

DUPLICATORS

Bogen Photo Corporation, 232 South Van Brunt St., P.O. Box 448, Englewood, New Jersey 07631 / Bowens Illumitran (slide duplicator).

Honeywell, Inc. / Repronar (slide duplicator). *See also* Projectors.

E. Leitz, Inc. / Reprovit copy stand with camera, slide duplicator. *See also* Projectors.

Sickles, Inc. / Slide duplicator. *See also* Mounts, Binding Materials.

FILING AND STORAGE CABINETS

Art Steel Company, Inc., 170 West 233rd St., Bronx, New York 10463 / Metal slide file cabinets (modified "card file").

Jack C. Coffey Company, Inc., P.O. Box 131, 104 Lake View Ave., Waukegan, Illinois 60085 / Luxor metal slide filing cabinets, projectors, stands, viewers.

Elden Enterprises, Inc., P.O. Box 3201, Charleston, West Virginia 25332 / Metal visual display rack slide cabinets.

Gaylord Brothers, Inc., Library Supplies and Equipment, P.O. Box 61, Syracuse, New York 13201 / Luxor metal slide filing cabinets.

General Fireproofing Company, 413 West Dennick Ave., Youngstown, Ohio 44505 / Metal slide filing cabinets.

Library Bureau Division of Sperry Remington, Division of Sperry Rand Corporation, 801 Park Ave., P.O. Box 271, Herkimer, New York 13350 / Wood 2" x 2" slide filing cabinets and metal slide files.

Multiplex Display Fixture Company, 1555 Larkin Williams Rd., Fenton (St. Louis County), Missouri 63026 / Metal visual display rack slide cabinets.

Nega-File, Inc., P.O. Box 78, Furlong, Pennsylvania 18925 / Carrying cases for 2" x 2" and 3¼" x 4" slides, wooden filing cabinets for 2" x 2", 2¼" x 2¼" and 3¼" x 4" slides.

Neumade Products Corporation, Box 568, 720 White Plains Rd., Scarsdale, New York 10583 / Metal slide filing cabinets.

Remington Rand, Inc. *See* Library Bureau Division of Sperry Remington.

Sandak, Inc., 4 East 48th St., New York, New York 10017 / Slide filing cabinets.

Steelcase, Inc., 1120 39th St., SE, Grand Rapids, Michigan 49508 / Metal slide filing cabinets.

Supreme Steel Equipment Corporation, 50th and Second Sts., Brooklyn, New York 11232 / "Conserva File" (metal file modified for slide storage).

Wallach and Associates, Inc., P.O. Box 18167, 1532 Hillcrest Blvd., Cleveland, Ohio 44118 / Metal slide filing cabinets.

H. Wilson Corporation, 555 West Taft Drive, South, Holland, Illinois 60473 / Metal slide filing cabinet.

FILE GUIDES

Demco Educational Corporation / Custom-ordered file guides, plastic card stock. *See also* General.

Koller and Smith Company, 160 Jay St., Brooklyn, New York 11201 / Fibreboard with plastic file guides.

Library Bureau Division of Sperry Remington, Division of Sperry Rand Corporation, 4175 Millersville Rd., Indianapolis, Indiana 46205 / Mylar slide file guides, Remington Rand Kardex cards, cardboard, 2¼" x 2¼" (blue, buff, echru, green, salmon, white).

LIGHT TABLES

Hamilton Manufacturing Company, Two Rivers, Wisconsin 54241 / Dial-A-Light tables; tracing tables.

Stacor Corporation, 285 Emmet St., Newark, New Jersey 07114 / Illuminated sorting tables.

MOUNTS/BINDING MATERIALS

AGFA Akteingesellschaft, Camera-Werk, Munich, Germany / Plastic slide mounts (Agfacolor Dia-Frames).

American Library Color Slide Company, 305 East 45th St., New York, New York 10017 / Plastic slide mounts (Lindia, Titania), slide labels.

Avery Label Company, 211 East 43rd St., New York, New York 10017 / Slide labels.

Chartpak Rotex, Division Avery Products Corporation, 2620 South Susan St., Santa Ana, California 92704 / Masking tape.

Dazor Manufacturing Corporation, 4455-99 Duncan Ave., St. Louis, Missouri 63110 / High intensity lamps, illuminated magnifiers, incandescent and fluorescent portable lighting fixtures, magnifying lamps for binding slides.

Eastman Kodak Company / Slide masks (tape and paper strips). *See also* Projectors.

Edwal Scientific Products Corporation, 12120 South Peoria, Chicago, Illinois 60643 / Anti-stat slide cleaner; chemical product for preventing fungus on slides (Permafilm).

Emde Products, Inc., 2040 Stoner Ave., Los Angeles, California 90025 / Aluminum and glass mounts, slide binders and masks for 2" x 2", 2-3/4" x 2-3/4", and 3¼" x 4" slides, slide supplies.

Erskine Company, 16-18 West 22nd St., New York, New York 10010 / Cases, plastic slide mounts (Lindia), slide masking tape, viewers.

Esco, 2141 N.W. 25th Ave., Portland, Oregon 97210 / Slide mounts (paper and cardboard).

Gem-Mounts and Gem-Masks Company, Box 630 Times Square Station, New York, New York 10036 / Paper masks, slide mounts.

Karl Heitz, Inc., 979 Third Ave., New York, New York 10022 / Reader-projector for rapid evaluation of 35mm slides, projection stands, plastic slide mounts (Lindia), table viewers, viewers, zoom pocket microscopes.

Kaiser Products, P.O. Box 7101, North End Station, Colorado Springs, Colorado 80907 / Plastic slide mounts, slide mounting materials.

Kindermann, Division of EPOI International, Ltd., 623 Stewart Ave., Garden City, New York 11533 / Plastic slide mounts.

E. Leitz, Inc. / Slide masks, aluminum slide mounts (Perrotcolor). *See also* Projectors.

Nuclear Products Company, P.O. Box 1178, El Monte, California 91734 / Anti-static glass cleaning brush, mounting materials, static eliminators.

Professional Tape Company, Riverside, Illinois 60546 / Permanent adhesive slide labels ("Time Labels").

Radio-Mat Slide Company, Inc., 444 North Peninsula Dr., Daytona Beach, Florida 32018 / Mounting materials (Radio Mat slides).

Seary Manufacturing Corporation, 19 Nebraska Ave., Endicott, New York 13760 / Slide mounting equipment (film cutters, mounting press, etc.).

Sickles, Inc., Photo Equipment Division, P.O. Box 3396, Scottsdale, Arizona 85257 / Plastic slide mounts (Gepe), slide duplicators, slide production equipment.

3M Company / Photographic tape No. 235 for slide masking. *See also* Projectors.

Wess Plastic Molds Company, 50 Schmitt Blvd., Farmingdale, New York 11735 / Plastic slide mounts.

PLASTIC ALBUM PAGES

Bardes Plastics, Inc., 5225 West Clinton Ave., Milwaukee, Wisconsin 53223 / Plastic holders for slides (for three-ring binder or file folder).

Plastic Sealing Corporation, 1507 North Gardner St., Hollywood, California 90046 / VIS slide file folios for three-ring binders.

Plastican Corporation, P.O. Box 157, Butler, New Jersey 07405 / Plastic slide frames for three-ring binders.

Richard Manufacturing Company, 5914 Noble Ave., Van Nuys, California 91404 / Plastic "Album Pages" for three-ring binders for 2" x 2" and 2¼" x 2¼" slides.

PROJECTORS AND STANDS

Airequipt, Inc., 20 Jones St., New Rochelle, New York 10802 / Automatic slide projectors.

Allied Impex Corporation, Division of AIC Photo, Inc., 168 Glen Cove Rd., Carle Place, New York 11514 / Projectors.

Applied Research and Engineering, Inc., 1475 Barnum Ave., Bridgeport, Connecticut 06610 / Rear projection screens, slide changers and controls, and projector dissolve units.

Argus, Inc., 2601 South State St., Ann Arbor, Michigan 48106 / Projectors, viewers.

Berkey Technical, Division of Berkey Photo, Inc. *See* Keystone, Division of Berkey Photo, Inc.

Charles Beseler Company, 216 South 18th St., East Orange, New Jersey 07018 / 3¼" x 4" projectors.

The Brewster Corporation, 50 River St., Old Saybrook, Connecticut 06475 / Projectors, screens (including Robo-Wall), viewers.

Brumberger Company, Inc., 1948 Troutman St., Brooklyn, New York 11237 / Screens, projectors.

Buhl Optical Company, 1009 Beech Ave., Pittsburgh, Pennsylvania 15233 / Projectors.

Compco Corporation, 1800 North Spaulding Ave., Chicago, Illinois 60647 / Projection stands, 3-D slide projectors.

Christie Electric Corporation, 3410 West 67th St., Box 60020, Los Angeles, California 90060 / Projectors, stands.

Jack C. Coffey, Inc. / Projectors and stands. *See also* Filing and Storage Cabinets.

Ken Cook Transnational Company, 9929 West Silver Spring Rd., Milwaukee, Wisconsin 53225 / Projectors.

Cousino Electronics Corporation, 1941 Franklin Ave., Toledo, Ohio 43624 / Projection stands.

Decision Systems, Inc., East 66 Midland Ave., Paramus, New Jersey 07652 / Dial-A-Slide random access projectors.

DuKane Corporation, 100 North 11th St., St. Charles, Illinois 60174 / Projectors.

Electronique Automation, Inc., 11 Vincent Massey, Quebec 8, P.Q., Canada / Projectors.

Fordham Equipment Company, 2377 Hoffmann St., Bronx, New York 10458 / Projectors, slide storage boxes.

Honeywell, Inc., Photographic Products Division, P.O. Box 1010, Littleton, Colorado 80120 / Preview projectors (no screen required, preview area is part of projector), projectors, slide duplicators.

Hudson Photographic Industries, Inc. / Projectors. *See also* Screens.

International Audio Visual, Inc. / Projectors, stands. *See also* Screens and Pointers.

International Education and Training, Inc., 1776 New Highway, Farmingdale, New York 11735 / Projectors.

Ken-A-Vision Manufacturing Company, Inc., 5615 Raytown Rd., Raytown, Missouri 64133 / Micro-projectors.

Keystone, Division of Berkey Photo Corporation, Keystone Place, Paramus, New Jersey 07652 / Projectors.

The Klitten Company, Inc., 1213 North Amalfi Dr., Pacific Palisades, California 90272 / Projectors, synchronizers and programmers.

Eastman Kodak Company, 343 State St., Rochester, New York 14650 / Projectors, stands.

LaBelle Industries, Inc., 510 South Worthington St., Oconomowoc, Wisconsin 53066 / Projectors.

E. Leitz, Inc., 468 Park Ave. South, New York, New York 10016 / Aluminum slide mounts (Perrotcolor), projectors, slide duplicators.

Optical Radiation Corporation, Azusa, California 91702 / Xenographic Model 500 high intensity slide projector.

Realist, Inc., P.O. Box 67, N. 93 W., 16288 Megal Dr., Menomonee Falls, Wisconsin 53051 / Projectors.

Smith System Manufacturing Company, 1405 Silver Lake Rd., New Brighton, Minnesota 55112 / Projectors, projection stands.

George R. Snell, Associates, Inc. / Projectors, stands. *See also* Screens and Pointers.

Spindler and Sauppe, Inc., 13034 Saticoy St., North Hollywood, California 91605 / A-V programmers, multi-speed dissolve controls, pointers (illuminated), projectors.

Standard Projector and Equipment Company, Inc., 1911 Pickwick Avenue, Glenview, Illinois 60025 / Projectors, viewers.

Strong Electric Corporation, P.O. Box 1003, 87 City Park Ave., Toledo, Ohio 43601 / Remote control changers, projectors.

Viewlex, Inc., 1 Broadway Ave., Holbrook, Long Island, New York 11741 / Projectors.

Sound Slide Projectors

Creatron, Inc., 36 Cherry Lane, Floral Park, New York 11001 / sound slide projectors.

Gruber Products Company / Sound slide projectors. *See also* Screens.

Hoppmann Corporation, 5410 Port Royal Rd., Springfield, Virginia 22151 / Sound slide projectors, rear screen projection systems.

The Kalart Victor Corporation, P.O. Box 112, Hultenius St., Plainville, Connecticut 06062 / Sound slide projectors.

Montage Productions, Inc., 49 West 27th St., New York, New York 10001 / Sound slide projectors.

Pro-Gramo, Inc., 44 West 44th St., New York, New York 10036 / Sound slide projectors (Slide/Filmstrip Sound Synchronizer).
3M Company (Minnesota Mining and Manufacturing Company), Visual Products Division, 3M Center, St. Paul, Minnesota 55101 / Sound-on-slide systems.
Victor Animatograph Corporation. *See* The Kalart Victor Corporation.

SCREENS AND POINTERS

Applied Research and Engineering, Inc. / Screens. *See also* Projectors and Stands.
The Brewster Corporation. *See also* Projectors and Stands.
Brumberger Company, Inc. / Screens. *See also* Projectors and Stands.
Da-Lite Screen Company, Inc., P.O. Box 629, Warsaw, Indiana 46580 / Screens.
Draper Shade and Screen Company, P.O. Box 108, Spiceland, Indiana 47385 / Screens.
Ednalite Corporation / Pointers. *See also* Viewers/Slide Sorters.
Graflex Division, The Singer Corporation, 3750 Monroe Ave., Rochester, New York 14603 / Screens.
International Audio Visual, Inc., 119 Blanchard St., Seattle, Washington 98121 / Black screens, pointers, projectors, screens, stands, xenon light sources.
Polacoat, Inc., 9750 Conklin Rd., Cincinnati, Ohio 45242 / Rear projection screens—table top units, screens.
Radiant Corporation, 8220 North Austin, Morton Grove, Illinois 60053 / Screens.
Raven Screen Corporation, 124 East 124th St., New York, New York 10035 / Screens.
George R. Snell, Associates, Inc., 155 U.S. Route 22, Eastbound, Springfield, New Jersey 07081 / A-V systems (automatic sequential front and rear screen projection system), lecturns, pointers, projectors, screens, stands.
Spindler and Sauppe, Inc. / Pointers. *See also* Projectors and Stands.
Trans-Lux News-Sign Corporation, 625 Madison Ave., New York, New York 10022 / Rear projection screens.

Rear Projection Screens—Table-Top Models

Burleigh-Cashman Company, West Franklin, New Hampshire 03235 / Rear projection screens (table-top).
Lester A. Dine, Inc., 2080 Jericho Turnpike, New Hyde Park, New York 11042 / Projectors, rear projection screens, stands, viewers.
GAF Corporation / Rear projection screens. *See also* Viewers/Slide Sorters.
Gruber Products Company, 5254 Jackman Rd., Toledo, Ohio 43613 / Projection stands, screen unit (table-top), sound slide viewers, viewers with stands.
Hudson Photographic Industries, Inc., 2 South Buckout St., Irvington-On-Hudson, New York 10533 / Projectors, rear projection screens (Caritel, HPI Telescreen).
Polacoat, Inc. / Rear projection screens (table-top). *See also* Screens and Pointers.

VIEWERS/SLIDE SORTERS

Argus, Inc. *See also* Projectors and Stands.
Baia Corporation, 9353 Lee Rd., R7, Jackson, Michigan 49201 / Viewers.
The Brewster Corporation. *See also* Projectors and Stands.

Jack C. Coffey, Inc. / Viewers. *See also* Filing and Storage Cabinets.
Ednalite Corporation, 210 North Water St., Peekskill, New York 10566 / Editor/
transviewer with magnifinder, electric projection pointer, magnifier.
GAF Corporation, Pictorial Products Division, 140 West 51st St., New York, New
York 10020 / Rear projection screens, viewers.
Karl Heitz, Inc. *See also* Slide Mounts.
Keystone Ferrule and Nut Company / Slide sorters. *See also* Carrying Cases.
Macbeth Daylighting Corporation, P.O. Box 950, Little Britain Rd., Newburgh,
New York 12550 / Previewers.
Seebamil Sales Corporation. *See* GAF Corporation.
Smith-Victor Corporation / Slide sorters. *See also* Carrying Cases.
Tru-Vue Company. *See* GAF Corporation.

MISCELLANEOUS

Diecrafters, Inc., Victor, New York 14564 / Princeton Slide Holder.
Edmund Scientific, 100 Edscorp Building, Barrington, New Jersey 08007 / Photo
and optical items (color wheels for slide projectors).
Pantographic Company, Department 91, 1310 S.E. Seventh Ave., Portland,
Oregon 97214 / "Slide Scriber Titles."

DIRECTORY OF SLIDE SOURCES

"See also" references refer to the source listing under which the complete address of a distributor and/or slide producer is provided.

GENERAL SOURCES

The American Institute for Visual Instruction, Pictorial Events, P.O. Box 858, Radio City Station, New York, New York 10019 / Art, history, science, travel.

American Library Color Slide Company, Inc. 305 East 45th St., New York, New York 10017 / Art, earth science, history, science.

American Museum of Natural History, Photography Division, Central Park West at 79th St., New York, New York 10024 / Animals, anthropology, archaeology, art, geography, science.

H. J. Ammeraal, Jr., R.I.C.C.P., dba Amoco Films, 710 Forest Ave., New Port Richey, Florida 33552 / Art (Asian and European architecture, painting, sculpture, and graphic arts), geography/travel, science.

Auslender Productions, Inc., 6036 Comey Ave., Los Angeles, California 90034 / Art (American sculpture), cats, distortion, mood, nature, people.

Avid Corporation, P.O. Box 4263, 10 Tripps Lane, East Providence, Rhode Island 02914 / Art, geography/travel, science.

Budek Films and Slides, Inc. *See* Avid Corporation.

Creative Arts Studio, Inc., 2323 Fourth St. N.E., Washington, D.C. 20002 / Produces slides from script to screen, any area, e.g., art, and care and treatment of diabetes.

Robert Davis Productions, P.O. Box 12, Cary, Illinois 60013 / Art (American, Asian and European architecture, painting and sculpture), geography/travel, history, music, science.

Demco Educational Corporation, Box 1488, Madison, Wisconsin 53701 / Art, geography/travel, history, science, etc.

Denoyer-Geppert Company, Times Mirror, 5235 Ravenswood Ave., Chicago, Illinois 60640 / Art, earth science, geography/travel, science.

Encyclopaedia Britannica Educational Corporation, 425 North Michigan Ave., Chicago, Illinois 60611.

Environmental Communications, 62 Windward Ave., Venice, California 90291 / Man's relationship to his environment, e.g., Paolo Soleri, urban crowd behavior, art, architecture videotapes, groups, social groups and environment, pollution, cities, communes, television.

European Art Color Slides, Peter Adelberg, Inc., 120 West 70th St., New York, New York 10023 / Art (American painting, European architecture, painting, sculpture, Egyptian, Central American, Mexico and Guatemala), geography/travel, history, science.

GAF Corporation, Pictorial Products Division, 140 West 51st St., New York, New York 10020 / Apollo moon landing, art, geography/travel.

Goldsmith's Music Shop, Inc., Language Department, 301 East Shore Rd., Great Neck, Long Island, New York 11023 / Art, geography/travel, history, science.

Harcourt Brace Jovanovich, Inc., 757 Third Ave., New York, New York 10017 / Biology, history, mathematics, science.

Keystone View Company, Meadville, Pennsylvania 16335 / Handmade lantern slide kits (biology, history, mathematics, music).

Learning Machines, Inc., Box 86, Pinos Altos, New Mexico 88053 / Educational administration, educational psychology, English, geography/travel, history, mathematics, science.

Meston Color Slides, 3801 North Piedras, El Paso, Texas 79930 / Art, geography/travel, history.

National Film Board of Canada, Canada House, 680 Fifth Ave., New York, New York 10019 / Arts and crafts, health, science, social studies (Canadian).

Playette Corporation, 301 East Shore Rd., Great Neck, New York 11023 / Art, geography/travel, history, science.

Roloc Color Slides, P.O. Box 1715, Washington, D.C. 20013 / Art, geography/travel, history, science (Apollo 14 slides).

Scott Education Division, 104 Lower Westfield Rd., Holyoke, Massachusetts 01040 /Art, geography/travel, history, science.

Secas International Company, 1350 Old Dixie Rd., P.O. Box 1475, Jupiter, Florida 33458 / Art, geography/travel, history, science.

Smithsonian Institution, Photographic Services, Washington, D.C. 20560 / Anthropology, art, geography/travel, history, science, and exhibitions at the Smithsonian Institution.

Society for Visual Education, Inc. (SVE), Subsidiary of The Singer Company, 1345 Diversey Parkway, Chicago, Illinois 60614 / Art, geography/travel, history, science.

State University of New York at Buffalo, Instructional Communication Center, Media Library, 22 Foster Annex, Buffalo, New York 14214 / Art, geography/travel, history, technology.

Universal Color Slides Company, 136 West 32nd St., New York, New York 10001 / Art, geography/travel, history.

G. W. Van Leer and Associates, 1850 North Fremont Ave., Chicago, Illinois 60614 / Custom design and production in all visual communication media internationally.

AGRICULTURE

Covalda Date Company, P.O. Box 908, Coachella, California 92236 / Date growing, desert culture, desert scenes.

The Fertilizer Institute, 1015 18th St. N.W., Washington, D.C. 20036 / Agriculture, agronomy, safety and maintenance.

NASCO, 901 Janesville Ave., Fort Atkinson, Wisconsin 53538 / Home economics, science, vocational agriculture.

Pan American Development Foundation. *See also* Housing.

U.S. Department of Agriculture, Office of Information, Photography Division, Washington, D.C. 20250 / Activities of the U.S. Department of Agriculture.

Visual Communication Office, New York State College of Agriculture and Life Sciences, Cornell University, Department of Communication Arts, 412 Roberts Hall, Ithaca, New York 14850 / Agriculture, human ecology.

Vocational Education Productions, California State Polytechnic College, San Luis Obispo, California 93401.

ART (INCLUDES ARCHAEOLOGY
AND ARCHITECTURE)

Harold C. Ambrosh Productions / Pueblo Indian arts and crafts, pottery. *See also* History.

American Crafts Council, 29 West 53rd St., New York, New York 10019 / American crafts.

ALESCO—American Library and Educational Services Company, 404 Sette Drive, Paramus, New Jersey 07652 / American and European Architecture, painting, and sculpture.

American Numismatic Society, Broadway at 155th St., New York, New York 10032 / Numismatics.

Ancora, Consejo de Ciento, 160, (Edificio Creta), Barcelona 15, Spain / Ancient, Asian, Egyptian and modern art, and Spanish architecture, painting, sculpture and decorative arts.

Archaeological Institute of America, 260 West Broadway, New York, New York 10013 / Archaeology, European and South American architecture, painting, and sculpture.

Art Color Slides, Inc. *See* Francis G. Mayer.

Art Council Aids, P.O. Box 641, Beverly Hills, California 90213 / African, American Indian, American painting, Pre-Columbian, and primitive art.

Art Now, University Galleries, Inc., Department 50, P.O. Box 222, Malverne, New York 11565 / Emphasis on contemporary art.

Art Slides BLAUEL, Rottenbucher Strasse 52, 8032 Graefelfing, Germany / European painting.

Arts in Society, University of Wisconsin—Extension, Room 728 Lowell Hall, 610 Langdon St., Madison, Wisconsin 53706 / Offers instructional research packages: The Arts and Crafts in Kenyan Society; Art and Environment; Art and Social Revolution, Art and Technology; The Street as a Creative Vision.

Audio Visual Archive, Museum of Modern Art, 11 West 53rd St., New York, New York 10019 / American and European painting and sculpture.

Austrian Institute, 11 East 52nd St., New York, New York 10022 / European art, geography/travel, history, science. Will loan to universities and colleges.

Barney Burstein, Photographer, Original Color Slides, 29 Commonwealth Ave., Boston, Massachusetts 02116 / Minor arts, painting, and sculpture. Emphasis on art in American museums and galleries.

Carman Educational Associates, Inc. / Modern typography. *See also* Geography/Travel.

Color Slide Enterprises, Box 150, Oxford, Ohio 45056 / Ancient Greek and Roman sculpture and works in the Louvre.

Cultural History Research, Inc., 20 Purchase St., Rye, New York 10580 / European architecture, painting, and sculpture and general French history.

The Eastin-Phelan Distributing Corporation. *See also* Geography/Travel.

Educational Audio Visual, Inc. (EAV), Pleasantville, New York 10570 / African, American, Asian, and European architecture, painting and sculpture.

Educational Dimensions Corporation, Box 488, Great Neck, New York 11022 / Nineteenth and twentieth century art, Chinese and primitive art, Black studies.

Embassy of the Polish People's Republic, Information Officer, Press Office, 2640 Sixteenth St. N.W., Washington, D.C. 20009 / Polish architecture, painting and sculpture.

FACSEA, Society for French-American Cultural Services and Educational Aid, 972 Fifth Ave., New York, New York 10021 / European architecture, painting and sculpture, geography/travel.

Four Continent Book Corporation, 156 Fifth Ave., New York, New York 10010 / U.S.S.R.: architecture, art, geography/travel (cities, gardens, resorts).

Graphic Arts Technical Foundation, Inc., 4615 Forbes Ave., Pittsburgh, Pennsylvania 15213 / Graphic arts.

Humanities, Inc., The Center for Humanities, Inc., Two Holland Ave., White Plains, New York 10603 / Art, history. "An inquiry into the nature of man," and "Man and his environment" (sound-slide sets).

Imago Color Slides, P.O. Box 811, Chapel Hill, North Carolina 27514 / Emphasis on ancient architecture, minor arts and medieval sculpture.

International Museum of Photography, Office of Extension Activities, 900 East Ave., Rochester, New York 14607 / The history of photography.

Kahana Film Productions / Central American architecture, painting, and sculpture. *See also* Geography/Travel.

McGraw-Hill Book Company, 330 West 42nd St., New York, New York 10036 / "Color Slide Program of Art Enjoyment."

McIntyre Visual Publications, P.O. Box 297, North Main Street, Champlain, New York 12919 / American and European architecture, painting, and sculpture.

Francis G. Mayer, Art Color Slides, Inc., 235 East 50th St., New York, New York 10022 / American, Asian, European architecture, painting and sculpture, and South American painting.

Miniature Gallery, 60 Rushett Close, Long Ditton, Surrey, England / African, American and Asian painting and sculpture, European and South American architecture, painting and sculpture and decorative arts.

The Museum of Modern Art, Museum Bookstore, 11 West 53rd St., New York, New York 10019 / American and European painting and sculpture, other slides from MOMA collection are available from Sandak, Inc.

National Gallery of Art, Extension Service, Washington, D.C. 20565 / Slides of National Gallery's collection.

William Rockhill Nelson Gallery of Art, Atkins Museum of Fine Arts, 4525 Oak St., Kansas City, Missouri 64111 / American architecture, painting and sculpture, Asian and European painting and sculpture.

Pan American Development Foundation / Pre-Columbian pottery and sculpture; South American architecture, painting and sculpture. *See also* Housing.

Philadelphia Museum of Art, Slide Library, Parkway at 26th St., Philadelphia, Pennsylvania 19130 / African, American, Asian, European, South American architecture, painting and sculpture.

William Protheroe, 2323 Vestal Ave., Los Angeles, California 90026 / Graphic art, sculpture, twentieth century painting.

Prothmann Associates, Inc., 650 Thomas Ave., Baldwin, New York 11510 / African, American, Asian, European architecture, painting and sculpture. Exclusive distributor for following slide producers: Bijutsu Shuppan-Sha, Tokyo; Editions Rencontre, Switzerland; Educational Productions, England; Hannibal, Athens; Kunsthistorisches Museum, Vienna; Polygoon, Amsterdam;

Publications of Art and Art History, Paris; Sans Vega, Madrid; Slide Center, England; Dr. Franz Stoedtner, Berlin; Valdagno, Italy.

Rosenthal Art Slides, 5456 South Ridgewood Court, Chicago, Illinois 60615 / Emphasis on contemporary American and European architecture, painting, and sculpture; advertising art; Australian Aboriginal art; Mexican and Mohammedan architecture.

Sandak, Inc., 4 East 48th St., New York, New York 10017 / Emphasis on eighteenth century to present American and European art. African, American, Asian and European architecture, painting and sculpture, graphic arts.

SASKIA, Photographic Services for Historians of Art, P.O. Box 440, North Amherst, Massachusetts 01059 / American and European architecture, painting and sculpture.

Scala Fine Arts Publishers, Inc., 24 West 45th St., New York, New York 10036 / European architecture, painting and sculpture.

Silvermine Publishers, Inc., Comstock Hill, Silvermine, Norwalk, Connecticut 06850 / Art instruction.

Taurgo Slides, 154 East 82nd St., New York, New York 10028 / African, American, Asian, European architecture, painting and sculpture, South American architecture and sculpture.

Tipi Shop, Inc., Box 1270, Rapid City, South Dakota 57701 / Organized by the U.S. Department of the Interior (Indian Arts and Crafts Board). Contemporary Indian and Eskimo crafts of the United States, "Contemporary Sioux Painting" and slide lecture kits.

The United Presbyterian Church, Mission Program Information, Commission on Ecumenical Mission and Relations, Room 1268, 475 Riverside Dr., New York, New York 10027 / African, Asian and South American painting and sculpture.

The Walters Art Gallery, 600 North Charles St., Baltimore, Maryland 21201 / American and European painting and sculpture.

Visual Resources, Inc. (Eva Wisbar), 1841 Broadway, New York, New York 10023 / Emphasis on twentieth century contemporary art.

The University Prints, 15 Brattle St., Harvard Square, Cambridge, Massachusetts 02138 / African, American, Asian and European architecture, painting and sculpture.

University of Washington Press / African sculpture. *See also* Science.

Architecture and Architectural Sculpture

Harold C. Ambrosh Productions / Mesa Verde ruins, prehistoric Indian ruins. *See also* History.

Wayne Andrews, 521 Neff Road, Gross Pointe, Michigan 48230 / American and European architecture.

Architectural Color Slides, 187 Grant St., Lexington, Massachusetts 02173 / American, Australian, Canadian, European, Mexican, and New Zealand architecture.

Architectural Delineations, 343 East 30th St., New York, New York 10016 / American, Asian, European and South American architecture and sculpture, art nouveau, European history.

Educational Art Transparencies, 27 West Summit St., Chagrin Falls, Ohio 44022 / American, Canadian, European and Mexican architecture, geography/travel.

FACSEA / French architecture. *See also* Art.
Robert F. McConnell, Producer of Travelslide Classics, 4447 Que St., N.W.,
Washington, D.C. 20007 / American, Asian, Central American, European,
Mexican, and South American architecture, geography/travel, history.
Joseph P. Messana, Photographer, 5574 Lakewood, Detroit, Michigan 48213 /
American, European, South American architecture and sculpture.
National Cathedral Association, Slides and Film Section, Washington Cathedral,
Mount St. Alban, Washington, D.C. 20016 / Washington Cathedral.
State Historical Society of Wisconsin / Wisconsin architecture. *See also* Costume.
U.S. Department of Housing and Urban Development / American and European
architecture. *See also* Housing.

Black Art

The Afro-American Slide Depository, The Department of Art, The University of
South Alabama, Mobile, Alabama 36608 / Includes practicing contemporary
artists and retrospective collections.
Educational Dimensions Corporation / Black studies. *See also* Art.
Harmon Foundation, Inc., 598 Madison Ave., New York, New York 10801.
Prothmann Associates, Inc. *See also* Art.
Sandak, Inc. *See also* Art.

CONSUMER EDUCATION

Architectural Aluminum Manufacturers Association / Home safety. *See also*
Industry and Industrial Management.
Olcott Forward, Inc., 234 North Central Ave., Hartsdale, New York 10530 / Busi-
ness education, consumer education, social studies.
The Superior Electric Company, Media Manager, Bristol, Connecticut 06010 /
"How to Decorate with Light."
Underwriters' Laboratories, Inc., 207 East Ohio St., Chicago, Illinois 60611 / Con-
sumer education: How the company tests products for the safety of the
public against hazards to life, limb and property.

COSTUME/FASHION

Fairchild Visuals, Division of Fairchild Publications, Inc., 7 East 12th St., New
York, New York 10003 / Display, fashion history, fashion and merchandis-
ing careers, retail trends, textiles.
Milady Publishing Corporation, 3839 White Plains Rd., Bronx, New York 10467 /
Cosmetology, fashion history, vocational education, etc.
State Historical Society of Wisconsin, 816 State St., Madison, Wisconsin 53706 /
Costume (major emphasis), history (Blacks in Wisconsin history), Wisconsin
architecture.

GEOGRAPHY/TRAVEL

Austrian Institute / Austria. *See also* Art.
BEE Cross Media, Inc., 36 Dogwood Glen, Rochester, New York 14625 / Emphasis
on the Philippines.
British Information Services, 845 Third Ave., New York, New York 10022.

Broadman Films, 127 Ninth Ave. North, Nashville, Tennessee 37203.

Carman Educational Associates, Inc., Box 205, Youngstown, New York 14174 / China, U.S.A., U.S.S.R. (comparative study slide sets).

Cine-Canada, Inc., 400 Notre Dame St., East, Montreal 127, Quebec, Canada / Canada.

Downtown Progress, 521 Twelfth St., N.W., Washington, D.C. 20004 / Will make available on loan basis a slide presentation and a film about downtown Washington, D.C.

The Eastin-Phelan Distributing Corporation, Davenport, Iowa 52808 / Landmarks and areas of interest in Europe.

Educational Art Transparencies / Europe, Mexico, U.S.A. *See also* Art—Architecture and Architectural Sculpture.

FACSEA / France. *See also* Art.

Four Continent Book Corporation / U.S.S.R.: cities, gardens, resorts. *See also* Art.

German Consulate General *(for Michigan and Indiana area only)*, 2200 Book Building, Detroit, Michigan 48226 / To obtain slides for a particular area, the other 12 German Consulates have to be contacted in order to provide a list of slides available within each jurisdiction.

Ginn and Company, A Xerox Company, 191 Spring St., Lexington, Massachusetts 02173.

Martha Guthrie Slides, Distributed through BEE Cross Media Inc., 36 Dogwood Glen, Rochester, New York 14625 / Japan and Korea.

Hispanic Society of America, Broadway between 155th and 156th Sts., New York, New York 10032.

Hubbard Scientific Company. *See also* Science.

Imperial Film Company, Inc. / Slide sets on Hawaii, Japan, Moscow and other Soviet cities, Washington, D.C. *See also* Science.

Kahana Film Productions, 1909 North Curson Place, Los Angeles, California 90046 / Central American architecture, painting and sculpture, geography/ travel with emphasis on Central America, East Africa, Europe, Israel and Japan.

Robert F. McConnell / Asia, Bermuda, Canada, Europe, Latin America, U.S.A. *See also* Art—Architecture and Architectural Sculpture.

Francis G. Mayer. *See also* Art.

National Park Service, Photo Library, Washington, D.C. 20240 / Loan only.

Rhode Island Development Council, Tourist Promotion Division, Roger Williams Building, 49 Hayes St., Providence, Rhode Island 02908 / Rhode Island (for loan only).

Scala Fine Arts Publishers, Inc. / Europe. *See also* Art.

Scientificom. *See also* Science.

South Dakota Department of Highways, Film Librarian, Communications Division, Pierre, South Dakota 57501 / Geography/travel, history. For tourism promotion only.

Swedish National Tourist Office, 505 Fifth Ave., New York, New York 10017 / Sweden.

John Wiley and Sons, Inc., 605 Third Ave., New York, New York 10016 / Physical geography (the Earth, Atmosphere and Oceans, Climate, Soils, and Vegetation, Landforms of the Earth's Crust).

World in Color, Box 392, Elmira, New York 14902.

HISTORY

Harold C. Ambrosh Productions, Box 3, Rancho Mirage, California 92270 / Indians
of the Southwest (Pueblo arts, crafts, life, prehistoric Indian ruins).
Architectural Delineations / European history. *See also* Art—Architecture and
Architectural Sculpture.
Austrian Institute / Austrian history. *See also* Art.
Humanities, Inc. *See also* Art.
Colonial Williamsburg Foundation, Film Distribution Section, Box C, Williams-
burg, Virginia 23185 / General history.
Cultural History Research, Inc. / General French history. *See also* Art.
FACSEA / French civilization. *See also* Art.
General Learning Corporation, Educational Affiliate of G.E. and Time, 250 James
St., Morristown, New Jersey 07960 / General history.
Harcourt Brace Jovanovich, Inc. / World history. *See also* Science.
Imperial Film Company, Inc. / American history. *See also* Geography/Travel.
Instructional Materials and Equipment Distributors, 150 Cotner Ave., Los Angeles,
California 90025 / California missions, general history.
Robert F. McConnell / American history. *See also* Art—Architecture and Archi-
tectural Sculpture.
Francis G. Mayer. *See also* Art.
Millersville Instructional Materials Service, Millersville State College, Millersville,
Pennsylvania 17551 / American colonial history.
Pan American Development Foundation / Latin American civilizations. *See also*
Housing.
Olcott Forward, Inc. / Social studies. *See also* Consumer Education.
South Dakota Department of Highways. For tourism promotion only. *See also*
Geography/Travel.
State Historical Society of Wisconsin / Blacks in Wisconsin history. *See also*
Costume.

HOUSING

National Association of Home Builders, National Housing Center, 1625 L St.,
N.W., Washington, D.C. 20036.
Pan American Development Foundation, 17th and Constitution Ave., N.W.,
Washington, D.C. 20006 / Latin America: agriculture, ancient civilizations,
art, housing, scenery, Pre-Columbian pottery and sculpture.
U.S. Department of Housing and Urban Development, 451 7th St., S.W.,
Washington, D.C. 20410 / American and European architecture. Publication:
U.S. Department of Housing and Urban Development, A Selected Bibliog-
raphy of Films, Filmstrips, Slides and Audiotapes, Washington, D.C.,
June 1969.

INDUSTRY AND INDUSTRIAL MANAGEMENT

American Institute of Timber Construction, 333 West Hampden Ave., Englewood,
Colorado 80110 / Timber industry.

Architectural Aluminum Manufacturers Association, 410 North Michigan Ave., Chicago, Illinois 60611 / The glass revolution for home safety.

Chamber of Commerce of the U.S., 1615 H St., N.W., Washington, D.C. 20006 / Explaining the American business system.

Hobart School of Welding Technology, Trade Square East, Troy, Ohio 45373 / Sets of slides about welding training.

Petroleum Extension Service, University of Texas, Drawer V, University Station, Austin, Texas 78712 / Petroleum industry: technical training, drilling and production.

MEDICINE

American Dental Association, 211 East Chicago Ave., Chicago, Illinois 60611 / Dentistry and dental health education.

American Dietetic Association, 620 North Michigan Ave., Chicago, Illinois 60611 / Food service in nursing homes.

The American Journal of Nursing Company, Educational Services Division, 10 Columbus Circle, New York, New York 10019 / Topics to aid nursing and allied health personnel.

American Optometric Association, 7000 Chippewa St., St. Louis, Missouri 63119 / Health care: vision.

American Podiatry Association, Audio-Visual Section, 20 Chevy Chase Circle, Washington, D.C. 20015 / Medical: foot disorders.

American Society for Microbiology, 1913 I St., N.W., Washington, D.C. 20006 / Microbiology.

Clay-Adams / Nursing. *See also* Science.

Cleveland Health Museum and Education Center, 8911 Euclid Ave., Cleveland, Ohio 44106 / Health education.

Guidance Associates, 41 Washington Ave., Pleasantville, New York 10570 / Human reproduction.

Harwyn Medical Photographers, P.O. Box 19787, Philadelphia, Pennsylvania 19143 / Photo-micrographic slides of medical subjects.

Hubbard Scientific Company / Human reproduction. *See also* Science.

Kenny Rehabilitation Instutute of the American Rehabilitation Foundation, A/V Publications Office, 1800 Chicago Ave., Minneapolis, Minnesota 55404 / Teaching care of patients.

Los Angeles Foundation of Otology, 2130 West Third St., Los Angeles, California 90057 / Otological surgery slides.

W. B. Saunders Company, West Washington Square, Philadelphia, Pennsylvania 19105 / Medical and nursing for education of students and continuing education of physicians and nurses. Science.

University of Washington Press. *See also* Science.

John Wiley and Sons, Inc. / Nursing instruction. *See also* Geography/Travel.

ORNITHOLOGY

Laboratory of Ornithology, Cornell University, 159 Sapsucker Woods Rd., Ithaca, New York 14850.

National Audubon Society, Photos and Film Department, 950 Third Ave., New York, New York 10022 / J. J. Audubon's birds and mammals, natural history.

SCIENCE

American Meteorite Laboratory, P.O. Box 2098, Denver, Colorado 80201 / Meteorites.

Audio-Visual Support Center, Building 1621, White Sands Missile Range, New Mexico 88002 / Missiles, science.

Austrian Institute / Austrian inventors. *See also* Art.

Carolina Biological Supply Company, Burlington, North Carolina 27215.

Clay-Adams, Division of Becton, Dickinson and Company, 299 Webro Rd., Parsippany, New Jersey 07054 / Biological, medical, nursing, science.

Harcourt Brace Jovanovich, Inc., 757 Third Ave., New York, New York 10017 / Algebra and geometry, earth and life sciences, world history. Designed for grades K-12.

Harper and Row, Publishers, Inc., College Department, 49 East 33rd St., New York, New York 10016.

Hubbard Scientific Company, P.O. Box 150, Northbrook, Illinois 60062 / Astronomy, biology, geography, geology, human reproduction, meteorology, science, space exploration.

Imperial Film Company, Inc., 4404 South Florida Ave., Lakeland, Florida 33803 / Animal tissue, bacteria, complex life forms, plant sciences, reproduction, simple life forms. Apollo XI. Geography, history (small selection).

Macalaster Scientific Company, Route 111 and Everett Turnpike, Nashua, New Hampshire 03060 / General physics.

Moody Institute of Science, Educational Films Division, 12000 East Washington Blvd., Los Angeles, California 90021.

NASCO. *See also* Agriculture.

National Teaching Aids, Inc., 120 Fulton Ave., Garden City Park, New York 11040.

W. B. Saunders Company. *See also* Medicine.

School Specialty Supply Company, Box 1327, Salina, Kansas 67401 / Earth sciences, life sciences, space exploration, weather.

Science Slides Company, Division of Communications International, 22 East 42nd St., New York, New York 10017.

Scientificom, Division of Mervin W. LaRue Films, Inc., 612 North Michigan Ave., Chicago, Illinois 60611 / Geography/travel, science.

Spitz Laboratories, Inc., Division of McGraw-Hill, Inc., Chadds Ford, Pennsylvania 19317.

Technamation, Inc., 112 Parkway Drive South, Hauppauge, New York 11787 / Anatomical series, physical and biological sciences, refrigeration.

University of Washington Press, Film Division, 1416 N.E. 41st St., Seattle, Washington 98105 / Art, medicine, science.

Ward's Natural Science Establishment, Inc., P.O. Box 1712, Rochester, New York 14603 / Biology, earth sciences.

MISCELLANEOUS

The Center for Curriculum Development, Inc., A Chilton Subsidiary, 401 Walnut St., Philadelphia, Pennsylvania 19106 / Foreign language slides.

Education and Training Consultants Company, Box 49899, Los Angeles, California 90049 / Education for professional educators, e.g., Systems Engineering of Education Series.

The Franklin D. Roosevelt Philatelic Society, Hyde Park, Secretary's Office,
     P.O. Box 337, Main Post Office (Dutchess County), Pleasant Valley, New
     York 12569 / Roosevelt postage stamps.
John Fraser Associates, P.O. Box 157, Alamo, California 94507 / Training for
     aides to libraries; "Library page training"; orientation for adult library helper.
Learning and Information, Inc., 315 Central Park West, New York, New York
     10025 / Training for hotels, motels, restaurants and clubs.
Vedo Films, 85 Longview Rd., Port Washington, New York 11050 / Anthropology,
     sociology.

DIRECTORY OF SLIDE LIBRARIES

The Directory includes approximately 240 slide libraries in the United States, Canada and other countries. References to countries other than the United States are at the end. Listings have been derived from correspondence, questionnaire responses and other contacts with the author.

Supervisory and collection titles when given are those provided by the individual in charge of the slide library. In a limited number of cases, the supervisor's title was not provided although a questionnaire was returned. For these individuals, the title "Slide Librarian" (in quotes) has been assigned.

As indicated in Chapter 3, the majority of slide libraries do not have detailed descriptions of their cataloging and classification systems available. For those collections known to the author to have a guide to their cataloging and/or classification procedures, the abbreviation (c) is placed at the end of the entry.

The following is an outline of entry format and abbreviations used in the Directory.

STATE (or **COUNTRY**)

City

INSTITUTIONAL TITLE, library, department, school and/or college, address, zip code.
Title of individual in charge of slide library. Collection title. Date of establishment (Estab.). Number of slides. Number of full-time staff (FT), and part-time staff (PT).

*   Questionnaire answered by individual designated.

**   Questionnaire not returned or inadequate information provided.

(e)   Slide library established within the last five years, i.e., during the period 1969 to 1973.

(c)   Cataloging and/or classification guide prepared for the collection.

unk. Information requested unknown by individual returning questionnaire.

UNITED STATES

ALABAMA

(Troy) Troy State University, Art Department, 36081. Chairman.* Estab. 1959. 30,300. 1 FT, 3 PT.

ARIZONA

(Tempe) Arizona State University, Architecture Library, 85281. Architecture Librarian.* Estab. 1959. 10,000. 1 FT, 3 PT. (c)
—Arizona State University, Art Department, 85281. Slide Curator.

(Tucson) University of Arizona, Department of Art, College of Fine Arts, 85721. Slide Technician.* Estab. 1953-55. 46,000. 0 FT, 2 PT.

ARKANSAS

(Fayetteville) University of Arkansas, Art Department, 72701. Slide Librarian. Slide Library.

(Little Rock) Arkansas Arts Center, Library, MacArthur Park, 72203. Slide Librarian.

CALIFORNIA

(Arcata) California State University, Humboldt, The Library, 95521. Art Librarian.

(Berkeley) University of California, Berkeley, Art History Department, 94720. Slide Curator.**
—University of California, Berkeley, Environmental Design Library, Department of Architecture, 231 Kroeber Hall, 94720. Assistant Head Librarian.* Unk. 50,000. 2 FT, 3 PT. (c)

(Davis) University of California, Davis, Art Department, College of Letters and Science, 95616. Slide Librarian.* Estab. c.1955. 33,000. 1 FT, 12 PT.
—University of California, Davis, Library, Memorial Union Art Gallery, 95616. Librarian.**

(Long Beach) California State College, Art Department, 90801. Slide Librarian. Slide Library.

(Los Angeles) Los Angeles County Museum of Art, 5905 Wilshire Blvd., 90036. Curator of Slides.
—University of California, Los Angeles, Department of Art, 405 Hilgard Ave., 90024. Curator—Slides and Photographs.* Slide and Photographic Collections. Estab. 1952. 164,000. 2 FT, 5 PT.
—University of Southern California, Architecture and Fine Arts Library, 824 West 37th St., 90007. Librarian.** c.62,000.

(Northridge) California State University, Northridge, Department of Art History, 93124. Slide Librarian.

(Oakland) Mills College, Art Department, Division of Fine Arts, 94613. Slide and Photograph Curator.** Estab. 1930s.

(Riverside) University of California, Riverside, Department of Art, 92502. Slide Librarian. Estab. 1956. 50,000. 1 FT, 5 PT.

(San Jose) California State University, San Jose, School of Humanities and The Arts, Department of Art, 95192. Slide Librarian.
—San Jose State College, Department of Art, 93106. Slide Librarian.* Estab. c.1938. 95,000. 1 FT, 3 PT.

(Santa Barbara) University of California, Santa Barbara, Department of Art, 93106. Slide Librarian.**

(Santa Cruz) University of California, Santa Cruz, University Library, 95060. Slide Librarian.* Slide Library. Estab. 1966. 58,000. 1 FT, 3 PT. (c)

(Stanford) Stanford University, School of Humanities and Arts, Department of Art and Architecture, 94305. Slide Librarian.* Slide Library. Estab. 1950s. 75,000. 2 FT, 12 PT.

(Valencia) California Institute of the Arts, School of Art, Library, 24700 McBean Parkway, 91355. Slide Librarian. Estab. 1960. 20,000. 1 FT, 1 PT. (c)

(Whittier) Whittier College, Art Department, 90608. Slide Collection. (e)

COLORADO

(Boulder) University of Colorado, Fine Arts Department, 80302. Slide Curator.

(Denver) The Denver Art Museum, 100 West 14th Avenue Parkway, 80204. Museum Apprentice. 30,000.
—University of Denver, Colorado Seminary, School of Art, University Park, 80210. Research Associate of Humanities. Slide Collection.

CONNECTICUT

(Hartford) Wadsworth Athenaeum, Colt, Morgan, and Avery Memorials, Education Department, 25 Athenaeum Square North, 06103. Education Director.** Estab. 1930s. c.35,000.

(Middletown) Wesleyan University, Art Department, 06457. Slide Librarian. Slide Library.

(New Haven) Yale University, School of Art and Architecture, Box 1605A Yale Station, 06520. Slide and Photograph Librarian.* Slide and Photograph Library. Estab. c.1924. 170,000. 5 FT, 6 PT. (c)

(Storrs) University of Connecticut, Art Department, School of Fine Arts, U-99, 06268. Slide Librarian.

DELAWARE

(Newark) University of Delaware, Department of Art and Department of Art History, 19711. Curator of Slides.**

(Wilmington) Eleutherian Mills, Historical Library, Greenville, 19807. Curator. Pictorial Collections.

(Winterthur) The Henry Francis du Pont Winterthur Museum, 19735. Cataloguer.* Slide and Photo Collection. Estab. c.1956. 40,000. 2 FT, 0 PT.

FLORIDA

(Gainesville) University of Florida, College of Architecture and Fine Arts, 32601. Audio-visual Librarian.* Estab. c.1952. 55,000. 1 FT, 3 PT.

(Orlando) Florida Technological University, Library, P.O. Box 25000, 32816. Assistant Director for Technical Services. (e)

(St. Petersburg) Museum of Fine Arts, 255 Beach Drive North, 33701. Assistant Director.* Estab. 1961. 5,500. 1 FT, 5 PT.

GEORGIA

(Atlanta) Atlanta School of Art, 1280 Peachtree St. N.E., 30309. Audio-Visual Librarian. c.10,000.

—Emory University, Department of the History of Art, 30322. Slide Librarian.* Estab. 1965. 52,000. 1 FT, 5 PT.

—Georgia Institute of Technology, School of Architecture, 30332. Catalog Slide Librarian. 24,000. (c)

HAWAII

(Honolulu) University of Hawaii, Art Department, George Hall, Room 131, 2560 Campus Rd., 96822. Slide Curator.**

ILLINOIS

(Chicago) Art Institute of Chicago, Ryerson and Burnham Libraries, Michigan Ave. at Adams St., 60603. Assistant Librarian.* Slide and Photograph Collection. Estab. c.1904. 82,000. 6 FT, 5 PT. (c)

—Northeastern Illinois University, Bryn Mawr at St. Louis Avenue, 60625. Slide Librarian. 40,000. 1 FT, 2 PT.

—University of Chicago, Department of Art, History of Art, 401 Goodspeed Hall, 60637. Curator of Slides.* Estab. 1938. 130,000. 1 FT, 1 PT. (c)

—University of Illinois at Chicago Circle, College of Architecture and Art, Box 4348, 60680. Audio-Visual Curator.* Slide and Photograph Library. Estab. 1947. 106,000. 2 FT, 20 PT. (c)

(De Kalb) Northern Illinois University, Department of Art, 60115. Slide Librarian.* Estab. 1961. 50,000. 2 FT, 3 PT.

(Edwardsville) Southern Illinois University, Lovejoy Library, Humanities and Fine Arts Library, 62025. Librarian.**

(Elmhurst) Elmhurst College, Memorial Library, 60126. Special Collections Librarian.* Estab. 1967. c.6,000. 1 FT, 2 PT.

(Evanston) Evanston Public Library, 1703 Orrington Ave., 60201. Assistant Librarian. (e)

—Northwestern University, Department of Art, College of Liberal Arts, 60201. Slide Librarian.** c.45,000.

(Glen Ellyn) College of Dupage, Learning Resources Center, 60137. Director of Materials Utilization. (e)

(**Park Forest South**) Governors State University, University Libraries, 60466. Assistant Director of Libraries. (e)

(**Urbana**) University of Illinois at Urbana-Champaign, Architecture Library, 202 Architecture Building, 61820. Architecture Librarian.* Estab. mid-1880s. 60,000. 1 FT, 3 PT. (c)
—University of Illinois at Urbana-Champaign, Department of Art and Design, 143 Fine Arts Building, 61820. Slide Curator.**

INDIANA

(**Bloomington**) Indiana University, Fine Arts Library, 47401. Slide Librarian.* Slide Library. Estab. c.1935. 190,000. 2 FT, 10 PT.

(**Fort Wayne**) Fort Wayne Art Institute, Museum of Art, 1202 West Wayne St., 46804. The Fine Arts Consultant.

(**Indianapolis**) Herron Museum of Art. *See* Indianapolis Museum of Art.
—Herron School of Art, Library, Indiana University-Purdue University at Indianapolis, 1701 North Pennsylvania, 46202. Assistant Librarian. Estab. 1971. 15,000. 1 FT, 2 PT.
—Indianapolis Museum of Art, Library, 1200 West 38th St., 46208. Librarian.* Estab. c.1920. 22,000. 1 FT, 0 PT.

(**Muncie**) Ball State University, Art Department, 47306. Chairman.**

(**Notre Dame**) University of Notre Dame, Department of Art, 46556. Curator.* Slide Library. Estab. 1953. 45,000. 1 FT, 5 PT.

(**Richmond**) Earlham College, 47374. Audio-Visual Services. Slide Librarian.**

(**South Bend**) Indiana University at South Bend, Department of Fine Arts, 1825 Northside Blvd., 46615. Slide Collection.

(**Terre Haute**) Indiana State University, Cunningham Memorial Library, Teaching Materials Center, 47809. Head, Teaching Materials Center.* Estab. 1950. 2,000. 1 FT, 10 PT.

IOWA

(**Grinnell**) Grinnell College, Department of Art, 50112. Assistant.* Slide Collection. Estab. 1920. 22,500. 0 FT, 2 PT.

(**Iowa City**) University of Iowa, School of Art, 52240. Curator of Visual Materials.* Estab. 1935. 94,000. 1 FT, 17 PT.(c)

KANSAS

(**Lawrence**) University of Kansas, Department of History of Art, Spooner Hall, 66044. Curator of Slides.** 100,000. 0 FT, 3-4 PT.

(**Manhattan**) Kansas State University, Department of Art, College of Arts and Sciences, 66502. Photographer I.* Estab. 1964. 15,500. 0 FT, 1 PT.

KENTUCKY

(**Louisville**) University of Louisville, Allen R. Hite Art Institute, Belknap Campus, 40208. Curator.* Slide Collection. Estab. c.1950. 33,000. 1 FT, 3 PT.

(Wilmore) Asbury College, Morrison–Kenyon Library, 40390. Slide Collection. (e)

LOUISIANA

(New Orleans) Tulane University, Newcomb College, Art Department, 70118. Slide Librarian.* Estab. c.1910. 90,000. 1 FT, 2 PT.

(Ruston) Louisiana Polytechnic Institute, Department of Art and Architecture, 71270. Slide Collection.

MAINE

(Orono) University of Maine, Art Gallery, Carnegie Hall, 04473. Slide Librarian.** 15,000.

(Portland) Portland School of Art, 93 High St., 04101. Slide Collection.
–Portland Museum of Art, 111 High St., 04101. Volunteer. Slide Library. 3,000.

MARYLAND

(Baltimore) Enoch Pratt Free Library, Films Department, 400 Cathedral St., 21201. Administrative Assistant.* Estab. c.1922. 24,000. 1 FT, 0 PT.
–Johns Hopkins University, Department of the History of Art, Charles and 34th Sts., 21218. "Slide Librarian."* Slide Collection. Estab. 1948. 60,000. 4 FT, 1 PT.
–Maryland Institute, College of Art, Library, 1300 Mt. Royal Ave., 21217. Slide Librarian.* Estab. 1963. 48,000. 2 FT, 1 PT.

(Catonsville) Catonsville Community College, AV Department, 21228. Library Technical Assistant.* AV Department. Estab. 1964. 20,000. 4 FT, 2 PT. (c)

(College Park) University of Maryland, School of Architecture, 20742. Curator of Slides.

MASSACHUSETTS

(Boston) Boston Architectural Center, Library, School of Architecture, 320 Newbury St., 02115. Librarian.
–Museum of Fine Arts, 465 Huntington Ave., 02115. Director of Slide and Loan Services.* Slide Library. Estab. 1905. 70,000. 2 FT, 5 PT.

(Cambridge) Harvard University, Fogg Art Museum, Library, Quincy Station, 02138. Curator of Photographs and Slides.* Estab. c.1927. 170,000. 2 FT, 6 PT. (c)
–Massachusetts Institute of Technology, Rotch Library, 02139. Assistant Rotch Librarian for Slides.* Estab. 1900. 90,000. 3 FT, 3 PT. (c)

(Northampton) Forbes Library, Art and Music Department, 01060. Slide Collection. (e)
–Smith College, Art Department, Hillyer Art Gallery, 01060. Curator of Slides.* Estab. 1920s. 92,000. 1 FT, 4 PT.

(Norton) Wheaton College, Art Department, 02766. Curator of Slides and Photographs.* Estab. 1931. 37,000. 1 FT, 2 PT.

(South Hadley) Mt. Holyoke College, Department of Art, 01075. "Slide Librarian."* Estab. c.1900. 20,500. 0 FT, 2 PT.

(Waltham) Brandeis University, Fine Arts Department, 02154. Librarian.* Estab. 1953. 60,000. 1 FT, 9 PT.

(Wellesley) Wellesley College, Department of Art, Jewett Arts Center, 02181. Slide Librarian.* Estab. 1892. 48,000. 2 FT, 2 PT.

(Williamstown) Sterling and Francine Clark Art Institute, South Street, 02167. Photograph and Slide Librarian.* Estab. 1967. 25,000. 1 FT, 1 PT.
—Williams College, Art Library, Main Street, 02167. "Slide Librarian."* Estab. 1910. 47,000. 1 FT, 2 PT.

(Worcester) Worcester Art Museum, 55 Salisbury St. at Tuckerman St., 01608. Librarian.** c.27,000.

MICHIGAN

(Allendale) Grand Valley State College, Department of Fine Arts, College Landing, 49401. Assistant Professor of Art. Slide Collection. (e)

(Ann Arbor) University of Michigan, Architecture Library, College of Architecture and Design, 240 Architecture and Design, 48104. Librarian.* c.50,000.
—University of Michigan, Department of the History of Art, Tappan Hall, 48104. Curator of Slides and Photographs.* Slide and Photograph Collection. Estab. 1911. 135,000. 5 FT, 4 PT. (c)

(Bloomfield Hills) Cranbrook Academy of Art, 500 Lone Pine Rd., 48013. "Slide Librarian."* Estab. 1949. 10,000. 0 FT, 1 PT.

(Dearborn) Henry Ford Museum and Greenfield Village, 48121. Manager. Audio-Visual Services. Slide Collection.

(Detroit) Detroit Institute of Arts, Research Library, 5200 Woodward Ave., 48202. Librarian.** 30,000. (c)
—University of Detroit, Library, 2001 West McNichols Rd., 48221. Head of Reference. Reference Department.
—Wayne State University, Department of Art and Art History, College of Liberal Arts, 48202. Curator of Slides.* Estab. 1966. 76,000. 1 FT, 5 PT. (c)

(East Lansing) Michigan State University, Library, Department of Art, 116 Kresge Art Center, 48823. Art Librarian.** c.30,000.

(Rochester) Oakland University, Department of Art, 48063. Assistant Curator in Art.* Estab. 1959. 37,000. 1 FT, 3 PT. (c)

MINNESOTA

(Marshall) Southwest Minnesota State College, Library, 56258. Catalog Librarian. (e)

(Minneapolis) Minneapolis Institute of Arts, 201 East 24th St., 55404. Slide Curator.* Estab. 1950. 15,000. 0 FT, 3 PT.
—Minneapolis Public Library, 300 Nicollet Ave., 55401. Head, Visual Aids Department.** c.45,000.

—University of Minnesota, Architecture Library, 160 Architecture Building, 55455. Librarian.** c.18,500.
—University of Minnesota, Department of Art History, 109 Jones Hall, 55455. Slide Librarian.* Slide Room. Estab. 1947. 100,000. 1 FT, 3 PT.
—Walker Art Center, Library, 1710 Lyndale Ave., South, 55403. Librarian.**

(St. Paul) The College of St. Catherine, Art Department, 55116. Art Assistant. Slide Collection. (e)
—School of the Associated Arts, Library, 344 Summit Ave., 55102. Librarian.** c.10,000.

MISSISSIPPI

(Hattiesburg) University of Southern Mississippi, Department of Art, Box 33.39401.

MISSOURI

(Kansas City) Kansas City Art Institute and School of Design, 4415 Warwick Blvd., 64111. "Slide Librarian."** 17,000.
—University of Missouri-Kansas City, Department of Art and Art History, 64110. Curator of Teaching Collections.* Estab. 1948. 35,000. 1 FT, 11 PT.

(St. Louis) City Art Museum of St. Louis, Richardson Memorial Library, 63110. Librarian.* Estab. c.1925. 11,000. 0 FT, 1 PT.
—Washington University, Department of Art and Archeology, 63130. Slide Librarian.** Slide Library.

NEBRASKA

(Omaha) Joslyn Art Museum, Library, 2218 Dodge St., 68102. Librarian. 15,000. (e)

NEW HAMPSHIRE

(Hanover) Dartmouth College, Department of Art, Carpenter Hall, 03755. Slide Curator.* Estab. c.1890. 80,000. 1 FT, 3 PT.

NEW JERSEY

(Mahwah) Ramapo College of New Jersey, Library, Ramapo Valley Rd., P.O. Box 542, 07430. Assistant Library Director. 2,000.

(New Brunswick) Rutgers University, Douglass College Art Department, 08903. Curator.* Slide Collection. Estab. 1920s. 22,000. 0 FT, 5 PT.

(Newark) The Public Library of Newark New Jersey, Picture and Print Collection, Art and Music Department, 5 Washington St., 07101. Supervising Art and Music Librarian.* Estab. 1958. 11,000. 1 FT, 0 PT.

(Princeton) Princeton University, Department of Art and Archaeology, McCormick Hall, 08540. Director of the Section of Slides and Photographs.* Estab. c.1900. 160,000. 5 FT, 0 PT. (c)

(Union) Newark State College, Fine Arts Department, Morris Ave., 07083. Coordinator of Slide Collection.

(Upper Montclair) Montclair State College, Fine Arts Department, 07043. Fine Arts Department. (e)

NEW MEXICO

(Albuquerque) University of New Mexico, Fine Arts Library, College of Fine Arts, 87106. Slide Curator.* Slide Library. Estab. c.1948. 65,000. 1 FT, 4 PT. (c)

NEW YORK

(Albany) State University of New York at Albany, Department of Art, 1400 Washington Ave., 12203. Curator.* Slide Library. Estab. 1958. 50,000. 1 FT, 3 PT.

(Binghamton) State University of New York at Binghamton and Harpur College, Department of Art and Art History, 13901. Curator of Visual Resources.* Estab. 1951. 70,000. 1 FT, 7 PT. (c)

(Brockport) State University College at Brockport, Department of Art, 14450. Chairman.* Slide Room (and Study Area). Estab. 1967. 15,000. 0 FT, 5 PT.

(Bronx) Fordham University, Department of Fine Arts, 10458. Associate Professor of Art. Slide Collection. 15,000.
—Manhattan College, Fine Arts Department, 10471. Slide Collection. (e)

(Bronxville) Sarah Lawrence College, 10708. Slides Library.

(Brooklyn) Brooklyn College of the City University of New York, Bedford Ave., 11210. Curator of Slides.* Slide Collection. Estab. c.1943. 30,000. 1 FT, 4 PT.
—Brooklyn Museum, Eastern Parkway and Washington Ave., 11238. Slide Librarian. Slide Library.
—Kingsborough Community College of the City University of New York, Department of Speech, Music and Art, Oriental Blvd., Manhattan Beach, 11235. Slide Curator.
—Pratt Institute, Library, 215 Ryerson St., 11205. Librarian.* Estab. 1959. 40,000. 1 FT, 4 PT.

(Buffalo) State University of New York at Buffalo, Art History Department, 325 Foster Hall, 14214. Curator of Visual Resources.

(Corning) Corning Community College, The Arthur A. Houghton, Jr. Library, 14830. Curator of Slides.* Estab. 1959. 16,000. 1 FT, 0 PT. (c)
—Corning Museum of Glass, Corning Glass Center, 14830. Assistant for Slides and Photographs. c.15,000.

(Geneva) Hobart and William Smith Colleges, 14456. Slide Librarian.

(Ithaca) Cornell University, College of Architecture, Art and Planning, 14850. Slide Curator.* Slide Collection. Estab. c.1880. 150,000. 1 FT, 5 PT. (c)
—Cornell University, Department of the History of Art, 35 Goldwin Smith Hall, 14850. Curator of Slides and Photographs.* Estab. c.1935. 100,000. 1 FT, 9 PT.

(New York) American Museum of Natural History, Slide Library, Central Park West at 79th St., 10024. Manager of Photography and Slides.** Slide Library. 20,000.

—The Archaeological Institute of America, 260 West Broadway, 10013. Slide
   Curator. Slide Archive.
—Barnard College, Art History Department, 606 West 120th St., 10027. Slide
   Collection. (e)
—City College of New York, Art Department, Convent Ave. and 139th St., 10031.
   "Slide Librarian."**
—The City University of New York, Graduate Center, 33 West 42nd St., 10036.
   Art Librarian. Slide Library.
—Columbia University in the City of New York, Department of Art History and
   Archaeology, Schermerhorn Hall, 10027. Curator.* Slide Collection. Estab.
   1934. 300,000. 1 FT, 15-20 PT. (c)
—Solomon R. Guggenheim Museum, 1071 Fifth Ave., 10028. Slide Librarian.
—Joseph H. Hirshhorn Museum and Sculpture Garden Library (temporary
   address): 135 East Sixty-Fifth St., 10021. (New building under construction
   in Washington, D.C. To be opened Winter 1973-1974.) Librarian.* Estab.
   1973. 4,000.
—The Metropolitan Museum of Art, Fifth Ave. and 82nd St., 10028. Chief Librar-
   ian.* Photograph and Slide Library. Estab. 1907. 270,000. 7 FT, 10 PT. (c)
—Museum of Modern Art, Library, 11 West 53rd St., 10019. Cataloguer and Visual
   Specialist.
—New York University, Institute of Fine Arts, 1 East 78th St., 10021. Curator of
   Slides and Photographs.* Estab. 1930. 200,000. 1 FT, PT not given. (c)
—The School of Visual Arts, Library, 209 East 23rd St., 10010. Slide Curator.*
   Estab. 1967. c.15,000. 2 FT, 0 PT.

(Niagara Falls) Niagara County Community College, Library, 430 Buffalo Ave.,
   14303. Librarian. (e)

(Poughkeepsie) Vassar College, Department of Art, 12601. Curator of Slides and
   Photographs.* Estab. 1915. 60,000. 1 FT, 9 PT.

(Riverdale) College of Mt. St. Vincent, Art Department, 10471. Slide Collection.
   c.15,000.

(Rochester) University of Rochester, Fine Arts Department, River Campus Station,
   14627. Slide and Photograph Curator.* Estab. 1900s. 40,000. 1 FT, 1 PT.

(Saratoga Springs) Skidmore College, Library, Art Reading Room, 12866. Curator
   of Slides.* Estab. 1933. 14,000. 1 FT, PT not given.

(Stony Brook) State University of New York at Stony Brook, Art Department,
   11790. Assistant Reference Librarian.**

(Syracuse) Syracuse University, Ernest Stevenson Bird Library, 205A, 13210. Slide
   Curator. c.90,000.

(Troy) Russell Sage College, Art Department, 28 First St., 12180. Slide Library.

(Utica) Munson-Williams-Proctor Institute, Library, 310 Genesee St., 13502.
   Librarian.** c.17,000.

(West Point) United States Military Academy, Library, 10996. Fine Arts Librarian.
   c.5,000.

NORTH CAROLINA

(Chapel Hill) University of North Carolina, Department of Art, The William Hayes Ackland Memorial Art Center, 27514. Curator of Slides and Photographs.* Estab. c.1940. 70,000. 2 FT, 5 PT.

(Durham) Duke University, The Department of Art, 6605 College Station, 27708. Chairman. Slide Collection. (e)

(Raleigh) North Carolina State University at Raleigh, Library, School of Design: Architecture, Landscape Architecture, Product Design, P.O. Box 5398, 27607. Librarian.* Estab. unk. 25,000. 2 FT, 0 PT. (c)

OHIO

(Athens) Ohio University, Fine Arts Library, Seigfred Hall, 45702. Curator of Slides.* The Slide Room. Estab. 1954. 34,000. 2 FT, 5 PT.
—Ohio University, School of Art, 45701. Slide Librarian.

(Cincinnati) Cincinnati Art Museum, Library, Eden Park, 45202. Librarian.* Estab. c.1937. 20,000. 2 FT, 0 PT.
—The Public Library of Cincinnati and Hamilton County, Films and Recordings Center, 800 Vine St., 45202. Head, Films and Recordings Center.* Estab. 1947. c.25,000. 13 FT, 2 PT (staff of Films and Recording Center).
—University of Cincinnati, College of Design, Architecture and Art, 45221. Director of Visual Aids Archives.* Estab. 1920. 100,000. 2 FT, 8 PT.

(Cleveland) Case Western Reserve University, Department of Art, 10940 Euclid Ave., 44106. Slide Librarian.**
—Cleveland Institute of Art, 11141 East Boulevard, 44106. Head.* A-V Department. Estab. 1960. c.15,000. 1 FT, 1 PT. (c)
—Cleveland Museum of Art, Art Reference Library, 11150 East Boulevard, 44106. Librarian.* Estab. 1916. 140,000. 6 FT, 9 PT. (c)

(Columbus) Ohio State University, Division of the History of Art, 126 North Oval Dr., 43210. Slide Librarian.* Slide Library. Estab. 1920s. 90,000. 2 FT, 23 PT. (c)

(Granville) Denison University, Department of Visual Arts, 43023. Slide Librarian.* Estab. 1938. 20,000. 1 FT, 0 PT.

(Oberlin) Oberlin College, Library, Department of Art, 44704. Curator of Slides.* Estab. c.1917. 130,000. 1 FT, 4 PT.

(Oxford) Miami University, Library, 205 Hiestand Hall, 45056. Departmental Librarian.* Estab. 1952. 24,000. 2 FT, 2 PT.

(Toledo) Toledo Museum of Art, Art Reference Library, Box 1013, Monroe St. at Scotwood Ave., 43601. Librarian.* Estab. c.1930. 36,500. 3 FT, 1 PT.

OKLAHOMA

(Norman) University of Oklahoma, Art Library, School of Art, Room 202 FJC, 73069. Slide Curator.* Estab. c.1946. 35,000. 0 FT, 3 PT.

OREGON

(Corvallis) Oregon State University, Department of Architecture, School of Humanities and Social Sciences, Gilman Hall, 97331. Slide Librarian.**

(Eugene) University of Oregon, Architecture and Allied Arts Library, School of Architecture and Allied Arts, 97403. Librarian.* Estab. c.1914. 93,000. 4 FT, 7 PT.

PENNSYLVANIA

(Bryn Mawr) Bryn Mawr College, Department of the History of Art, 19110. Curator of Slides and Photographs for Departments of: History of Art and Classical and Near Eastern Archaeology.* Estab. 1905-1908. 100,000. 1 FT, 10 PT. (c)

(Clarion) Clarion State College, Department of Art, 16214. Slide Collection.

(Collegeville) Ursinus College, Library, 19426.

(Philadelphia) Community College of Philadelphia, Educational Resources Center, 34 South 11th St., 19107. 8,000.
—Moore College of Art, Library, 20th and Race Sts., 19103. Librarian.
—Philadelphia City Planning Commission, Library, 13th Floor, City Hall Annex, S.E. Corner, Juniper and Filbert Sts., 19107. c.6,500.
—Philadelphia College of Art, Broad and Pine Sts., 19102. Director.* Slide Library. Estab. 1959. 95,000. 3 FT, 3 PT.
—Philadelphia Museum of Art, Slide Library, Parkway at 26th St., 19101. Curator of Slides. Estab. 1939. 89,000. 4 FT, 6 PT. (c)
—Tyler School of Art, History of Art Department, Temple University, Beech and Penrose Aves., 19126. Chairman.* Slide Collection. Estab. c.1940. 25,000. 0 FT, 3-4 PT. (c)
—University of Pennsylvania, Graduate School of Fine Arts—G.2, 34th and Walnut Sts., 19104. Head of Slides.* Slide Room. Estab. 1925. 114,000. 3 FT, 4 PT. (c)

(Pittsburgh) Carnegie-Mellon University, Carnegie Institute of Technology, Hunt Library, Schenley Park, 15213. Librarian. 42,000. (c)
—University of Pittsburgh, Department of Fine Arts, Faculty of Arts and Sciences, 15213. Curator of Slides and Photographs.* Slides and Photographs. Estab. 1927. 70,000. 1 FT, 5 PT.

(University Park) Pennsylvania State University, Department of Art History, College of Arts and Architecture, 229 Arts II, 16802. Curator of Slides and Photographs.* Estab. 1930s. 90,000. 1 FT, 1 PT.

(Villanova) Villanova University, Department of Fine Arts, 19085. Slide Librarian.

RHODE ISLAND

(Providence) Brown University, Department of Art, 02912. Curator/Slides and Photographs.**
—Rhode Island School of Design, Library, Box B, 2 College St., 02903. Slide Librarian.* Estab. 1915. 46,000. 0 FT, 1 PT.

TENNESSEE

(Memphis) Memphis State University, Department of Art, 38152. Slide Curator.

TEXAS

(Austin) University of Texas, Department of Art, 78712. Slide Librarian.* Estab. 1938. 85,000. 3 FT, 15 PT.

(Dallas) Southern Methodist University, Meadows School of the Arts, Division of the Arts, 75222. Slide Librarian.

(Denton) Texas Woman's University, Fine Arts Library, College of Fine Arts, 76204. Librarian.** 13,000.

(Fort Worth) Kimbell Art Museum, Library, 76107. Slide Librarian. 5,000. (e)

(Houston) Rice University, Fine Arts Department, 6100 Main St., 77025. Slide Curator.** Slide Library.
—University of Houston, Architecture Library, Cullen Blvd., 77004. Architecture Librarian.
—University of St. Thomas, Art Department, 77006. Slide and Photograph Curator.

(San Antonio) The University of Texas at San Antonio, College of Fine and Applied Arts, 4242 Piedras Dr., East, 78228. Curator of Slides. Slide Library.

UTAH

(Salt Lake City) University of Utah, Audio-Visual Department, University Libraries, 84112. Audio-Visual Librarian. (e)

VIRGINIA

(Baileys' Crossroads) North Virginia Community College, Learning Resources Center, 3443 South Carlyn Spring Rd., 22041.

(Charlottesville) University of Virginia, McIntire Department of Art, Cocke Hall, 22903. Slide Curator.
—University of Virginia, School of Architecture, Fayerweather Hall, 22903. Slide Librarian.** 20,000.

(Norfolk) Old Dominion University, Department of Art, 23508.

WASHINGTON

(Seattle) Seattle Art Museum, Volunteer Park, 98102. Supervisor. Photograph and Slide Library.
—University of Washington, Art Library, School of Art, 105 Art Building, 98105. Preparator/Slide Collection.* Estab. unk. 66,000. 3 FT, 1 PT.

WISCONSIN

(Eau Claire) Wisconsin State University-Eau Claire, Department of Art, Park and Garfield Aves., 54701. Slide Library.

(Green Bay) University of Wisconsin—Green Bay, Instructional Services, Library, 54305. Librarian.

(La Crosse) University of Wisconsin—La Crosse, Art Department, 54601.

(Madison) University of Wisconsin, Department of Art History, Elvehjem Art Center 314, 53706. Slide Librarian.* Slide Library. Estab. 1923. 137,000. 1 FT, 2 PT.

(Menomonie) Stout State University, Art Department, 54751. Slide Librarian. Slide Library. 25,000.

(Milwaukee) Milwaukee Art Center, 750 North Lincoln Memorial Dr., 53202. Curator.* Estab. 1957. 11,000. 2 FT, 0 PT.

—University of Wisconsin—Milwaukee, Art Department, 53210. Slide Curator.

WASHINGTON, D.C.

—Georgetown University, Department of Fine Arts, College of Arts and Sciences, 20007. Chairman.* Estab. 1959. 12,000. 1 FT, 2 PT.

—Joseph H. Hirshhorn Museum and Sculpture Garden. *See* New York City.

—Howard University, Department of Art, College of Fine Arts, 6th and Fairmont Sts., N.W., 20001. Librarian.* Estab. 1926. 15,500. 1 FT, 1 PT.

—The Library of Congress, Prints and Photographs Division, Reference Department, 20540. Picture Cataloging Specialist. Collection of a few thousand lantern slides—no inventory list of all slides available. For approximate number and content, see listings in the *Guide to the Special Collections of Prints and Photographs in the Library of Congress*, Washington, D.C., Government Printing Office, 1955.

—National Gallery of Art, Smithsonian Institution, Sixth and Constitution, N.W., 20565. Curator in Charge of Educational Work.* Estab. 1941. 53,000. 1 FT, 0 PT. (c)

OTHER COUNTRIES

CANADA

(British Columbia) Simon Fraser University, University Library, Burnaby 2. Head, Cataloging Division.

—The University of British Columbia, Fine Arts Department, Vancouver 8. Slide Librarian.* Art Slide Library. Estab. 1949. 55,000. 1 FT, 1 PT. (c)

(Manitoba) University of Manitoba, Faculty of Architecture, Winnipeg 19. Slide Librarian. 60,000. (c)

(Nova Scotia) Nova Scotia College of Art and Design, 6152 Coburg Rd., Halifax. Slide Library.

(Ontario) The University of Western Ontario, Department of Fine Art, Fine Art Building, London 72. Slide Librarian.

—University of Ottawa, Communications and Instructional Media Centre, 100 Laurier Est, Room 106, Ottawa 2. Slide Librarian.

—City Hall, Sarnia. Planning Technician. (e)

—Rothmans Art Gallery of Stratford, 54 Romeo St., Stratford. Slide Collection. (e)

(Saskatoon) University of Saskatchewan, Department of Art.

GREAT BRITAIN

(London) Victoria and Albert Museum, Cromwell Rd., S.W. 7. Officer in Charge, Slide Loan Service.

LEBANON

(Beirut) American University of Beirut, Department of Fine and Performing Arts.

NEW ZEALAND

(Auckland) The University of Auckland, School of Architecture, Private Bag. Architecture Librarian. 10,000.

PAPUA

(Boroko) The University of Papua and New Guinea, The Library, P.O. Box 1432. University Librarian.

INDEX

Page numbers in bold refer to pages having photographs. Specific names of distributors and manufacturers of equipment, slides and supplies are cited only as they appear in the text. Direct reference to the directories is necessary for complete addresses and information on types of material handled by each source.